WHY DO I FEEL SO SAD?

WHY DO I FEEL SO SAD?

Your pathway to healing depression

DR SHEFALI BATRA

JAICO PUBLISHING HOUSE

Ahmedabad Bangalore Chennai
Delhi Hyderabad Kolkata Mumbai

Disclaimer

The opinions expressed and treatment methods suggested in this book are the author's own and do not reflect the opinions of Jaico Publishing House. The publisher or the author does not intend to cause any offence to any medical practitioners or their treatment methods by publishing this book. No responsibility is assumed by the publisher or the author for any injury and/or damage to persons or property as a matter of product liability, negligence, or otherwise, or from any use or operation of any methods, instructions or ideas contained in the published material. Please consult with your own physician or healthcare specialist regarding the suggestions and recommendations made in this book.

Published by Jaico Publishing House
A-2 Jash Chambers, 7-A Sir Phirozshah Mehta Road
Fort, Mumbai - 400 001
jaicopub@jaicobooks.com
www.jaicobooks.com

WHY DO I FEEL SO SAD?
ISBN 978-93-93559-86-9

First Jaico Impression: 2023
Third Jaico Impression: 2023

Page design and layout by Inosoft Systems, Delhi

Printed by
Trinity Academy For Corporate Training Limited, Mumbai

To my father, Ashok Batra (1950–2021),
whose name translates to "never sad". His attitude,
demeanour, and life are living proof of this book.

Contents

PART 3: Pave the Way for a New Style of Thinking (Techniques to Break Cognitive Distortions)

PART 4: To Start Making It Better, Stop Making It Worse (Lifestyle and Behavioural Contributors to Depression)

PART 5: This Is the Beginning of Your New Life

Foreword

The COVID-19 pandemic brought in its wake a tsunami of mental health concerns. Children and older people, frontline health workers, and people with existing mental health issues were among the worst affected. Over 40% of Indians reported feeling depressed during the pandemic in 2020.

Many of us have experienced stress, anxiety, insomnia, denial, anger and fear without realising what's actually happening to us. Many of us have asked ourselves 'Why do I feel so sad and angry?' or 'Why am I so exhausted all the time?' It is very likely that we have all struggled to find answers to these questions.

Scarcity of available resources, unequal distribution and inefficiencies in utilisation pose serious obstacles to better mental health. For a country of over 1.3 billion people, India has only about 8,000 psychiatrists. Moreover, the shame and stigma associated with mental illness make it difficult for even those who are actively trying to seek help from reaching out to mental health professionals. Many often end up consulting general physicians or family doctors.

The pandemic has made evident the critical need for information to support those seeking resources on stress, anxiety, depression and other mental health-related problems.

This is exactly what Dr Shefali Batra seeks to do through her insightfully well-written book *Why Do I Feel So Sad?*

Dr Batra provides practical and useful advice on dealing with depression which has tremendous credibility, coming from a mental health practitioner with over 20 years of experience in medicine and psychotherapy.

The first step to dealing with depression is understanding exactly what it is. This book explains the many facets of depression and how readers can identify patterns of self-doubt and diffidence that are holding them back from their goals and instilling in them a lack of purpose and a sense of hopelessness. What Dr Batra's writings aim to do is to move them from helplessness to happiness and from aimlessness to pointed pursuit.

She bases her advice on cognitive behavioural therapy (CBT), which is a form of therapy that seeks to modify thought patterns through time-tested practices that have their basis in modern brain research.

One of the sections of the book also dwells on how certain lifestyle choices and behavioural patterns can contribute to depression, and what we as individuals can do to prevent a bad situation from getting worse.

She provides readers with practices and habits one can adopt to curb intrusive thoughts from triggering negative emotions. She suggests easy to follow techniques to guide readers to new ways of thinking: 'Arrest your negative thought, and put it in the witness box'; 'Quit blame and shame, play the "what if?" game' and 'Change your locus to gain better focus.'

The book keeps you engaged through its use of real-world anecdotes, humour, and analogies.

While the written word shouldn't be a substitute for treatment options like therapy and medication, this book written by a veteran mental health practitioner contains useful advice for those who want to understand, handle and cope with depression.

As someone who is deeply interested in neuroscience, mental illness is a complex maze of chemical and neurological interactions. Cognition and behaviour are the result of synaptic connections and disconnections which mirror human social interactions. Often it is a sensitive understanding of an individual's situation or circumstances that can have a healing effect on mental illness. Dr Shefali Batra's book is a must read for everyone as I can't think of anyone who has not been through a phase of depression or acute stress in their life. After all, life is far more challenging today than it ever was.

Kiran Mazumdar Shaw
Executive Chairperson, Biocon Limited

PREFACE

Why I Wrote a Book on Depression

"Mental pain is less dramatic than physical pain, but it is more common and also harder to bear. The frequent attempt to conceal mental pain increases the burden: it is easier to say, "My tooth is aching" than to say, "My heart is broken."

—C.S. Lewis, *The Problem of Pain*

Have you lain in bed some mornings, finding it hard to motivate yourself to get going, even though the day was all chalked out? Maybe you snoozed the alarm, a few, or many times. Because waking up meant confronting what felt to *you* like another avoidable day. A day *you* anticipated to be full of annoyance—boring people, tedious chores, frustrating commitments, and unresolved conflict. Maybe at some point, you wondered how others manage to wake up enthusiastic, invigorated, and rejuvenated—confident about their capacities and motivation to make it a fulfilling, satisfying and productive twenty-four hours. Yet, there you were in bed, feeling hopeless, thinking that nothing was going to get better. It's also possible that you were aware of none of this being indeed *as bad* as how you were imagining it in your head. But you could not brush off the feeling.

If you've felt any of this, you're not alone.

Sadness, frustration, lethargy, gloom, despondency, and emptiness could plague all our minds and lives from time to time. But when it lasts over a period of time and interferes with daily activities, it could be a sign of more serious concerns like depression. Depression is a grave health condition that causes one to suffer deeply. If untreated, at its worst, it can unfortunately push people to commit suicide. It disallows you to live optimally, prevents academic and career success, and takes away much of colour and meaning (depending on its severity) from life. I've seen so many people with depression suffer incessant emotional pain. The daily battles they fight, the wounds they nurse by themselves, and the tussle they bear for just existing are agonising.

But before we talk about depression–a mental illness, we need to talk about mental health. In particular, poor mental health awareness. Conversations about it with family, friends, colleagues, mentors, partners and even children need to be normalised so that seeking help when needed becomes easy. According to the World Health Organization (WHO), in low to middle income countries, up to 75% of people with psychological problems do not receive any treatment. This can be attributed to a deficit in resources, inadequate expertise of treating professionals, lack of awareness, as well as the sufferer's unwillingness to seek assistance. If we don't see the problem, we are less likely to do something to resolve it. The last 30 years have momentously highlighted the gravity of depression with mounting statistics based on recent reports—principally it's long-suffering nature, emphasis on the fact that it is not always acute or self-limiting, and that it could lead to suicide.

According to the WHO (2019), more than 28 crore people in the world are depressed. Nearly half of these people live in South-

East Asia and the Western Pacific Region (which includes India and China). Depression is ranked as the single largest contributor to global disability. Sadly, it is also the major reason for suicide deaths across the world, which are close to 7,04,000 per year. In fact, suicide is the fourth leading cause of death in 15–29-year-olds.

In 2017, 19.7 crore Indians were suffering from mental disorders, of whom 4.57 crore had depression. Based on this, one in every 7 people in India has a mental disorder of varying severity. By 2030, depression is predicted to be the second leading contributor to the global burden of disease.

Even though it is classified as a medical disease, depression is not as unassuming as a cough, cold, malaria, blood cancer or other medical problems which may be due to viruses, bacteria, parasites, or genetic abnormalities. Very few people are aware of why they get depressed. Additionally, stigma in society doesn't help. People are often culturally misguided and may perceive depression as weakness of character or a personality flaw. That is why in some cases they caste out the sufferer as if depression was a punishable crime or offense.

Also, depressed people are not always lonely and crying. The visibly happiest and friendliest people you know could be very close to the edge without a safety net to catch them if they fall. You may have been there too. There isn't a soul that hasn't felt that pang of enduring sadness—an eagerness to overcome a nagging low mood, or an anticipation of rejection that shook your confidence and self-worth, and made you think, "Am I worthy of anything good?"

When I was 10, my classmate Anisha (name changed to safeguard her identity) told me in passing that she was not a "good enough" person. At that age, I thought that I and my life were perfect. When I asked why she felt so, she replied, "My mother is better than me in every way." I thought, "My mother is better than me in all ways too, because she is my mother—older, wiser, and more experienced. Besides, I must still work hard and long in life get to where I want to be." It was not of the essence to base my self-worth on a scale measuring me against *any* other person, even if it was my own mother. But Anisha thought differently. We were only 10. What could either of us do about how she felt?

I now remember that in no time, Anisha had put on a lot of weight, wasn't doing well in studies, and got into squabbles with everyone in class. She was branded as self-centred and uninteresting. If you ask me objectively, this did seem true—she had few friends, cried by herself often, and seemed disinterested in everything that the other kids engaged in. I tried being there for her, asked her to join us in the playground because it would be something fun, but she wasn't happy. I gave up trying at some point.

Things stayed the same.

During the occasional parent–teacher meeting I recall Anisha's mother as an achiever—a high-ranking official in the government, good-looking, charismatic and intelligent. Nothing suggested that she did not care about her daughter or that she belittled her. Anisha eventually dropped out of school. Back then, I was 10, not sufficiently aware or empowered to make much of a difference in her life. I had no idea what was wrong, so how could I set it right? But did her parents have no clue either? Or did they know, but ignored it?

Subsequently in life, I witnessed more of this. Some in friend circles, few in the family, many in the neighbourhood and among acquaintances—all combating sadness, turmoil, unrest, self-harm and a few who contemplated suicide too. Of all, another person who has remained wedged in my head was a medical school colleague. Though bright and accomplished in his work, he was often ostracised for being odd, sad, boring, and depressed.

I concluded that depression is practically everywhere.

In January of 2000, when I walked into the rural medical centre for mandatory training after medical school (MBBS), I approached this colleague for guidance for my work. He didn't make any eye contact or speak much. Something was amiss, but I asked him more about operational issues. He started responding and connected with me as a co-worker and friend. I listened and talked to him as much as I could within my capacity.

He said nobody spoke much to him or took him seriously—not even patients. "Why do you feel so?" I asked. No one I knew seemed to really complain about his work. It was delightful to clarify subject-related questions with him as he was methodical and his conceptual explanation was spot-on. During one such interaction, he recounted a painful childhood incident. His father, a labourer in a factory, had died unexpectedly in a machine-related accident. He was only eight years old when this happened. His mother had a rough time raising three children. He was the youngest. He began to cry and said he felt like he was the "loneliest person alive". At this time, I was older and more aware than I was when I witnessed Anisha's struggle. I suggested professional help on one such occasion, but he never followed up on the advice.

One morning two weeks later, he wasn't at the centre. He'd dropped out of the course at the home base. I had no way of connecting with him. It made news in the medical centre because throughout his career, he'd excelled consistently. A medical doctor, seemingly so well-informed about the body and mind, had given up at the final stage of reaching his career dream. It did leave me riddled with thoughts of remorse, of not having done something to make a bigger difference in his life than I thought I was capable of. Maybe I could have convinced him more assertively to seek professional help?

This was my second close encounter with psychological suffering in someone I knew which had gone unnoticed, undetected, and unattended. I'd been around, but I felt more helpless as a silent spectator who was so minimally involved.

All these experiences reminded me how we are constantly told to excel in life. The purpose of life is to believe, conceive, and achieve—all of which is wise and well-intended. I have the most caring, supportive, and loving family who were a source of strength to me in achieving the highest goals that I set for myself. Nevertheless, I knew people who faced situations that made them feel less aspirational, almost incompetent, and challenged. Not all had caring and supportive environments that nurture and contribute to positivity. Hardly anyone else I knew was being imparted basic or advanced life skills to make sure that we each feel content and happy in the long run. It worried me, because life isn't a 100-meter sprint, we all need to prepare for the marathon.

I wondered, *"Is there a way for me to make a difference?"*

Back then, books, news, billboards, and advertisements—all emphasised physical health and wellness. Committed to the same, I'd pursued the MBBS degree, completed the rural internship I described earlier, and was eagerly awaiting the mandatory education counselling session. Based on my rank, I'd be offered a seat in my desired subject for post graduate medical specialisation.

After a prolonged four-hour wait that morning, I hopped excitedly onto my seat and said one word to the education counsellor, "psychiatry". He looked dismayed as he said, "Doctor, you are getting an MS (Masters in Surgery) admission, why would you not take that?" "Umm, because I want to be a psychiatrist," I'd replied. In those brief minutes, I couldn't narrate to him all that motivated and inspired me to choose psychiatry as a specialty. In his opinion, there was an ocean of other "real medicine" branches to pursue and practise.

My close experiences with anguish, misery, and loss, and my helplessness in making a difference even though I intended to, motivated me to strive towards a career that could empower me to do so. The invisible, uncertain, and unknown intrigues me. I am captivated by how people give you just a tiny peek, but hide the mammoth remainder of the iceberg of their emotions. I wanted to explore how they truly feel, what they experience, and what could be done to make it better. Unlike climbing the tip of the iceberg where symptoms of an illness are obvious, I wanted to dive to the bottom to see what lay there, how it disturbed people's peace, and change it if I could. I knew I wanted to bring about a change, be it little or big in magnitude. Hence the post graduate degree in psychiatry.

Today, after almost two decades of practice, I think about those expressions of the classmate, colleague, and others I knew as being obvious signs of depression, across different stages of life. When we give a name to feelings, it lessens the power of the problem, and offers us the reins of control. So, we seek meaningful solutions to mend it. When we do that, we seek a cure for a documented medical problem, unlike centuries ago when depression management lay in the hands of priests instead of physicians.

I say to my patients as well as their families, "depression is a medical illness". But I also insist, "it's *incredibly* different". Unlike other medical problems where the sufferer pre-emptively runs to a professional, requests tests and seeks medication or alternative therapies to get better, many people with depression avoid seeking help owing to the stigma. I am often faced with these questions in my practice, "How come others deal with similar issues effortlessly? Why is my brother confident but I am feeble? Why is this endless struggle uniquely crafted for me? Am I fragile and incompetent? Why can I not handle this like others do?"

The answer to these questions lies in their oblivion to emotional wellness, and hence, illness too. Whether people recognise it or not, everyone around is battling an emotional war. However, some are armed with superior psychological defences, a stronger biological make-up, and better social support systems. Some people are immune to depression while others aren't. They just need to acknowledge it and do something about it, instead of hiding from their emotions.

Even today, in some segments of society and culture, depression is dreaded and feeds the irrational fear that talking about it to someone and seeking help will make you appear weak. I tell people, "You could be at a huge cocktail party with three hundred people around you who seem fine on the outside but are fighting the same battle inside. You just don't know because like you, they *too* don't talk about it. Ask anybody you feel close enough to, confidentially, if they have felt the way you do, and I bet they'll all affirm. That is why it's important to discern which thought is real and valid and realise that the voice in your head that calls you a freak–heightening your sadness and hopelessness and making you blame yourself is an unnecessary and false intrusion. It's not the truth. And it's not helpful. You are not your diagnosis. Your negative phase shall not last if you address it with the right treatment and care.

Depression treatment has long endured much analysis by spiritual healers, philosophers, doctors, and more. Written accounts of depression from 2000 B.C. attribute demoniac possession, imbalanced body fluids, weakness in temperament, and symbolic of failure. The eighteenth and nineteenth centuries saw depression as an unmodifiable weakness. Those with its severe aftermaths were shunned or locked up. In the latter part of the nineteenth century, treatments like exercise, diet, music, and drugs were advocated. Doctors suggested that it was important to talk about your problems with your friends or a physician. Benjamin Franklin suggested an early form of electroshock therapy for depression too, during this time.

It was the twentieth century that finally saw depression as a medical diagnosis. That is when Major Depressive Disorder (MDD) was added to the third edition of the *Diagnostic and Statistical Manual of Mental Disorders* (DSM-III, 1980). Psychoanalytical, behavioural, and cognitive theories were gradually proposed. Psychiatry became a stronger science and the illness model of depression explained that it deserved *timely* and *respectful* treatment. Antidepressants flooded the market. Outpatient departments (OPDs) buzzed with pharmaceutical representatives. Research aimed at the hunt for newer medication became rampant. I was involved in six such international clinical drug trials seeking medicines with better side effect profiles than their predecessors. Electroconvulsive therapy (ECT), which is an electrical shock applied to the scalp to induce a controlled seizure, was frequently used for patients with depression in the hospital ward I worked in. Because of the long-standing and chronic nature of depression, I noticed that exposure of patients to the side effects of biological treatments is long. This had to be addressed. Everything medicinal *did* make a difference, but *something*, in my opinion, wasn't just *enough*.

Since the focus of training has incessantly been so extensively placed on pharmacological (medicines and other biological means) management, discussing thoughts, emotions, behaviour, and lifestyle is often left to counsellors and social workers. But as I started to independently practice psychiatry in the real world, I observed that people's attitudes, personality, self-concept, time management, perfectionism, tolerance to frustration, interpersonal communication, feelings of guilt, excessive empathy, coping styles, sense of purpose and most importantly, long-standing beliefs about themselves, others, and the world—all influenced the quality of their mood. One tablet wasn't going to change all this magically. I had the medical know-how. Even today, I emphasise the role of medication in depression management. But I'd started to see dramatic results when a combination approach (of biological and psychological means) was applied. I had to change the way I was taught to practice.

Cognitive theories of depression had emerged in 1960s and 70s. Theorists Aaron Beck, Albert Ellis and David Burns insisted that the way in which people interpret negative events in their life, could contribute to their symptoms of depression. Also, Martin Seligman's work on helplessness and hopelessness reflected depressed people's internalisation of pessimism, which continues to leave them powerless, leaving them stuck in their status quo. I was delighted by these concepts which were time-tested and seasoned by the time I was practising in 2001. They helped me restructure people's cognitions about themselves and their world as I applied these understandings during my consultation sessions. Both medical and psychological intervention were working well for my patients.

As I grew to learn and further apply behavioural and cognitive therapy principles, it became even more obvious how depression can cloud rational judgment and dull out a brightly coloured world to a boring and listless grey. Based on its severity and type, I saw that it made patients feel irrationally pessimistic, in varying degrees. It often said to them, "You are a loser, people won't understand you, the world is a miserable place, and no matter what you do, nothing will get better". These self-defeating negative thoughts were flawed. But to my patients, they seemed deceptively real. That is why they believed that things were as bad as their mind perceived them to be. Cognitive therapy and mindfulness became my instruments to help people attack such negative thoughts, and replace them with positive, meaningful, and convincing attitudes. Awareness of these principles was key, because it was impossible to know how to set things right without knowing why and where they were going wrong.

During the pandemic when Jaico Publishing House connected with me, I was pondering over the years 2020 and 2021–how much had transpired through that time. Global statistics on the prevalence and burden of depression through the COVID-19 pandemic were revealing an alarming depression escalation–a count of 5.32 crore people worldwide. Depression had risen in the population by 27.6%. These were frightening numbers. UNESCO declared that the pandemic had caused the severest education disruption the world had ever endured. Children were stressed, parents were hassled, young couples were strained, elderly parents were losing hope, and the economy was unstable.

Depression isn't new to the world. But these numbers were. This book addresses the impact of depression in general, as well as the specific crisis generated during the pandemic, and its aftermath. We knew that a book on combating depression would surely help. More so, during my research I found that there was no book in India that clarified how cognitive methods which change one's thoughts, can better one's mood, irrespective of the environment or disrupted brain biology. The traditional medical model of depression had steered attention away from the power of the mind to control one's own emotions. We decided to collate content that could address this issue and contribute towards bettering lives.

Use of self-help books is called bibliotherapy and I am a strong proponent of its application. Jaico and I believed we needed an advanced book that could hand-hold, guide and encourage the reader in a step-by-step fashion. We knew there are many books on the shelf for depression, written by sagacious authors to cultivate a better mood and fuller life. But it was fundamental to make the reader inculcate changes which would result in improved self-management, rather than just providing bland information. I wanted to pave a way to help people realise that if they are depressed, it is critical to change, how it could be brought about, and what they needed to do to bring that transformation. This approach fits well with cognitive therapy (CT) and mindfulness, which has consistently shown marvellous results in my patients and clients. I believe there is tremendous potential to slow the rising numbers in clinical depression with the approach taught in this book. It tells you candid stories about real people I have seen over two decades in my practice, who wrestled their personal demons of sadness, self-deprecation, and depression. I have selected these accounts because their prevailing themes are so common among people, almost predictable. They highlighted their skirmishes with loved ones, battles they fought at work and in life, their distorted motivations, negative emotions, and self-defeating behaviours. This book emphasises how scientific, yet practically applicable cognitive and mindfulness techniques above and beyond the traditional use of psychiatric medication are instrumental in changing one's mood and life for the better.

This book is designed to provide thinking tools that nourish the incentive to morph yourself into the best version of your own being. In the pages to follow, you will see more examples of real people—read their stories, identify with their experiences, and walk on their path to self-enhancement. I've gone to reasonable lengths to protect their identities. Different examples might often seem alike. Yet most will be distinctive from each other. You will notice common threads in their weaving, and you might feel one with them too.

A perfect self-help handbook creates a seamless experience of bibliotherapy by coaching you to translate *your* troubled state of mind into a meaningful life. This can only happen if you apply the learnings from the book every day to full capacity. Absorbing even a little bit will be a step towards the end of the dark tunnel of depression, where I assure you, there is light of hope.

Hope itself can change life—eternally.

INTRODUCTION

YOU CAN BEAT DEPRESSION: THIS BOOK WILL TEACH YOU HOW

> "Depression has been called the world's number one public health problem. In fact, depression is so widespread it is considered the common cold of psychiatric disturbances. But there is a grim difference between depression and a cold. Depression can kill you."
>
> —David D. Burns, Stanford University School of Medicine.

Depression is much better understood today than ever before, and the scientific wakefulness about its causality is explained in the next few chapters. The *bio-psycho-social* illness model (Engel, 1977) explains how depression has biological, psychological, and social causes, and integrates these treatments to heal it. Biological management with antidepressants continues to remain a breakthrough, while Electroconvulsive Therapy (ECT) that gives a brief electrical shock to the brain under anaesthesia, Repetitive Transcranial Magnetic Stimulation (rTMS) that uses a magnetic pulse to realign nerve cells, and vagus nerve stimulation which activates the cranial nerve electrically; all of whose description is beyond the scope of this book—are all well-meaning and admirable medical efforts to help people with depression.

Yet a seamless integration of depressed people into society has not occurred. The psychoanalytical school seeks resolution of unconscious conflicts; behaviourists say that undesirable actions need to be unlearned and replaced; and biological theorists want to alter brain chemicals. Nonetheless, the focus is still largely on a cocktail of pills and brain stimulation procedures. Ever since cognitive, behavioural and mindfulness approaches emerged in the 1970s, I believe there are methods that can make you feel better, and make it last longer, without any adverse effects of biological therapies.

In this light, I have grown to believe that talking, listening, reading, and consequently, modifying your lifestyle and behaviour, are promising and approachable ways to change your reality. Cognitive Therapy (CT) techniques that this book will describe in the pages to follow, focus on reworking your thoughts. Hence, they are free of side effects. CT is as effective as medication, but in the longer term, it helps you stay depression-free for a longer time. This is because once you change the way you think, you will most likely not think negatively again. CT impact also supersedes relaxation, and psychodynamic approaches linking mental processes to early childhood experiences, both of which are otherwise routinely advocated in depression.

Brain scans [Magnetic Resonance Spectroscopy (MRS) and Single Photon Emission Computed Tomography (SPECT)] have spotted a modulation of brain chemicals (neurotransmitters) associated with depression and confirmed improvement in brain cell (neuron) functioning following cognitive therapy. Connections between cells and areas in the brain (neural networks) change following classic CBT (Cognitive Behaviour Therapy), mindfulness-based CBT as well as other interventions. When depression is severe and unrelenting with thoughts of self-harm, medication *is* needed. But even at that time, augmenting medicine with cognitive approaches prevents relapse and assures lasting wellness.

Isn't that promising?

Nobody likes to feel depressed. And yet, one who does, continues to feel so endlessly. CT is designed to defy some or many methods you've used to rid your negative reactions in the past. The "my depression is the biggest problem in my life" mentality tends to generate a circle of hostility towards depression, which is not actually a consequence of external forces. It emanates from your own mind. If you "blame" depression, you end up fighting with your own self, and nobody wins. You must change the relationship you have had with your emotions. This is the main objective of cognitive therapy.

When you learn something new, it challenges your pre-existing beliefs. In one of his interviews, psychiatrist Dr David Burns (stalwart in CBT and professor at The Stanford School of Medicine) mentioned how he had laughed off this new *cognitively inclined* approach innovated by Dr Aaron Beck (founding father of cognitive therapy) back in the 70s. He went on to be one of the first few students of Dr Beck. After attending his seminars, Burns gave up biological brain research, to practise cognitive therapy approaches, many of which he continues to innovate even today. Life is easier when change is welcomed.

How To Make This Book Work For You

This book is designed to be interactive, as if you were talking to your own therapist. Through this book, I offer you a perspective which is different from traditional medicine and counselling approaches. The suggested practices are like a supporting hand which guides you on a path to *actively* beat your negative thoughts, deal with negative emotions, and change negative lifestyles that contribute to and maintain depression. Many books offer instructions and theoretical knowledge only, but you could consider this as a practical 101 for depression. I will walk you through the visible signs of the problem and how to recognise symptoms, and then offer a structured, stepwise path towards the solution. The book is one of its kind, in that it offers applicable, actionable, and practical support. The DIY (do-it-yourself) techniques are easy to incorporate into your life whether you are on medication for depression, or even have a diagnosis of it. It has statistics, medical data, case studies and real-life stories of people who implemented this advice and accomplished their goal of living happier lives. We'll use worksheets and checklists to monitor perceptions, thoughts, feelings, and behaviours. While your moods are an effect of your genetic composition, brain chemicals, thinking styles and the environment, the easiest thing to change here is *the way you see your problems*. Hence the focus on mindfulness and cognitive processing.

This book will nudge you to evaluate how you think, pinpoint ways in which this thinking may be flawed, and direct you to change with adaptive techniques. These will help you analyse life's worrisome situations so that you see events for what they are, and not colour perceptions with a pessimistic mind's deceitful outlook. It will offer scholarly insights that are well-referenced, and have been applied over decades, with fruitful outcomes. You'll *have* to put the learning into action if you want to see a difference. How do you think that can happen?

Use this book with the right mindset

You may think, "Oh I don't need so much active work, and besides, this looks too tedious." You can start with skimming through the book but it will be enlightening only if the suggestions presented here are imbibed completely and acted upon. Putting your mind and soul into it, will make it work for you.

Make your emotional health a priority

There is always so much to do, and the clock is ticking too fast. I request you to ration out time in your day to think about what is underneath the surface to recognise how the mind can get trapped in stress, worry and rumination. A gentle prod to the rational path can transform your inner world. Just as your daily to-do list must involve physical exercise, you also need to spare time for an efficient mental workout. If not every day, it could be once in every week. But you must try to listen and follow what the book is trying to tell you.

Be persistent, and be willing to change

We all fall prey to unconstructive thoughts and feelings when we are distressed. It feels like the end of the road with nowhere to go. We are blinded by the obliviousness created by our negative beliefs. If you use a different lens, you'll see that the path to happiness is right in front of you. New skills take time to build, and old habits could take even longer to break. Be patient and let persistence carry you through. Running uphill may be difficult. But when you stay steady (even if slow), you will get up there, soon enough.

Understand the theme subjectively and objectively

Your personal experiences are unique. Some examples in the book may mirror your life completely while others may reflect behaviours in stark contrast to your own. You may or may not relate to all experiences mentioned here. But I hope as you read through them, you will build an awareness and understanding of the dysfunctional approaches they point to, and adopt the basic and advanced life management skills that this book teaches, to overpower negative thoughts.

Use the book for helping yourself or in addition to therapy

This book is written with *you* in mind. Focusing on how *you* think, feel, and behave, it unlocks a basic understanding of concepts like sadness, helplessness, hopelessness, pessimism, cognitions, cognitive therapy, and more. Anyone can benefit from this book. If you are already seeking therapy or medication, the book will complement the self-change journey you've already embarked upon. If you are aware of concepts like cognitive therapy, rational emotive behavioural therapy, acceptance and commitment therapy and mindfulness, you will find the terms familiar. If not, you'll learn and master these in no time.

I trained as a psychiatrist, worked for a while as a researcher, assessed minds and created wellness measurement tools like a psychologist, and offered solutions to change perspectives and thinking like a psychotherapist. But what I have enjoyed the most is understanding and connecting with people around me as a human being. I've spent a significant portion of my time as a professional in understanding depression and its numerous co-existent disorders. My goal in writing this book is to offer approachable, applicable, and accessible means for nurturing psychological health and wellness, and steering focus away from illness.

I've seen people get better. And I have seen them slide back into their lows. The question often is, "Why can't any method be foolproof and cure me completely?" I have said it before and I will say it again, it's not an easy battle against negativism. And if we see depression as an outside entity, we give it power over us because we label ourselves as helpless. But when we visualise depression as rooted largely in our own thoughts, it comes more under our control.

Nobody is perfect, no technique is seamless, no teacher is flawless, and no book is an answer to all of life's problems. But we can and should begin somewhere. If you use this book well, it *will* guide you to dig deeper and occupy those blank spaces in your own mind that were previously uninhabited. And you will start asking yourself the right questions so that you find meaningful and useful answers to fill up that emptiness and meaninglessness. You simply must begin thinking, feeling, and behaving in a way that equals your fundamentals and matches your core.

I have learned, observed, and practised humanistic, cognitive, behavioural, existential, mindfulness-oriented, and many other methods with patients over the past twenty years. Patients have been my best teachers as their tribulations as well as resistance to treatment has offered me the highest motivation to seek newer and more innovative answers to their (and all our) life's puzzling questions. All these techniques were devised many decades ago by stalwarts in the field like Soren Kierkegaard and Friedrich Nietzsche in existentialism, Abraham Maslow and Carl Rogers in humanism, Jon Kabat Zinn and Thich Nhat Hanh in mindfulness, Skinner and Lewinsohn in behaviourism, and Albert Ellis, Aaron Beck, and David Burns in the cognitive domain. To all these people, I offer my heartfelt gratitude, as these methods are life-changing when people embrace them. A delightful truth about reading, imbibing, and applying such deep metacognitive, behavioural, and emotive processes is that like a flower, you cannot rub the scent on others without being blessed with it yourself. It is such an unexpected and fulfilling added advantage.

If someone asks me, "Do you really believe that talking and listening to someone or reading a book that recommends changing your thinking style, *can* change your life forever?", my answer is a resounding "Yes!"

Let's begin.

PART - I

KNOW THE ENEMY IF YOU WANT TO FIGHT IT

"If you know the enemy and know yourself, you need not fear a hundred battles. If you know yourself but not the enemy, for every victory gained you will also suffer defeat. If you know neither the enemy nor yourself, you will succumb in every battle."

—Sun Tzu

EVERYONE IN THE WORLD *KNOWS SOMEONE WHO HAS DEPRESSION*, yet hardly anyone really *knows depression (in the way that they could actually help them heal)*. Doctors and patients both, still don't have all answers to intriguing questions like: "Why did I alone get depressed? How come this treatment hasn't worked? How come that pill helped my friend but not me? Am I not trying hard enough? When will I become okay?"

This section of the book will open your eyes to the nature of this cruel illness, how it is different from everyday sadness, why some people unfortunately get afflicted it while others don't, how it could masquerade in different forms to fool you, and how we need a structured approach to combat it. If you know depression, you will be empowered to fight it.

1

You Can't Beat Depression without Beating Its Stigma

> "No one would ever tell a cancer patient to 'just get over it.' Why people think they can tell those with depression as much, is baffling."
>
> —Sara Ella, *Coral*

Aryabhatta knew that zero matters, even though it appears insignificant. The stigma about depression is that seemingly trivial zero—an invisible, lurking, unfortunate wanderer in a depressed person's journey, that's worsening an already merciless struggle. Therefore, this chapter discusses stigma.

Societal stigma about depression is a negative, rather unreasonable and unfair social attitude attached to those who are depressed. It oftentimes places shame and humiliation on them, as if they are deficient compared to the rest of the world. Frequent open societal disapproval ensues. For example, people stereotype depressed people as lazy, weak, emotionally fragile, cowardly as well as attention-seekers and shunners of responsibility. Some feel that such a person would make an unworthy friend, incomplete partner, inefficient worker, or an incapable parent.

Imagine if this were true for a physical illness. Losing a job because of arthritis, a marriage proposal failing because of gastritis, or friends boycotting you because of appendicitis. And this is when depression *is* a medical illness. Wouldn't it be horrifying to think that if you met with an accident or woke up being afflicted by a parasitic disease caused by a mosquito bite, the world would treat you differently, misunderstand you, or reject you? In fact, in such a case, everyone usually tends to coax you to take tests, see the best experts in the field, and even suggest multiple medical opinions from different professionals to get the best possible help available. They care even more and offer additional assistance to help you get back on your feet, to live the full and wholesome life you deserve.

At the dinner table, a man announces: "I have an endoscopy in three days, guys. This gastritis a nuisance. I'll let you know how I do." Immediately others ask, "Hey do you need me to drive you to hospital? Should I arrange for bland food after the endoscopy? I'll cover for you at work if needed". But the other guy doesn't say, "Friends, I'm depressed and I'm seeing my psychiatrist tomorrow. I need your support to feel better, to live a happier life." And yet, the truth is that depression is a bigger killer than gastritis.

Why the disparity in mental and physical illnesses?

Depression Stigma: Then And Now

In 2016, Rossler said "There is no country, society, or culture wherein people with mental illness have the same societal value as people without a mental illness". Stigmatisation of mental illness has a tradition. In ancient Greece, stigma was a bad word that branded slaves and criminals. Depression and other mental illnesses weren't treated any different. Sufferers were imprisoned, banished, and tortured. The Middle Ages called it 'a punishment of

God' and 'possession by the Devil'. The penalty was to burn them alive, or chain them to the wall or their beds, in 'madhouses'.

During the peak of the Nazi reign, Germany reinforced manslaughter and sterilisation as a potential solution for mental illness. True, society today no longer imprisons, burns, or kills people for being psychologically ill. But some current attitudes could still be deemed unworthy of modern welfare. American sociologist Erwin Goffman's book *Stigma: Notes on the Management of Spoiled Identity* published in 1963 really laid the foundation for stigma research as a scientific discipline.

These findings from a 2020 review published in *BMC Psychiatry* about stigma associated with mental health problems in India are alarming. One-third of young Indians display poor knowledge of mental health problems and hold negative attitudes towards people suffering from them. An astonishing one in five show actual or intended stigmatising behaviour. In general, many Indians believe that individuals with mental illness are:

- Unable to control their problem
- Likely to be dangerous or criminal
- Cowards who lack willpower
- Difficult to like as human beings
- Blameworthy for their problems
- Less intelligent than normal people
- Impulsive, prone to changing minds
- Unable to keep up commitments
- Capable of only minor responsibilities
- Significantly responsible for divorces

The review also emphasised that youth in India are unaccepting of the autonomy of those suffering from mental illness and did not consider them capable of managing their personal and professional lives. When the young population feels this way, the hope for a better attitude towards depression begins to diminish.

Public Stigma

We assume that developing countries harbour prejudiced attitudes, which fade as we progress to developed ones. Contrastingly, stigma-researcher JianLi Wang, PhD (University of Calgary, Canada, 2010) observed that in Canada 43.3% people assumed "weakness of character" as a likely cause of depression, 45.9% believed depressed people were "unpredictable" and 21.9% feared that they are "dangerous". PhD scholar Pescoscolido, (stigma researcher at Indiana University, 2008) noted that 68% of US individuals did not want a person with a mental illness to marry into their family, and 58% would not like them in their workplace. In another research conducted in Germany in 2014, 47% of people endorsed that they would think lesser of an individual who had been admitted to a mental hospital. In Great Britain (2012), it was observed that depression does not conform to the hegemonic masculinity notion that asserts strength. So, they believe that men cannot and do not get depressed. Therefore, if they do, they don't seek help.

Courtesy Stigma

Another perception to worry about is courtesy stigma. This is transferred from the depressed person to family, like parents, siblings, spouses, children, and other relatives. Family courtesy stigma surfaces as shame and guilt for being responsible for the person's depression or it could reflect in anger and rebuke towards them, which arises out of embarrassment. Family reactions could range from distress and frustration to over-sympathising and badgering. Depressed people I know have repeatedly expressed how they wish their own family acknowledged that this is an illness and supported their treatment, instead of treating them like mutant aliens who need constant nagging and supervision. A Swedish study (Ostman, M., & Kjellin, L, 2002) on family members had reported how they wished their afflicted relative had never been born. How people perceive depression really decides the way they react to those who have it.

EXERCISE: How I Perceive Depression In Others

Look at the list of statements below. They reflect how you might think and feel. A large part of human motivation is subconscious. We can only change it if we bring this to conscious awareness. You can't set things right if you don't know where they are going wrong. Let's see how your subconscious mind might think about depression. Do put a check mark (√) against the statement if you have ever thought or felt this way.

- ☐ People with depression should just snap out of it.
- ☐ Depressed people are dangerous and unreliable.
- ☐ Depression is contagious.
- ☐ I wouldn't confide in a friend who has been depressed.
- ☐ If a friend is depressed, I won't take her opinion seriously.
- ☐ I can't see a depressed person the same way I see others.
- ☐ I would be apprehensive to employ a person with a history of depression, to be my child's nanny or caretaker.
- ☐ I would not feel like hiring a manager if I knew they had been depressed.
- ☐ I would worry about the capability of my child's schoolteacher if I knew that they had a history of depression.

- ☐ I wouldn't choose a life partner who's had depression.
- ☐ I wouldn't be comfortable dating someone with depression.
- ☐ I feel that depressed people don't try hard enough.
- ☐ I wouldn't seek advice from a depressed relative.
- ☐ I think I would not see a person who's been admitted to hospital for depression, the same way I see someone else.

Were any of these true for you? Many of you might feel, "Oh I've heard that, but I don't think like that". You might be aware of the public stigma but don't nourish it, live by it, or endorse it. Yet, you may not always oppose it. Even subtle stereotyped thinking and prejudiced emotionality can outcaste someone who's already feeling so low about their life.

SELF-STIGMA

For depressed persons, emotional trauma is twofold. First, they battle the limitations that depression poses on a day-to-day basis, alongside juggling negative thoughts, which in severe cases may question the validity of existence itself. Second, they agonise over the stereotypes, prejudice, and discrimination, not just from an aloof and ignorant society at large, but also from friends, family, partners, and other near and dear ones whom they trust most. *Self-stigma is a disease.* Initially there is internalisation of misconceptions about depression. This is then followed by shattered self-esteem, further limiting prospects for recovery.

EXERCISE: HOW I PERCEIVE DEPRESSION IN ME

Look at these statements. These too, reflect how you think and feel. Depression tends to push you in a self-defeating vicious cycle. You need to be aware of how you think about your low mood. Put a check mark (√) if you have thought or felt this way.

- ☐ Emotionally weak people get depressed, so I must be weak.
- ☐ I should stay away, else my low mood will rub off on people.
- ☐ Nobody will want to be friends with me if I'm depressed.
- ☐ People will think I'm unpredictable. I should avoid them.
- ☐ If I am depressed, then I must be feeble-minded.
- ☐ Depression makes me feel like an unworthy person.
- ☐ Others won't let me see their kids if I'm depressed.
- ☐ I have depression, so I'm incapable of applying for that job.
- ☐ People will disregard my opinion if I am depressed.
- ☐ If I speak about depression, normal people will mock me.
- ☐ I'd rather not speak to anybody about how I really feel.
- ☐ Talking to an outsider about my problem cannot help me.
- ☐ My depression is something I've created in my mind.
- ☐ I should stay away from people and get okay on my own.
- ☐ If people know I'm depressed, they'll think I'm crazy.

How many of these were true for you? Nobody is immune to depression, or its stigma. The impact of stigmatising beliefs isn't just directed externally towards others, but also inwards towards oneself. The fact is, if you have held stereotypical beliefs about depression, you are more likely to apply them on yourself and feel more stigmatised. These beliefs rob you of your basic human rights–to be socially engaged, involved, and to belong. Because you believe in hiding depression, you become more isolated.

Stigma and ignorance make you believe that depression is *a phase* that you must fight, and that it would not have occurred if you were a little stronger. That is why you might give up on healing opportunities in anticipation of denial, break social connections fearing rejection, and refrain from seeking treatment, believing that there's really no hope. Shame and guilt innate to depression are already big demons to tackle. This added to the disgrace and embarrassment of having a feeble character clearly cannot help. Depression isn't half the enemy, as the stigma surrounding it is. You can't beat depression without beating its stigma.

It was March 2016. Initially, it seemed like just another late Sunday afternoon. I'd left my cousin's house after a family brunch to head back home. I immediately found myself party to a crowd that the local police were gently requesting to disperse. I heard an undesirable chatter about Sheila. People did not know much about how Sheila felt, at least not while she was alive. It was all assumption anyway. Neighbours watched in horror through the huge glass window, as the police lowered Sheila's body and removed the dupatta which she'd used to tie around her neck to hang herself from the ceiling fan. Sheila had committed suicide.

The medical staff were talking to her 9-year-old boy who had witnessed this horrific event. Some bystanders mocked, "How did that ceiling take her weight?" Many cried in furore, "How weak can a woman be to do this to herself?" Yet another spoke, "I wonder how people can be so narcissistic. She only thought about herself. Could she not think about her little son or husband?"

I stood there aghast, pensively reflecting on their attitude. As a frequent visitor to the neighbourhood, I'd known of Sheila being withdrawn and less communicative. Was there no acquaintance or friend or family member who was aware of her struggle? Or did they know, and not have the time or inclination to understand how she felt?

I heard from a friendly neighbour that Sheila was most likely battling depression since the time she had been married, 10 years ago. Her husband was chronically alcohol dependent, and evidently, support from him had been minimal. Her own family was very traditional in their thinking and did not favour a separation or divorce. They also did not think that depression was a "real thing" nor support the idea of Sheila seeking help. On a little probing, I learned that her father had a long-standing history of depression too. She struggled to make ends meet and bore the wrath of an alcoholic partner and his daily beatings. Yes, she had a child, and he was her responsibility. Her suicide note mentioned that she was guilty of doing this and hoped that somehow her son would have a better future without a mother as "horrible" as her.

Sheila evidently had severe major depressive disorder that culminated in suicide. She wanted to be a good mother. She tried to be the best employee. She toiled to be a worthy wife. But her biological predisposition, lack of social support, her current situation, and essentially clouded judgment with lack of timely help most likely coaxed her into what she thought was the best solution to end her life's suffering.

Which was, to end life itself.

If she had perceived less of self, as well as public stigma, she'd probably be alive, happy, and well today. According to the World Health Organisation (WHO), one person in the world commits suicide every 45 seconds and the largest contributor to this is depression. In fact, suicide is the fourth leading cause of death in 15-to-29-year-olds worldwide. Ironically, many people continue to believe that depression is not a worrisome illness.

If Sheila was upset, she may have not been thinking straight to make the best judgment call. If she had thought carefully, the outcome might have been different. The problem is that self-defeating thoughts always seem so deviously logical, that one ends up believing them, and spirals down the black hole of ambivalence. We've all felt this way at some point, maybe in a lesser magnitude.

Each one of us needs to know this, understand it, and do something to change it. Sheila could have reached out. She could have sought help. She could have felt happy. But she didn't.

Can Stigma Be Fought?

To defeat the many forms of stigma, you need to stop getting caught up in what "they say" and focus on how "you feel". The fear of being outcast promotes illness secrecy. That is why you hide your "depression secret" in the closet. This way it gets buried deeper and the world stigmatises it more. When more people speak about it, the statistical normalcy becomes apparent. Selective disclosure can be a good start. Your depression does not have to be a status update on social media. However, sharing your feelings with a close friend, reliable family member, peer support group or empathic mental health professional for a start, will make you realise that you're not alone.

Stigma to Acceptance (feeling the worst to getting better)

Isolate very well

↓

Conceal, don't tell

↓

Selectively confide

↓

Majorly, still hide

↓

Universally reveal

↓

Broadcast and heal

EXERCISE: I Can/ Will Beat Depression Stigma

Stigma isn't your doing, not even self-stigma. It's indirect and involuntary conditioning that needs to be broken. Stigma is a social creation—so subtle and sinister that bringing it out is itself vexing. An unfortunate internalisation of a discriminatory mindset by a segment of a less informed society, stigma prevents you from accepting the normalcy of depression like any other medical illness. So, to combat it, you must change existing faulty theories, fight ignorance, get facts straight, be open to suggestion, build faith, preserve hope, gain perspective, and assess ways in which depression can be beaten. It all starts with overcoming the self-defeating unhealthy beliefs around depression and collectively transforming thoughts to vanquish it.

Read these affirmations and try to internalise them. Put a check mark (√) on the statements that already mirror your beliefs. And in time see if you can check *all* of them.

Depression

- ☐ is an illness, and not a personality or character flaw
- ☐ is not a mysterious or demoniac possession
- ☐ is not evil, dangerous, or threatening
- ☐ doesn't make people weird, creepy, or crazy
- ☐ does not make people weak, feeble, or delicate
- ☐ is not the sufferer's fault and isn't a cry for attention
- ☐ co-exists with talent, aptitude, and other positive traits
- ☐ does not have anything to do with intelligence
- ☐ does not take away the skill to be a good partner
- ☐ does not lower the potential to excel in one's life
- ☐ does not make a person an incompetent friend
- ☐ does not take away the ability to be compassionate and kind
- ☐ is an illness and can be treated, just like any other

- ☐ is not contagious, and does not rub off on people
- ☐ deserves my care, understanding and attention
- ☐ can be beaten if I work towards beating its stigma
- ☐ has biological, psychological, and social treatments
- ☐ can be overcome, and my world can be a better place

The first six statements stamp the shame about the causation of depression. The next six break the misconceptions about a depressed person being incompetent, and the final six beat the disgrace related to depression treatment.

Stigma of depression is unnecessary in your life's journey. But you don't *have* to let it worsen your already choppy voyage. You don't have to fight the entire world. You can start with defeating the demons that gnaw *you* from within. Don't feed them by absorbing pessimism from the outside. Make yourself a priority and stay projected towards your recovery goal.

Depression is ***not*** your fault. When you believe that, the walls of stigma you've built in your mind, will start to crumble. And your battle against depression will be half won.

2

Sadness versus Depression: Know the Difference

"When you're lost in those woods, it sometimes takes you a while to realize that you are lost. For the longest time, you can convince yourself that you've just wandered off the path, that you'll find your way back to the trailhead any moment now. Then night falls again and again, and you still have no idea where you are, and it's time to admit that you have bewildered yourself so far off the path that you don't even know from which direction the sun rises anymore."

—Elizabeth Gilbert

Normalcy And Abnormality

Sadness is a common emotion, fleeting over a few seconds to sometimes hours, days, weeks or more. Evolutionally, it functions rather adaptively—it helps us cope with loss, overcome failure, learn new skills, and engage in rewarding actions. We understand sadness by how it affects our body, mind and behaviour. At a physical level, sadness is drooped eyelids, downcast eyes, a typical central forehead frown, lowered corners of the lips with an inability to smile, and frequently, a slouched posture and slowed body movement. At an emotional level we use complex linguistic terms to describe sadness as dullness, anguish, grief, loneliness, agony, guilt, sorrow, distress or melancholy (in graded intensity). And at the behavioural level, sadness could encompass stagnation, inertia, withdrawal, irritation, unproductivity, inactivity, or crying. Sadness is one of six 'basic' emotional expressions, along with happiness, anger, surprise, fear, and disgust.

So why the fuss over sadness if it is such a routine and fundamental human emotion?

Because depression as we discussed earlier, is the single largest contributor to global disability. Such a high prevalence of this condition exists only because most of us are unable to prevent everyday sadness from progressing to depression. Sadness is uncomfortable, unhelpful, uninvited, and unwanted. According to the depression continuum explanation, sadness and major depression lie on a spectrum, with long-standing sadness sitting somewhere in between. The brain and neurochemical mechanisms for both are essentially the same.

Repeatedly thinking about sadness makes it build on itself, allows it to become long-standing, and finally cements it to a depressed mood state. Even when extreme, sadness is just *one* of the many symptoms that reward you with the diagnosis of depression. Clinical depression diagnosis requires the presence of at least five out of nine major symptoms for a minimum duration of *two weeks*. These are: depressed mood or extreme sadness, reduced interest or pleasure in usual activities, sleep difficulties, changes in weight or eating, retardation or agitation in the body or mind, fatigue, feelings of worthlessness or guilt, lessened concentration span, and thoughts about death or suicidal ideation.

The internet has expanded the general awareness about every medical illness to such an extent, that people find it hard to resist the urge to self-diagnose. Medicalisation of sadness means concluding minor symptoms into a major diagnosis. If you assess yourself online with unsubstantiated tests, you could misconstrue all sadness as clinical depression. On the other hand, the stigmatisation of real depression could make you wary of admitting to a low mood, so much that you anticipate people judging you negatively for being sad, and making you hide it. This way, you never appropriately realise how you're feeling and how you need to make it better.

We need a valid boundary to separate *major* depression from *normal* sadness.

Every human being is conditioned to react in specific ways to situations. Some of this is innate (nature) which is not in your control, and a large part of this is acquired (nurture), which is how you have learned to react, from previous life experiences. The distress you feel in response to life events is a dialectical balance between these two constructs. Some examples include grieving the loss of someone you love, joblessness, interpersonal stress, conflict, divorce, failure, abuse, violence, broken dreams, unmet goals, and general doubts about life and the future. We're all likely to feel bad, lose our sleep and/ or appetite, avoid people, and even cry endlessly in these situations. An occasionally fleeting feeling of meaninglessness could also set in. We ignore it because it usually passes. But depression is enduring, and you deserve to wade your way out of it, to live life wholesomely. For that you need to know what demon you're fighting. Let's see how you can do this.

EXERCISE: Make Sense of Your Sadness

Sadness is subjective. This means, it is an emotion that *you* feel, acknowledge, and convey. Another person in the same setting may not sense it the way you do. And so, your dialogue with yourself decides your emotional state. Imagine someone asking you the question "how are you doing?" Contemplate whether these statements pop in your head as a response. Please put a check mark (√) on ones that you feel have been true for you.

- ☐ I'm feeling low.
- ☐ I'm down in the dumps.
- ☐ I am lonely.
- ☐ Everything is appearing bland.
- ☐ I feel miserable.
- ☐ I just don't feel good.
- ☐ I'm going through a difficult phase.
- ☐ I feel something snapped in my brain.
- ☐ I feel a nagging pressure.
- ☐ I'm experiencing a dip in my mood.
- ☐ My mood is 'dark'.
- ☐ I am stuck in a black cloud.
- ☐ I feel pathetic.
- ☐ I am blank.
- ☐ Something is not right in my head.
- ☐ I am a bit depressed.

All these statements create a narrative for you and the people you communicate with. Your answers help you make meaning of what you are feeling. For example, if you realise that "something is not right in my head", then it's a sign that this is more than a normative sadness in response to a stressor (however usual or unusual this stressor may be). Let's learn from the conversation of two characters, Meera and Jaya.

Meera and Jaya were chatting at the informal office party one evening in late December. "We've missed you. Why have you not made an appearance these last few months?" Meera questioned. Jaya said, "I've been feeling down for nearly a month now. I don't sleep or eat too well and nothing's fun anymore. I've been wanting to stay home all day and thankfully working from home helps me isolate. I feel I should hibernate. Meera, I absolutely like you, that's not the issue. But I don't like talking to *anyone*. So, I've stayed away. I just thought I'd try and reconnect today for a change. So, I'm here"

Meera was concerned, "Oh, but your work has been great and we discussed it the other day at the annual review meeting too. Is this the winter blues? Or your hormones by any chance?" Jaya got emotional. "The problem is that nobody understands. I spoke to my sister, and she said I might need antidepressants and should seek therapy. How can she say that? She doesn't even know what's going on. I think nobody has a clue about how I feel. I'm not going to talk to anyone about my feelings anymore."

Both Jaya and Meera, could not make sense of Jaya's mood. To me as a professional, the depression is starkly evident. Jaya's sad mood, loss of interest in previously pleasurable tasks, sleep and appetite disturbances, agitation, and fatigue—all lasted for more than two weeks. Jaya had narrated the diagnostic criteria for major depression as per the Diagnostic and Statistical Manual for Mental Disorders – 5th Edition (DSM-5) like a checklist without even intending it. But like Meera and Jaya, most people do not decipher this complex emotional code to see the depression exhibiting itself so obviously. Maybe neither was ready for a depression label. Hence Meera suggested "winter blues" and "hormones" as the probable cause, and Jaya was upset with the "antidepressant" or "therapy" proposition by her sister, because it would have labelled her as a "depressed" person.

It is true that treatment with antidepressants is not the complete answer. It's also a fact that an impulsively offered depression label from a loved one seems stigmatising. But this is a question of making sense of *how you feel.* Jaya's clouded mind led her to altered emotional reactivity; so, she retorted negatively. She failed to do what was right, which was to see that this was more than ordinary sadness and seek the right guidance to help her out of a likely depression. She didn't even want to consider it. Her colleague, too, did not direct her to this idea. Jaya needed to investigate her feelings, make sense of them, and know that these weren't normal.

Have you been able to do that?

EXERCISE: See The Context of Your Sadness

Sadness is likely to occur when you're in a situation that is challenging, demanding, or draining. Also, this tends to happen when people are rejecting, judging, and denying. But what about the times when situations have been rewarding, and people around you have actually been welcoming and nice? What is the dialogue in the mind at that time? Is there a negative tweak? Put a check mark (√) on the statements that have crossed your mind at a time when something good happened, but you didn't trust it would last.

- ☐ This is just a fluke.
- ☐ It's not going to last for long.
- ☐ They're pity rewarding me.
- ☐ I don't deserve this promotion.
- ☐ This 5-star rating is a mistake.

- ☐ She's being nice out of pity.
- ☐ A party won't help me feel better.
- ☐ That's not my favourite anymore.
- ☐ Life isn't going to be happy again.
- ☐ The pain is here to stay.
- ☐ My favourite comedy show isn't funny anymore.
- ☐ I'll be unhappy no matter what.
- ☐ It's too effortful to feel anything.
- ☐ Life has lost its vibrant colour.
- ☐ Life is black and white now.
- ☐ This isn't about you, it's just me.

What does this narrative say about the context of sadness? It is clearly announcing that "something is not right and it's not going to become right," and that "it doesn't matter why this negative feeling surfaced, it's here to stay". This signals more than a situational sadness, that has now crisscrossed your existence and isn't restricted to a stressful situation that may have brought it on. Sadness might be a passing state, but depression tends to be like a persistent trait.

If you remember Meera and Jaya's conversation at the party, at some point Meera had complimented Jaya's performance. To which Jaya replied, "You're being nice, and I appreciate it. Truth is, I am not really doing a great job. In fact, I wonder if you're saying this just to make me feel good. It embarrasses me because I don't want people's mercy. One freak chance might just have been a good streak of luck. I doubt it will strike me again."

Meera didn't know what to say and she tried to change the conversation, "Oh well, we're here at the party finally so let's have a good time!" Jaya countered it with "This isn't making me feel better. My mood doesn't really change even with the usual fun stuff that I enjoyed in the past. I'll just go home, I guess. Why be a bother to happy people? You guys have a good time. Bye for now."

What's going on inside the brain in depression can be so intense, that a situational change is unable to transform how you feel in a snap. Humans aren't machines. Jaya could not sense the situational context. She was in a fun space, with a good friend who was trying to help, but her sadness was so pervasive that it had engulfed her, and she lost voluntary control over her mood. She was almost aggressive, but passively so. She felt like she had no power to make it better.

EXERCISE: Spot Check on Sense of Control

When you take personal accountability for events in your life, you tend to deal with them responsibly. In depression, this knack may be lost and you seem to lose control. Put a check mark (√) on the statements that may have crossed your mind when something unfortunate happened to you.

- ☐ This only happens to me, somehow.
- ☐ I'm the only one who's got problems.
- ☐ Other people are luckier than I am.
- ☐ Nothing goes my way.
- ☐ I'm cursed.
- ☐ Others have it easy.
- ☐ I try, but it never works.
- ☐ I have a black destiny.
- ☐ If only I was lucky.
- ☐ This is unfair.
- ☐ This sadness hit me from nowhere.
- ☐ I can't do much about how I feel.

- ☐ The feeling isn't going to leave me.
- ☐ I can't manage this.
- ☐ Nobody can help me.
- ☐ I can't go on like this.

This kind of narrative discounts personal responsibility. It pronounces that "things are wrong but they're not in my control," and "it doesn't matter what I do, the sadness is not going away". These statements could outwardly express themselves as helplessness with or without resentment. Both unfortunately don't help.

In time, Jaya was increasingly frazzled at work. Meera was a co-worker, but also a good friend, so she made some internal considerations and eased off her responsibility to some extent. But gradually, Jaya's performance became erratic. Some days her work was good and on others, improper. She was sleeping less, eating junk food, and had isolated socially. She said to Meera once, "Since I am working from home, somehow pressure has risen. There's no margin separating day and night, or bedroom and office. I haven't been able to exercise. I'm getting frequent colds as these come when I don't sleep enough. My usual food delivery places have shut down and I don't see any nutritious options available. You have your husband and kids to make you feel better; I must endure this pressure all by myself." There was some bitterness in her voice. And yet, she did not wilfully intend to sound that way.

It didn't matter what the reality was. Jaya felt powerless. Her loss of control was feeding into helplessness, passivity, anger, frustration, disinterest, and meaninglessness. She didn't see the point in being proactive and continued to blame her situation. It was as if she didn't realise that there *were* options and alternatives for everything that she deemed was a problem. Depression was discounting all liability, and she was defenceless. Have you felt powerless like this? Did you realise that this was not normal?

All sadness is not depression. But all depression could start with, and/or entail enduring sadness. Let's see what we can do about it.

Depression DSM-5 Diagnostic Criteria

The DSM-5 outlines the following criteria to make a diagnosis of depression. The individual must be experiencing five or more symptoms during the same 2-week period and at least one of the symptoms should be either (1) depressed mood or (2) loss of interest or pleasure.

- Depressed mood most of the day, nearly every day.
- Markedly diminished interest or pleasure in all, or almost all activities most of the day, nearly every day.
- Significant weight loss when not dieting or weight gain or decrease or increase in appetite nearly every day.
- A slowing down of thought and a reduction of physical movement (observable by others, not merely subjective feelings of restlessness or being slowed down).
- Fatigue or loss of energy nearly every day.
- Feelings of worthlessness or excessive or inappropriate guilt nearly every day.
- Diminished ability to think or concentrate, or indecisiveness, nearly every day.
- Recurrent thoughts of death, recurrent suicidal ideation without a specific plan, or a suicide attempt or a specific plan for committing suicide.
- To receive a diagnosis of depression, these symptoms must cause the individual clinically significant distress or

impairment in social, occupational, or other important areas of functioning. The symptoms must also not be a result of substance abuse or another medical condition.

American Psychiatric Association. 2013. Diagnostic Criteria from DSM-5 (R). Arlington, TX: American Psychiatric Association Publishing.

3

Why We Get Depressed: Know the Depressed Brain

"That's the thing about depression: A human being can survive almost anything, as long as she sees the end in sight. But depression is so insidious, and it compounds daily, that it's impossible to ever see the end. The fog is like a cage without a key."

—Elizabeth Wurtzel, Author

Have you observed how siblings, born to the same parents, gone to the same school, and had similar opportunities in their early years, reacted differently when they were made to suddenly shift school during teenage? One welcomed it and the other was angry, upset, and depressed? Have you noticed two friends, both having gone through their own relationship breakups in early adulthood coped contrarily? One went on to find a better partner and was happily married; and the other was heartbroken, sullen, and sad for the longest time ever? Or how diverse people diagnosed with cancer, or subjected to sexual assault or physical and emotional trauma responded to these misfortunes in unique and unconnected ways? Some used the experience positively and grew through them, while others went down the path of dejection?

That's the truth about depression. It's not a one-size-fits-all illness. There are striking similarities in the cause, presentation, and treatment of all kinds of depression. In the coming chapters, I will show you how all of these can be so distinctive to the observing eye that they appear to be independent disorders. For now, let's peek inside a typical depressed brain with a magnifying glass, to see how it works or doesn't.

It's My Brain Chemicals

Serotonin, dopamine, and adrenaline (epinephrine) have become common lingo today. We know from movies, novels, and hearsay that depression is caused by a chemical imbalance in the brain. While this is scientifically sound, it oversimplifies the complex causality of this seemingly modest illness.

The brain (like every organ in the human body) is made up of several smaller units (brain cells or neurons). The human brain is estimated to comprise 10,000 crore neurons and 5,00,000 crore glial cells (neuronal assistants) that support them to function. An average human brain weighs 1,500 grams and hence based on how much your body weighs, this forms 2 to 3% of your body weight. Yet, your brain uses 20% of your body's energy budget. Human cognitive (thinking) abilities have surpassed that of all other mammals, defying evolution. It is this dynamic system of your brain that determines how you see things, perceive emotions, and make meaning of your life's experiences.

All depression *is* biological. This means some neurochemicals are always deranged when you feel sad. But depression is more than the seesawing of one or two haphazard brain chemicals. A genetic predisposition, faulty neural connections, impaired information processing, stressful life events, reduced coping capacity, defective thinking styles, unsatisfactory social support, dysfunctional family environment, poor friendships, psychoactive substances of abuse, and medical illnesses; countless forces interact with each other before the bubble bursts, and depression makes its presence known in your life.

This is exactly the reason why those siblings I mentioned earlier, the friends with breakups, as well as other people who go through traumatic experiences, react differently. On the outside every depressed person could feel sad, lose interest in pleasurable tasks, lack motivation, sense inexplicable fatigue, endure hopelessness and want to end his or her life. But on the inside the depression story is different for each one. And so is the treatment.

MY HEART ACHES

We've long believed that we think with our brain and feel from the heart. We've even said it out loud in conversation, "He uses his brain for everything, he doesn't have a heart!" or "She's so soft-hearted, she'd cry at the drop of a pin!" or "My son carries his heart on his sleeve, I wish he was stronger!"

Truth is, we don't feel from the heart; we do so from the emotional part of our brain. Specific portions of our 1,500-gram brain are designated to sense, monitor, modulate, regulate, and express emotions. These specific brain segments constitute the "limbic system" or the "emotional brain". We can't unfortunately see this section directly on an X-Ray, CT scan or MRI. However, in research settings, newer scanning techniques like positron emission tomography (PET), single-photon emission computed tomography (SPECT), and functional magnetic resonance imaging (fMRI) allow us to see which area of the brain gets active when we think in a particular way, or what chemical gets released when we feel a specific emotion. This makes it easier for us to understand and correct what goes wrong inside a malfunctioning brain.

Consider your favourite comedian for a moment, who you find funny. He always makes you chuckle. But if you were at a funeral and someone messaged you his video clip, you wouldn't laugh then, would you? Also, a snide remark from a best friend usually seems like banter, but the same from an office colleague seems offensive and gets you upset. And then, if you had to spend all your time with a friend, partner, boss, neighbours, or family member who repeatedly gets you frustrated, you might begin to feel depressed over time. And that favourite comedian will not be able to make you laugh anymore, no matter what. Have you noticed this happen to you?

Connections between neurons (neural circuits) inside your brain have different brain chemicals driving them. With time some neurons grow, multiply or even regress. If over an extended period, you've had multiple rejections, frustrations, and setbacks, your neural circuits change, chemicals transform, growth of the neurons alters, and the whole brain could get transformed. That is why a single low mood does not change your disposition, but after a long period of sustained low moods, your brain resets the mood centre to "stay bad" always. That is when depression has announced its unwelcome arrival.

More About The Emotional Brain

All research on depression points to three brain segments that I will introduce here. The thalamus (chamber), hippocampus (sea horse), and amygdala (almond). These words are of Greek origin. I have reasonably oversimplified this information to help you understand the depressed brain. This does not express complex neurological connotations that would otherwise be shared in medical and research settings. Yet, this will scientifically help you understand the powerhouse of your life, your brain, better.

Thalamus, the word means "chamber". Like a sorting ground, the thalamus receives sensory information and sends it around to different parts of the brain to organise, analyse and scrutinise, for the next plan of action. Thalamus is hence relaying important proprietary information to the amygdala and hippocampus. But before that, it's sending it to higher parts of the brain that think and reappraise whether this information is useful or harmful, happy or sad, productive or unproductive, and so on. When the brain gives the thalamus its verdict, the thalamus sends it out to the amygdala and hippocampus.

Amygdala is a small almond like brain structure that makes you responsive to any emotion. This could include positive and upbeat, as well as negative and undesirable emotions. Especially when you're feeling an upsetting or frightening emotion strongly, the amygdala becomes very active. If you get stressed and are unable to modulate or tone down emotions, your amygdala is most likely misbehaving in response to an elevated stress hormone. With long-standing depression, the size of the amygdala may change too. To feel better, it becomes important to bring the amygdala back to normal functioning and behave itself.

Hippocampus is a curved brain structure that resembles a sea horse, hence the name. It's where we keep all our memories, positive as well as negative. If we recall our life's positive memories all the time, we'll never feel unhappy. But if we choose to ignore delightful moments and focus on the adverse happenings of our day; we'll eternally sense sadness. Imagine a situation in which the misbehaving and hyperactive amygdala connects with a selectively filtering hippocampus that chooses to place the spotlight on negative memories? This blows negativity and pessimism out of proportion. And unsurprisingly, you become depressed.

This explanation makes it clear that emotion-laden information is received by the brain-sorting chamber (thalamus) and sent out to an executive centre where a decision is made at the higher level to reappraise it as positive or negative. Then it is relayed to the emotional processing unit (amygdala) and finally warehoused into a long-term memory store (hippocampus).

All this information can be brought out *anytime* for future use. Different chemicals facilitate this process. They decide what message to send out from one neuron to the other. And in an evolutionally determined smooth flowing brain system, this happens for the positive. We were designed to be habitually *not* depressed, *not* negative and *not* pessimistic.

Back To Chemicals: The Fuelling Force

We are chemically-run electrical creatures. Chemical substances generate electric potentials that drive our body systems. Several thousand chemicals are at play, while you read this book too, for example. Here is a table showing the effect of just a handful of brain chemicals or neurotransmitters that could be involved in depression (there are many more, but these are significant and top the list).

Acetylcholine	Happy and sad memories, recall of past events
Serotonin	Sleep, appetite, pain, impulsivity, suicidality
Dopamine	Reward, happiness, wellness, motivation
Norepinephrine	Reward, motivation, anxiety, apprehension
Glutamate	Feeling in extremes, catastrophising, reacting
GABA	Sense of control, calmness, retaining inhibitions

Like all machines, body systems occasionally fail, chemicals get deranged (quantity or quality), and the human brain falters. At such a time, for many diverse reasons, the brain chemicals or neurotransmitters cannot keep the normal mood going. The mind's homeostasis or status quo gets broken. Neurotransmitters are suddenly not enough; signals between cells hence don't process rightly, the amygdala overreacts, and hippocampus recalls bad memories. How would you not feel depressed, with this entire muddle inside you?

Bringing It Together

I would be surprised if this thought hasn't run through your brain yet.

"So, what's really making ***me*** so depressed? Why did only ***my*** brain malfunction?"

At least I am hoping that you have clarity on the chemicals in your brain, the neural circuits, and the relaying mechanics between the processing centres. But the golden question still is, "*why you*?"

- It could be your genes.
- It could be your life events.
- It could be early trauma.
- It could be loss you endured.
- It could be the season.
- It could be medical problems.
- It could be your temperament.

There is definite power to genetics. People who are depressed tend to often have a family member who may have had depression too. Suicide is also known to run in families. An identical twin has 50 to 80% chance of having depression if the other twin has it. And yet, genes may not always govern your existence. Even in the case of physical illnesses like diabetes and hypertension, if you modify your lifestyle, keep your weight in check, watch your diet, avoid stress, and stay happy, chances are that the physical illness won't engulf you. So is the case with depression. You can beat it before or after it surfaces if you know the right strategy.

Likewise, the effect of stress. Stress arouses a cascade of physiological changes. The stress hormone, cortisol, wreaks havoc putting the body on high alert, preparing it for combat. Persistently elevated cortisol levels can alter the amygdala which you know, regulates emotional perception. Like if the stressor started long ago during childhood. We've heard of people who've had a troubled upbringing; maybe emotional, physical, or sexual abuse in the early years or been neglected by figures who ideally should have been sources of love and support. All these events generate long standing stress that obstinately alters your nervous system in destructive ways. The resultant change in neurotransmitters, neural circuits and neural signalling can contribute to depression.

Everybody's life is stressful. Many may have endured childhood trauma, death of a loved one, job layoffs, financial setbacks, relationship turmoil, challenging kids, business failure, or theft for that matter. But everybody does not always *get stressed* even though they could have *faced the same stressor*.

Another biological metric we cannot arguably challenge is seasonal affective disorder (SAD) or seasonal depression which is uniquely influenced by sunlight. When sunlight is limited, serotonin influence diminishes, and the additional exaggeration of melatonin (released in darkness to induce sleep) can make one lethargic, disinterested, and depressed. But is everybody who is far off from the equator, depressed?

Some medical conditions have a direct influence on the brain too; like Alzheimer's disease, Parkinson's disease, Huntington's disease, multiple sclerosis, stroke, or brain infections like encephalitis; that impair the brain's structure and function. Vitamins B_{12} and D deficiency could contribute too. Similarly, thyroid diseases, parathyroid illnesses, diabetes, hypertension—all are linked with depression.

The golden question still is "What came first? The illness or depression?"

I've given you all these explanations to enhance your information, build awareness and offer answers that create understanding and disengage your misconceptions about depression. The medical model of depression is rooted in neurochemicals. These are justifications and explanations for having depression but aren't defences for *staying* depressed. Medicines that correct neurotransmitter deficits help ease depression symptoms, but how come they do not heal depression completely? There is still an untouched underlying denominator that can potentially challenge all these pretexts. And answer your question, "Is there a way to not be depressed in spite of all of the above?" It's the last, but surely not the least contributor to your depression.

It's the way you think.

4

Many Masks of Depression: Are You Wearing One?

"The worst type of crying wasn't the kind everyone could see--the wailing on street corners, the tearing at clothes. No, the worst kind happened when your soul wept and no matter what you did, there was no way to comfort it. A section withered and became a scar on the part of your soul that survived. For people like me and Echo, our souls contained more scar tissue than life."

—Katie McGarry, *Pushing the Limits*

Depression can express itself on a spectrum, ranging from mild to moderate to severe intensity, or present itself in unrelated, bizarre dimensions, seemingly distinct from each other. Ordinarily the classic landscape of depression involves sadness, crying, fatigue, and being unable to concentrate at work or enjoy with friends. You might believe that a depressed person even *looks* depressed. And yet, that may not always be true. Depression affects everybody differently. Some people have a few symptoms that span a longer duration, while others have many symptoms all at once. Depression is a felonious perpetrator. Understanding the many faces of this devil helps you find the real culprit behind the pretence it masquerades in.

Major (Unipolar) Depression

My patient Anjali's complaint catalogue listed headaches and tiredness at the top. She felt perpetually drained and didn't sleep well. In fact, she'd sleep as soon as she went to bed, but woke early—just within a few hours, and couldn't sleep again. The headaches were dull and generalised. All these obscure symptoms began five weeks ago and were getting worse. She was disinterested in her usual everyday activities. She also missed work as she felt tired in both body and mind. She couldn't concentrate on anything at all – work or home chores, not even the Netflix shows that took up her usual downtime.

Anjali's children were at school all day. She worked part-time, cooked the day's meals in the evening, and they all ate 'family dinner' together. It was routine. Yet, she felt guilty that she wasn't spending quality time with family. In fact, both kids were teenagers who hardly had any time from their schedule to spend with her. She was increasingly uncomfortable being intimate with her husband and felt guilty about that too, though he understood and acknowledged how she felt. She worried that "something bad" was going to happen to her and her family and would cry uncontrollably often. She didn't want to live anymore because she was a "bad person" but didn't have a logical explanation for the same. She wasn't feeling hungry and had lost six kilograms of weight, all in the last four to five weeks.

Anjali had major depression. Low and sad mood, guilt, decreased sleep and appetite, slowness in thought and action, lack of energy, fatigue, inertia, helplessness, hopelessness, and thoughts about death or suicide. The hallmark of major depression is that every little day-to-day task or activity becomes nearly impossible to accomplish. Colour is wiped out from life's palette, and all you see is a dull and aching grey. Life seems unworthy, bland, and unliveable, even though on the surface everything seems alright with no reason to complain. You feel empty, remorseful, sad, angry, frustrated or occasionally irritable. Everything mundane seems like a burden—even brushing teeth, bathing, and dressing. You may lose enthusiasm for life, and struggle to enjoy things that would otherwise make you happy. With so much anguish, you could wish you did not exist or that something mystical would happen to make it all stop in some way—the pain or life itself.

Atypical (Bipolar) Depression

Rohan's mother came in to discuss his behaviour. His father had left them eight years ago when Rohan was ten. It wasn't a pleasant divorce. "He's grown to become such an angry young man," she complained. He'd stopped going to college. He would leave home some days but wouldn't be at college, and on others he would stay in his room, sleeping. On rare occasions, he'd go to her room, hug her, and cry like a baby. She never really figured out what was going on. He'd get upset if she suggested studying, meeting friends, or working out. His food schedule was erratic. Online pizza orders had gone up, he'd visibly gained weight, and yet, refused to exercise or listen to anyone.

Rohan said his friends were "no good" and it was "pointless" keeping in touch with them. He was increasingly irritable and intolerant of anybody who disagreed with him. On a rare occasion when an old friend whom he liked came home, he would be social, play video games, gorge on the snacks his mom prepared for them, and seemed to enjoy himself. One day, from the opposite side of the living room, she saw him standing on the ledge of their 20th floor apartment balcony (patio), smoking weed. Around the same time, she had discovered a suicide note in her drawer saying the world was "unfair and unjust" and he didn't wish to live anymore.

When Rohan's mother confronted him, he got angry. He slammed the door and said he did it to get her attention. She was at a loss for words and had no idea what to do to help. When I told her he sounds depressed, she was rather shocked by the diagnosis. "He's manipulative, insolent, disobedient, aggressive, disrespectful, and a liar. How is this depression?" She retorted, "He is the one making *me* depressed!"

Rohan is among the 1% of the world's population that suffers bipolar or atypical depression. If you suffer from this, your brain processes emotional information poorly. You could become sensitive to frustration and react to criticism astronomically. Without sufficient evidence, your brain anticipates failure and humiliation, so you ruminate–as if it's already happened and react in accordance – with scorn and contempt. You feel sad but you express anger. People with atypical depression lack the capacity to be persistent, so they feel they have underachieved and might discuss their feelings and experiences in a showy manner, oftentimes to seek attention. If you behave in this manner, you might also get labelled as touchy, moody, and passive-aggressive. Atypical depressive behaviour troubles people around you significantly.

Particularly the neurotransmitters serotonin and norepinephrine are dysfunctional in atypical depression. If you've had this, chances are that when you first visit your doctor, it was not diagnosed. Such depression is part of the bipolar spectrum and occasionally alternates with episodes of extreme happiness or intense irritability, alongside talkativeness, and racing thoughts. Usually, atypical or bipolar depression strikes at an earlier age and if left untreated, it can precipitate more severe mood swings as age advances.

Premenstrual Dysphoric Disorder (PMDD)

Sonya sat before me and gorged on the bowl of chocolates lying on my desk. She said they calmed her. She insisted that the world was evil and chocolate was irresistible. She kept giving in. At 33, she'd worked her way up the corporate ladder, broken the glass ceiling and bagged the position of managing director at her company. And yet, sitting before me, she felt hopeless and self-deprecating. She sounded tense. I could see how keyed up she was.

Sonya couldn't focus on work, said she was "no good", and insisted she didn't deserve her recent promotion. She was sleeping too much the past few days, and couldn't resist cheese and sugary temptations. An occasional smoker, she was now puffing 15 cigarettes a day. Her incessant thoughts of suicide worried her. She had suffered from an occasional low mood and intermittent frustration earlier. The feelings would come and go. But her visit schedule exposed a pattern – a similar time each month for the past 4 months. It became clear that these symptoms were occurring just prior to her monthly period. That could not be discounted.

Sex hormones oestrogen and progesterone interact with neurotransmitters that regulate mood and behaviour. As these hormones wax and wane each month, so do the brain chemicals, affecting the mood. Usually these appear a few days prior to the monthly period, but could surface up to two weeks beforehand too, and become extremely severe just one or two days prior.

If you (or people, you know) have endured "period blues" you would be familiar with the symptoms. You may get irritable, and argue with family, your partner, neighbours, or co-workers unnecessarily. Without apparent reason, you feel sad, hopeless, and worthless. At the physical level, breast swelling and tenderness, headache, muscle and joint pains, and a vague stomach bloating makes you feel "sick". You feel "lazy" and don't want to work even though you know you should. What gets to you most is the edginess and the "I am losing control" feeling. Worst of all, overeating foods rich in tryptophan (a serotonin precursor) like cheese and chocolate cause bloating and unwanted weight gain. Previously labelled as premenstrual syndrome, this is today better known as Premenstrual Dysphoric Disorder (PMDD).

Peripartum Depression (PPD)

Family and friends mistakenly assumed that Nandita was unhappy about the birth of a girl child given the patriarchal society she existed in. But Nandita always *wanted* a girl, and was anyway ecstatic about having a baby, throughout her pregnancy. She was a happy go lucky, ever-smiling, sporty and enthusiastic young lady–the go-to person for friends and family, who thought she was most level-headed and sane in this "mad world".

Somewhere around the beginning of the ninth month of her pregnancy, Nandita had begun to feel tired, low, and occasionally agitated. She didn't speak about it to anyone at home. "Everyone is so enthusiastic about the upcoming birth of the baby, how can I tell them I feel miserable? They'll think I'm crazy."

When the beautiful baby girl arrived, Nandita became increasingly disinterested in feeding, nursing, or caring for her. She knew she had to eat well to breastfeed but couldn't bring herself to. The baby would cry and keep her up at night, but even when she had the chance, Nandita couldn't sleep. She'd become fidgety and restless. She was tired and run down (over and above how usually new mothers feel after delivery). One day, while bathing her daughter she got a fleeting thought of drowning the little one in the tub and ending her own life too. Nandita had always been a firecracker of positivity. This wasn't normal, she realised. That instant, she decided to seek help.

As many as one in seven women endure depression symptoms after they've delivered a baby, just like Nandita. These could start before delivery too, or surface up to a year after the baby is born. Previously regarded as a post (after) partum (delivery) mood disorder, this is now better known as peri (around) partum (delivery) depression. While the hormonal effect of oestrogen, progesterone, and testosterone has repeatedly been held culprit, many factors like family conflict, poor relationship with the husband, inadequate help at home, emotional turmoil, and ongoing stress also seem to contribute. This depression variant is dangerous and impairs mother–child bonding leading to inadequate care of the baby. Many new mothers may be driven to suicide (20% of all post-partum deaths) as a result. PPD is a serious depression variant and is one that responds well to help, if brought to light in time.

Agitated Depression

Shankar was labelled as "the angry old man" at office. At the review meeting, he'd flung the white board eraser at a subordinate who was presenting the quarterly sales statistics. It gashed the 27-year-old's forehead, just about missing his eye.

Shankar was summoned by human resources (HR) right away and issued a final warning to tame his anger. Two days later, his secretary saw him sobbing profusely and muttering under his breath, "My life is not worth living. Nobody understands!" She took the brave chance to go in (nobody dared to do that with Shankar) and speak to him about it. Shankar's face was flushed, he was pacing around the room, wringing his hands, and clenching his fists, intermittently banging his head on the wall. Afraid for her safety, she summoned the security guard who had to escort Shankar to their in-house medical facility.

When I evaluated Shankar over the next few weeks, I confirmed this to be agitated depression. Although agitation can be caused by alcohol or other drugs, lack of sleep, specific brain infections, and several other medical problems. In this case, I gathered it was not medical.

Shankar had long-standing relationship turmoil with his wife. He didn't speak much to anyone about it. He hid it from friends and colleagues, only to displace the frustration on his workplace subordinates. Nobody would have suspected he was depressed. But he was sad, hopeless, fatigued, indecisive, distracted, guilty, angry, and suicidal.

Agitated depression is symbolic of a greater severity of illness, as sufferers have a higher risk of self-harm or suicide. Not everybody gets this frantic when depressed but knowing that this can be the only visible symptom, helps acknowledge this variant better. Remember, agitation and sadness *can* co-exist.

Melancholic Depression

Rita was a patient who avoided video calls and clinic visits. She did telephone appointments. During one session, she sat inside the closet. "It's dark, smug and secure" she said. "I spend eight hours of my day here and occasionally take a break to sit under my home office desk." "How does that make you feel though, Rita?" I asked. "Oh, I feel safe. I like the quiet. I feel pain, but the darkness eases it. I only get out of here at night."

Rita lived alone. She'd taken a break from work since this "dark mood" hit and started "sucking the living life" out of her as she described it. She felt small and preferred to be cocooned inside the closet. That's the only time she felt that the darkness *outside,* matched the darkness *inside* her. It was a grotesque description of how low she felt. Rita knew that this behaviour was not normal.

She didn't share her feelings with anyone else, afraid that nobody would understand.

One out of every three to four depressed individuals, endures melancholia. In 400 B.C., Greek Philosopher Hippocrates proposed, that melan (black) cholē (bile) gets released from the gall bladder of the depressed person, which spreads through the body and darkens the mood to murky black, like a dusky cloud dimming any glimmer of light. There is a distinctive quality to this low mood (it has been described as the lowest of all lows) and is associated with an inability to perceive pleasure in anything at all. Nothing seems to have the capacity to change this pitiful disposition. Rita's mind was slow, her morning mood was the worst, and sleep and hunger were almost absent. Her inertia was so pronounced that she expressed once that she wished to die but lacked the drive to get up and out of the closet to plan a suicide. Melancholic depression is strongly biological and rigid as a prison's blank stone wall that appears impassable to the sufferer.

Seasonal Affective Disorder (SAD)

When Jenny got into the University of London for her graduate programme, she was excited. She'd moved there in August, two years ago. At 22, this was the first time Jenny had moved away from home and was understandably homesick. Three months passed, and she was lethargic, didn't want to study, overslept, avoided friends and felt worthless. She was eating more than before and gained seven kilos during this time. For a fitness enthusiast like Jenny, this was abominable. This was her dream scholarship programme. Not enjoying it was very uncharacteristic.

Jenny was clearly depressed. She visited the school counsellor in London, was referred to a psychiatrist and initiated on medication. She sought therapy, began exercising, and eating healthy. She improved in time and got on with her education. She even visited home (India) next June during summer break. But when she returned to London in August, the story repeated itself.

Jenny was born and raised in the heart of tropical, warm climate. For two decades of her life, she'd been used to bright sunny days, with a large amount of time spent outdoors. She wasn't prepared for the short and dark winter days of London—far away from home as well as from the equator. Lack of sunlight played havoc with her mood.

Jenny had Seasonal Affective Disorder (SAD). The hallmark of SAD is serious depression symptoms that come at very specific time periods every year, and remit completely in the interim. Sunlight is known to control serotonin release through specialised neurochemical pathways. Reduced exposure to the sun can reduce serotonin. Likewise, melatonin, which is released in the dark makes you sluggish. Less sunlight enhances melatonin secretion from the pineal gland and can make you sleepy and lethargic all the time.

When you have SAD, you feel sad, irritable, tearful, tired, lethargic, distractible, and lazy. You tend to eat and sleep more than usual, and lack energy to do pretty much anything. You can't fight this, and hence might get irritable. Carbohydrates and sugar cravings, with weight gain due to overeating are common. Sometimes these symptoms are mild, and people call them "winter blues". But at other times these are incapacitating and could cause frustration, agitation, violence, or suicide. Women are four times as likely as men to suffer SAD. It is interesting how exposure to real or artificial light can prevent SAD. But each time it strikes, it can appear stubborn and doesn't leave you in peace.

Persistent Depression (Dysthymia)

Marc said that his depression hadn't left him for nine years. He had a history of alcohol abuse, which was the reason for his divorce, six years ago. Alcohol was not a concern right now, however. Since the divorce, he'd been feeling increasingly empty, guilty, and sad. He dated on and off but didn't have any serious relationship as he couldn't connect, he said. He went to work every day but wasn't very productive.

On further questioning he revealed, "I've been lonely and sad for as long as I can remember." Coming from a broken home, he'd always missed his father but hadn't discussed it openly. When asked about school and college, he offered, "I managed to study, get fair grades, and land a decent job. But I know one thing—I have never been happy." Presently Marc sensed no enjoyment whatsoever, felt tired and purposeless, and sometimes wished he wasn't alive. He used the word "empty" a lot. His days, mood, and life seemed bland. "This is just how it's always been, so I assume this is how it will always be," he insisted.

Marc's depression was nagging, enduring, and vexing. But he was able to live with it. It was a bland and flavourless existence though. This variant of depression also known as "dysthymia", was earlier called "characterological depression" in which depression becomes a part of your character or persona, such that you cannot recall a time when it was not a part of you. Frequently, dysthymia gets complicated with serious episodes of major depression that do not allow you to function at all. This clubbing of major depression with a persistent depression is called "double depression". People neglect persistent depression simply because they have not known any state other than this.

Recurrent Brief Depression

Sameer was 30 years old, married, manager of a restaurant. He loved his job and family and didn't have many complaints from life. But he had frequent interfering thoughts of not being good enough, despite personal and professional success. He compensated for this perceived inadequacy by taking on more assignments, joining online courses, and working out intensively. On an occasion or two, he had become overwhelmed with how much he had set himself up to do and lose sleep over it. He said, "the feeling comes and goes but when it's there it's nerve-wracking. I know it'll go away in a week (as usual), but sometimes I'm convinced that nothing will get better." A pep talk from a friend would help. But this would repeat. His friend said to him one day, "Mate, you've been feeling this ever so often. Are you doing alright? I mean your life seems okay to me, but you dip very low intermittently. I worry about you."

Sameer had recurrent brief episodes of major depression. But because they were not lasting too long, he thought that these ups and downs were normal. The truth is, each time, he did get better. But what if one day it didn't happen? Time is always lost in "not feeling optimal" and there's a possibility that someday many recurring tiny episodes could add up to very serious major depression.

All Types Of Depression Have Much In Common

It's evident that all these types of depression are distinct, but they are not isolated disorders either. Depression is one face with many masks. Let's see their common threads.

All depression

- doesn't let you function normally

- feeds on your past, present, and the future
- involves sadness, whether it shows or not
- makes you feel, and want to be isolated
- comes and goes, but it could stay too
- can be internal, or a reaction to triggers
- is not just a feeling, it can also be a thought
- can cover itself up well, it can fool you.
- has some commonality in its management

This list comes from my personal experience over two decades. Whatever its nature, intensity, or duration, depression chews into your existence and eats a fair share of your happiness, preventing you from feeling fulfilled. That is why the word "empty" is often used by someone who is depressed. Accomplishment isn't about laurels, it's the ability to keep, and see your cup as full. Otherwise, there is a sense of persistent deficit and you're always thirsty. Don't dehydrate yourself of happiness. Don't neglect depression.

EXERCISE: Depression Symptom Checklist

These are some common symptoms seen in depression. "Yes" or "No" responses do not reveal a diagnosis. But they give you an idea about whether you have any depression symptoms. If you do, you will benefit from professional evaluation. Put a check mark (√) if you have thought or felt this way even occasionally.

In the last two weeks, I

- ☐ felt sad (without any obvious reason)
- ☐ felt low (without explanation)
- ☐ thought life wasn't worth living
- ☐ felt like eating more (or less) than usual
- ☐ lost (or gained) weight unintentionally

- ☐ didn't enjoy my favourite food
- ☐ didn't enjoy things that usually give me pleasure
- ☐ didn't want to talk to people
- ☐ wanted to stay alone
- ☐ felt agitated without any trigger
- ☐ felt like I was not motivated for anything
- ☐ saw no meaning in anything I did
- ☐ couldn't push myself out of bed
- ☐ didn't sleep well
- ☐ felt guilty
- ☐ felt empty
- ☐ felt worthless
- ☐ felt out of control
- ☐ thought nothing was going to get better
- ☐ cried (without a real trigger)
- ☐ couldn't focus
- ☐ couldn't do anything properly
- ☐ felt like I was being punished
- ☐ felt like I should be punished
- ☐ felt like a loser

How did you score? A check mark on some or many of these could point to depression, sadness being the chief qualifier. All humans have the capacity to feel sad. And sadness is *one* of the six normal human emotions. It is painful to be experiencing all these symptoms together. But when you know how you feel, and to what extent, you are more driven to do something about it.

This is not a textbook describing and educating you on depression taxonomy. Labelling yourself with a diagnosis won't bring back lost smiles, neither will the obsession, "I have a life-shattering disorder". The goal is to become aware of your struggles, gain clarity over your goals, point energy towards pressing concerns, and grow through the process. We will not play the label game. Instead, we'll walk you through your struggles on a personalised path, in the direction where *you* see *your* light.

5

Why You Can't Snap Out of Depression

> "In a strange way, I had fallen in love with my depression. I loved it because I thought it was all I had. I thought depression was the part of my character that made me worthwhile. I thought so little of myself, felt that I had such scant offerings to give to the world, that the one thing that justified my existence at all, was my agony."
>
> —Elizabeth Wurtzel, author

The following narrative was posted to me on a public forum. It is noteworthy of sharing–caked with emotion, pain, agony, frustration all together–and a cry for help.

"It's been 3 weeks of antidepressant pills every night, long wait times at the therapist office, emotionally taxing discussions about my childhood, and narrating my current painful feelings—none of it has been easy. I am consistently trying to change my perspective and see life differently. I exercise every day, force myself to eat, and even call a friend when I feel low. I bought a new car, adopted a dog, and got a new hairdo. But look at the world outside. It's bursting with energy, while I simmer slowly. Why is my vigour inadequate? In a twisted way, I was comfortable with my loneliness. I'm accustomed to it. Why can't I snap out of this now that I am on a recovery path? Why the long wait?"

This is how the mind impatiently yearns for wholesomeness, right after you wake from the hibernation of depression. While you were hiding, you had given up. But now that hope has surfaced, so has the desperation for immediate splendour. Oftentimes this eagerness can be counterproductive.

When you make up your mind to work on yourself, you immediately feel uplifted (placebo effect). But cognitive, emotive and behavioural transformation may have not commenced yet. Depression is a deeply ingrained behavioural health condition that changes the neurons, neurochemicals, and the circuitry in the emotional brain. Change at a molecular level takes time. That is why, the desire to live life full throttle, and resultant disappointment when you see you can't, can make you frustrated, nagging you with the question: "Why baby steps, why not a long jump?"

Wellness is an ongoing journey. It is true that depression is dark, painful, pale, bland, and hollow. But how do you sustain a happy life that is bright, painless, colourful, flavourful, and full? Many people who are depressed, may have subtly been so all their lives and not realised it. How then can a happiness masterpiece be painted overnight without any instruction? Let's break the myths around your desire to snap out of the low, so that you realise how consistency and commitment can get you to your happiness summit.

Snap Out of Depression Myth 1

"If you do things that make you happy, your depression will vanish."

Friends, family, and colleagues who say this, mean well. They insist that to not be depressed you must do things that make you happy.

There are many meaningful methods like exercise, movies, stand-up comedy, cooking, eating, traveling, and more that feel good. But these could be transient distractions. The brain is designed to adapt. With passing time, it seeks change. That is why the same person, sport, food, or job can't keep you continually happy unless you grow through the process. If you do not evolve, you stagnate and so does your happiness graph. When you're depressed, the low mood tends to continue despite external change, until the time you take active steps to change something internally.

Otherwise you keep wondering, "What even happened? I was so excited to get this new car, job, partner, home, yacht, or horse. I'm not happy about it anymore. The depression is back."

Quick fixes don't get you far. The race against depression isn't a sprint. This marathon calls for endurance, diligence, and perseverance. The happiness mountain cannot be climbed in a day, but every step upwards is a stride closer to the peak.

Snap Out of Depression Myth 2

"Stop thinking. See the glass as half full and you won't feel as bad."

Thinking helps when it is focused and purposeful. Perspective matters most. In fact, perspective change is the premise of cognitive therapy. But it requires application, more than rote learning. That is why a bland affirmation that your glass if half full, may not work. Depression is maintained by distorted perceptions and thinking models of yourself, others, and the universe. So, if you push the problem under the carpet by not thinking about it, and merely repeat to yourself that the problem isn't there, it won't go away. Thinking, analysing, making meaning of, and reappraising what you think, will help.

When someone tells you to stop thinking negatively, you tend to think that way even more. In fact, you also wonder, "This person does not understand me". You get entangled in a new negative circle of loneliness and abandonment, alongside the already existent depression.

Ruminating is destructive, but the opposite of not thinking is dysfunctional too. You must think about how you think. And change your thinking for the better. This is a time-consuming process, but once initiated, new connections in the brain are formed to retain the learned positivity. Cognitive, existential, and mindfulness techniques described later, will guide you to think differently. You *have to* think.

Snap Out of Depression Myth 3

"Your problem isn't that big. Get a grip, it will be okay."

Depression isn't a race. It's a personal experience. Everybody's mind is different, so is their perception of sadness. When you fracture your hand, it hurts. Just because the other person has a dual fracture, along with an abdominal injury, your pain may not lessen, even though you can now empathise better.

When you're told to get a grip, it implies that you reset your brain chemicals, neural circuitry, genetic disposition, thinking style and faulty perception—just like that—in an instant, instead of a structured and directional process. Your mind then poses an innocent question, "How do I get a grip, when my fingers are broken?"

People don't always understand. Not because they don't care, they just don't know better. Some sections of society have long branded depression as weakness of character, lack of grit, and a façade for feebleness, maybe even a self-indulgent ploy to attract attention.

Some people tend to absorb these stigmatising statements. Their snide remarks about depression are a learning opportunity for you to build your grit, and make you realise that *you* must navigate yourself to see the light at the end of the tunnel. If you internalise their negative beliefs, you might wonder if you're frail and push your limits till you break. When you do weight training, you cannot lift 100 kilograms on the first day. Slow and steady is the only way.

Myths to Facts: Learning to Be Patient

"You may have to accept that some things in life happen in a different order and pace than what you had in mind."

Feeling a strong urge to come out of depression sounds motivating. This is in stark contrast to the inertia of nihilism and scepticism that depression inherently rouses. If you had no goals, you'd never be impatient to meet them. But the goal to overcome depression deserves time, commitment, and motivation. Very often when you realise that the path to attain happiness is effortful, you could grow impatient. Would you then take a shortcut that envelops you in sadness, or choose a structured but effortful road that leads you to positivity?

Rethink. You can't *beat* depression with one shot. Because this devil has so may appendages, you'll have to disengage each one of them. It will happen, with direction, planning and implementation. Depression inherently makes you believe there is no way out. And as soon as you see a single ray of light, you want to embrace the sun. When you see the time, effort, commitment, money, energy, and emotion it takes; you might get so impatient that you think of giving up. Depression isn't your fault, and yet you feel like you're being punished. Give yourself the time, energy and opportunity to change.

EXERCISE: Is My Eagernenss Useful?

Ask yourself these questions when you sense annoyance, apprehension, or restlessness about depression recovery. Write down your response points as they come to your mind.

- ☐ Does my behaviour conform to my goal of healing?
- ☐ Have I thought about what I need to get to my goal?
- ☐ How have I anticipated this healing process to be?
- ☐ How much more do I need to give, than I already am?
- ☐ How much more is this costing me than I'd assumed?
- ☐ Will it be worth it, going through this whole process?
- ☐ Is there another, better option for me to feel happier?
- ☐ Do I want to get better the easy way or the right way?
- ☐ Am I picking laidback options? What might these be?
- ☐ Can I distance myself from quick fixes to do what is right?
- ☐ Am I on the verge of abandoning my goal of happiness?
- ☐ Is this approach the right choice for me?
- ☐ How much is my happiness worth, and should I work for it?

This exercise is important to help you realise that the impatience to recover may not serve you well. If you really want to heal, you will need to draw on your ability to understand, analyse, and then disintegrate the roots of your depression. You'll have to be patient as you go through this book. And remember the lines below. Write it down on your mirror or desk if you like.

"Good things take time. So, I must wait, or settle for less. I will wait, and in time I'll reach where I need to be."

Part - II

THOUGHTS RULE YOU, BUT WHEN TWISTED, THEY COULD FOOL YOU

(Cognitive Behavioural Model of Depression)

"When we feel bad, we often automatically decide that either we are bad, or another person is bad. Both of these moves cause damage and distort the truth; which is that we are all navigating difficult conditions the best we can, and we all have a lot to learn, and unlearn."

—Dean Spade, Mutual Aid: Building Solidarity in This Crisis

THIS SECTION OF THE BOOK WILL HIGHLIGHT THE COGNITIVE model of depression. This is what had brought to light the application of Aaron Beck's cognitive therapy (CT), to correct depression.

We have noted in the earlier chapters that depression has a multifaceted causality. We read about the biological predisposition brought on by brain chemicals and identified how environmental influencers and stressful events trigger negative emotions. And yet we postulated an underlying broad denominator that could influence the ultimate impact of all the above – *the way you think*. It is only when you identify the irrationality in your thinking, can you correct the distortions, and enjoy the emotional benefits of rational thinking.

In these chapters, I have narrated a series of events that occurred in the life of a single person, Jaya (a character I introduced in the previous section). I have recounted her perception of these occurrences—what she thought about them, how she felt as a result, and subsequently the way she reacted—all of which led her to feel depressed. I focused on her alone, to make you realise how a person–smart and intelligent, and leading a life as regular as any other, can hold a wide range of cognitive distortions which influence mood so significantly. Through her story and alongside explanation, I want you to understand how cognitive errors that twist your thinking can make you depressed.

Each chapter will talk about one specific cognitive error. As you read, you will realise that many of these co-exist with one other and even enhance the others' expression. Your thoughts drive everything, and if you don't take charge of how you think, your mind can fool you and take you down the depression road.

6

This Is What Happens When You Become a Slave to Your Negative Thoughts

"Take charge of your life! The tides do not command the ship. The sailor does."

—Ogwo David Emenike

Your emotions, actions, and reactions–all are a reflection of your thinking. Oftentimes negative thinking happens subconsciously, secretly programming your brain's circuitry. This hazard expresses itself ultimately as clinical depression.

Overcoming depression with cognitive change requires you to think. But thinking too much about thoughts without appropriate guidance and direction can be dangerous. If you have been avoiding negative thoughts and are made to bring them up, you awaken unhappy emotions. This could reinforce the fact that your negative thinking was already valid.

When you think about your thoughts in a structured therapeutic way with cognitive therapy principles in place, you stop focusing on the problem and place attention on solutions. Until then, negative thoughts could keep growing in power while positivity and optimism could get feebler. Cognitive theory reveals how the seeds of negativity are sown with negative events, and how they could sprout to powerful negative thoughts.

EXERCISE: Have You Endured Agonising Experiences?

These statements describe stressful events. Even though you may not have gone through these, some could simulate your broad experiences. Please put a checkmark (√) on what may have been true for you at any time in life.

- ☐ I was bullied badly in school (or at some point in life).
- ☐ My father (or mother) passed away when I was young.
- ☐ I grew up in a broken home (or disturbed household).
- ☐ This is my third breakup in two years (a single one too).
- ☐ It's impossible to keep pace with my friends.
- ☐ I wasn't born pretty, and I know that's not changing.
- ☐ My monthly period drains my happiness. It's painful.
- ☐ My pregnancy hormones govern my behaviour.
- ☐ My mood seems more volatile than the stock market.
- ☐ My wife behaves like she's not interested in me anymore.
- ☐ My husband seems to have no time, I'm not a priority.
- ☐ I have the least cooperative colleagues at my workplace.
- ☐ I have a critical boss who only sees my shortcomings.
- ☐ Running my own business is too strenuous and demanding.
- ☐ I don't have what it takes to succeed like everyone does.
- ☐ My long-standing illness won't leave me. It's disillusioning.

All of these could be excruciatingly painful realities. Each one sounds like a justifiable plea for feeling bad or sad. As humans, we continue to be influenced by what happens around us. Negative events can disillusion anybody. What matters, however, is whether the discouraging thoughts are transient or lasting, and whether you let them define your state of mind or not. It's only *your* mind which can decide what thoughts you choose.

We have already discussed at length about how sadness is biological, and how the deranged chemicals and faulty neural networks create a signal malfunction in the brain's emotive processing and memory centres. All this together results in gross breakdown of the emotion management system that expresses itself as a sad mood. When left untreated over time, this could transmute into long-standing sadness, or depression. Yet, the biological theories–all of which are outcomes of scientific advancement, could work counterproductively if they are misconstrued by extrapolating as: "Depression has nothing to do with how I think. It's all about the chemicals in my brain".

If emotions are purely biological reactions, you might believe that your mood is a result of chemicals changing because of *what happens to you*. But the truth is, your mood is a result of *what you do with what happens to you*. Emotional growth or breakdown ensues in accordance. Facing pain may be out of your hands, but how you react to it, can be a matter of choice. Your realisation, understanding and the practice of being conscious about the way you respond, can change your outcome. Then you won't be a slave of your negative thoughts anymore.

Do you remember Jaya's conversation with Meera at the office party? Jaya had been low and gloomy–unfocused at work, unable to enjoy social interaction–and yet, she was oblivious of the fact that this could be pathological sadness which would improve if she sought help. Let's analyse a few of Jaya's emotional interactions to understand the *root cause* of her feelings and whether her thoughts had any role to play.

Jaya was dating her boyfriend, Veer, for over a year. In her mind, she felt this relationship could move to the next level, implying that they should deliberate a long-term commitment like marriage. When she broached the idea, he seemed slightly unforthcoming. He said, "It's a little hasty for me to discuss this right away. Can we keep things the way they are, and plan this sometime next year? I really like you and I don't mean to belittle our commitment. I want to be with you. But I have a career to focus on, and family financial issues to sort out. Once those get resolved, I could give our relationship deeper thought, and a better chance."

The same day, Jaya sobbed her heart out and was sad. She was thinking, "He doesn't really love me." A few hours later, she was angry, "He's not faithful. He's flippant in his commitment." The next morning, she woke up with self-doubt, "Maybe I'm not good enough? Does he find me unattractive? Does he not like my friends? Was my mom rude to him when we met last?" Another time, she was ridden with guilt, "I've been ranting too much about my work. Maybe my work stress is getting to him?"

The flurry of emotions made her restless, impatient, and edgy. Veer couldn't comprehend—she'd been a happy person all along—emotionally independent and a go-getter in life. They'd enjoyed their time together and it had been a respectful give and take.

He was surprised by her reaction and told her that he was not exactly prepared for this heavy-duty retort to what he deemed was a "reasonable" request. In response, she'd felt dejected, sad, and guilty, and was behaving inconsistently every day. He thought she needed some time to process, so he suggested they take a break from talking with each other for a while, until she had a hold over her intense emotional reactions. He made it very clear that his commitment was utmost. Her reactions were rather out of place and concerning.

Jaya's emotional bustle concluded with despair. "I have messed up this relationship and lost out on a really good guy."

Do you notice that *every* emotion Jaya felt, was *preceded* by a negative thought and she was captive to it? Someone she loved and wanted to spend her life with, had just refused to commit to her. How would Jaya feel?

- She felt *dejected* when she thought the love of her life didn't love her anymore.
- She felt *angry* when she told herself that he wasn't serious about the relationship.
- She sensed *inadequacy* when she suspected that she didn't look good enough.
- She experienced *shame* when she assumed her family had wrongly snubbed him.
- She suffered *guilt* when she sensed she'd been burdening him with her stresses.
- She felt *depressed* when she believed she had lost out on a superb life partner.

In life, we all respond to events or situations in accordance with what we think and feel about it. That's what makes everyone unique. When things are going as planned, you enjoy the status quo. It is the times of change (which you might sometimes deem as crisis) that determine how you really feel. Do you feel confident, or do you get confused?

This is what happened with Jaya too when she was faced with something unexpected. If only she had recognised that Veer loved her deeply, and not misunderstood his intentions and words, she would feel differently. She would not have got into the loop of negative emotions like anger, rejection, and dejection. If only she could *believe* that he really needed some space and time as he was bogged by family pressures and career uncertainty, she would have not felt the negative emotions she did.

Was Jaya innately sensitive to rejection? Had she endured multiple experiences in which her loved ones had betrayed her? What was her inner working model? What thoughts was she slave to, and how were they ruling her mind and reactions, now?

Slowly but steadily, Jaya sunk deeper in a negative loop. Her self-esteem dipped. She was doing her best at work, but she thought she was incompetent. Jaya thought that the world pitied her. She disregarded her sister's suggestion to seek professional help. Jaya had become caged in her negative thoughts. What could she do? Who could free her?

Similarly, in your life, everything that you feel in any situation is an outcome of how you are thinking about it. The constant narrative and repetitive messages you send to your brain have a colossal impact on your emotions. And if you could change these thoughts, your emotions can, and will, undoubtedly change.

You may think, "I tend to think negatively when I am feeling sad. Is my emotion then a result of my thoughts? Or are my thoughts an outcome of my negative feelings? What do I really need to sort, in order to start feeling better?"

Cognitive behavioural therapy theorised by Aaron Beck, is based on the premise that you can learn how to control how you think, and effectively how you feel and behave. A large part of your sadness and depression is rooted in your thoughts. If you change how you think, you *will* feel differently.

EXERCISE: Have You Ever Felt Like a Slave to Your Thoughts?

Put a check mark (√) on any statement that may have traversed your mind when life didn't seem good, and your stress was mounting. This does not reflect on the stressor–it expresses how you *thought* about *yourself* when you faced it.

- ☐ I am no good.
- ☐ I'm silly.
- ☐ I'm uninteresting.
- ☐ I am incapable.
- ☐ I am being punished.
- ☐ I've wronged.
- ☐ I made a fool of myself.
- ☐ I messed it up.
- ☐ I ruined everything.
- ☐ I broke a good relationship.
- ☐ I will appear stupid.
- ☐ I will goof up.
- ☐ People will mock me.
- ☐ I deserve to be punished.
- ☐ Life will never be okay.

Even if you haven't thought any of these ever, what did you notice about them? The first five reflect misery of the present moment, the subsequent five are an adverse reappraisal of a past occurrence, and the last five are hostile predictions about the future. Even though you may have believed that these are not true, you still could not help getting sucked into the idea that they are. You were fighting with your own thoughts. Who won eventually?

Cognitive theories insist that *thoughts cause you to feel sad or depressed.* The golden truth holds—thinking optimistically makes you feel positive emotions and rationalising negatively makes you feel depressed or anxious. It's not people, events, or streaks of bad luck but your thoughts that shackle you. You've got to break free from negative thoughts to avoid the vicious cycle of depression.

Life can be chock-full of negative events and difficult situations. When faced with these, do you tend to feel sad, angry, guilty, humiliated, attacked, helpless, hopeless, worthless, and depressed?

Let's establish a clearer connection between your thoughts and emotions, to better estimate how and why you feel low in the first place. To change how you feel, you will need to understand the thought that feeds into that feeling first.

NOTE: YOUR THOUGHTS INFLUENCE YOUR FEELINGS

Thoughts that run through the mind	**Emotion felt**
- I gave up on a good prospective life partner. - I'll never be okay without my deceased father. - I didn't get the promotion. I'm a loser. - My business isn't ever going to get better.	Sadness
- I'll never be able to buy that palatial home. - I don't earn enough money to live a good life. - I haven't been on any dates. I'm unattractive. - I'm wearing make-up. I'm not actually pretty.	Inadequacy
- I'm not a fun person. I'll never have friends. - I'm not pretty enough. I'll always be single. - I wasn't invited. Nobody cares about me. - I'm single. How can I go to that party?	Loneliness

Thoughts that run through the mind	**Emotion felt**
- My partner never seems to understand me. - My team never makes it to the meeting in time. - I should have taken that job offer back then. - The neighbours are noisy only during my exams.	Frustration
- I didn't get promoted. I'm a loser. - I delayed the proposal. I always mess up. - My cake flopped. I'm good for nothing. - I fumbled in the interview. I'll always be jobless.	Incompetence
- He saw me but *chose* to ignore me. - He overcharges *only* me. - She's too *vain* to ever compliment me . - He raised *my* rent because he knows I like it here.	Annoyance
- I didn't get any calls. I'll always be jobless. - I messed the appraisal. I'll never get promoted. - I cheated on my diet again. I'll be fat forever. - I have tried enough. I'll be depressed forever.	Hopelessness
- I work too much. The divorce is totally my fault. - I couldn't help my cousin. I'm totally useless. - I have been very busy. I'm a horrible mother. - I can't pay mom's medical bills. I'm awful.	Guilt

You might say, "I have never thought any of the things mentioned above and yet, very often I feel some or many of these negative emotions. I have no idea why I am so sad, lonely, hopeless, angry, or depressed. This is not about my thoughts. I am not even thinking them!"

Many of you might agree that at times you did think this way. But then you might wonder, "If these thoughts are not true and they aren't helpful either, why would I be thinking this way again and again? I guess these *are* true, and so, my misery *is* justified!"

EXERCISE: YOUR THOUGHTS DRIVE YOUR EMOTIONS

Here is an exercise to discern that your negative emotions would *not* occur without negative thoughts. Think of something important that you lack in life which makes you restless, eager, impatient, or unhappy. (This could be a job, partner, children, money, health, fame, a home, car, appreciation from your boss, respect from your subordinates, a promotion, bonus, or anything that according to you is overtly conspicuous, by its absence)

Do you feel you are unhappy because you do not have this?

Yes?

Wrong.

You are unhappy because you *think* you are unfortunate without this, and that you *think* you need this to be happy. You might now think: "This is the whole problem. Nobody else seems to understand how this deficit in my life is *genuinely* and *indisputably* driving my unhappiness."

Okay. So, let's reason with this a little more.

- Have you been unhappy throughout your life without this?
- Have you ever been happy in life despite not having this?
- Do you know of other people who are happy without this?
- Do you know of people who have this and are still unhappy?
- If you had this, but didn't care about it, would you be happy?
- If you didn't have it and didn't care, would you be unhappy?
- If you were not thinking about it, would you be unhappy?
- If you learned that this was bad, would you be unhappy?

It seems a little boggling but read these questions once again. If what you lack is a *real* deficit then you would have *never* in your life been happy without it, and neither would anyone else in the world, who has a similar deficit like you. It's how you *think* about it which makes you believe that you are unhappy without it.

EXERCISE: Your Thoughts Drive Your Actions

Imagine another hypothetical situation. Have you, or someone you know ever done something risky, irrational, unsafe, or unreasonable? I will list out some such actions. Please put a check mark (√) on whatever applies.

- ☐ Overeaten when you were on a strict diet?
- ☐ Smoked even though you had cough or asthma?
- ☐ Had alcohol despite negative health effects?
- ☐ Had sex with the wrong person and thought, it's alright?
- ☐ Had fatty food despite high cholesterol or triglycerides?
- ☐ Tried dangerous drugs (cocaine, LSD, amphetamines, etc.)?

What might have been driving the motivation when you (or someone you knew or imagine) were doing all these things? Please put a check mark (√) on whatever thought may have applied to you.

- ☐ This will do me good, I'm quite sure of it.
- ☐ I will feel better after I eat, or drink, or smoke up.
- ☐ Nah, I won't get cancer, I don't smoke much.
- ☐ I'll use the drug occasionally, it's not an addiction.
- ☐ Life is boring. This will surely spice up things.
- ☐ What matters most is that right now, I deserve this.

You may assume that you (or the person who did so), *felt* like eating or smoking or drinking. And so, you did. But now you can see that each of these actions and the resultant behaviours are *also* fuelled by some dysfunctional thinking, which makes you believe that the faulty behaviours are appropriate. Thoughts lead to action. They drive almost *everything*. If you become more aware of your thoughts instead of passively identifying with them, you can control your inner world. Your emotions are a significant part of that universe.

Much of depression is also an outcome of feeling oppressed. When subjugated, you could feel two principal emotions – anger and dejection. In the earlier narrative about Jaya's sister suggesting she seek therapy for depression, Jaya had construed being depressed as a victimised identity–like a permanent adjective rather than an emotional state that she needed to work on. That is why she felt oppressed, even when it was not the case. Of course, this has everything to do with the way she conceptualised anyone's struggle with depression. Possibly her own stigmatising mindset, lack of awareness of the neurobiological basis of her condition, and misconceptions about what people would think of her—all contributed to her negative defence. It's all about what Jaya *thought*. Her thought was negative, dysfunctional, and twisted, and she was almost a slave to it. She had no other way to think.

Dealing with a diagnosis of depression isn't easy. Even though depression awareness has heightened over the past years, the emotion of 'feeling depressed', gets equated with the 'identity' of a victim. Again, this identity is not a valid one; it's the way you *think* about it.

EXERCISE: How Do You *Think* About Your Depression

If you were ever sad or depressed, would you assume these statements? Put a check mark (√) on what resonates with your thinking.

- ☐ Strong people don't get depressed.
- ☐ I'll be labelled with low willpower.
- ☐ Others might see me as dangerous.
- ☐ People will not take me seriously.
- ☐ I'll be considered incapable at work.
- ☐ Workwise I'll appear unreliable.
- ☐ I'll seem like an attention-seeker.
- ☐ I won't be considered for the promotion.
- ☐ People will say I am self-absorbed.
- ☐ They'll all say I have no gratitude.
- ☐ People will call me a downer.
- ☐ They'll call me a bad omen.
- ☐ They'll say I'm unmotivated.
- ☐ It'll seem like I have no drive.
- ☐ It'll look like I'm childlike and naïve.

All these adjectives tend to get permanently associated in the mind with depression. Instead of being an emotional state, depression becomes an identity. These statements are biased, discriminatory, and unpleasant. It's not a perfect world. Your life wasn't as perfect before depression hit you either. But the mind tricks you into believing many things about depression that are not true. The problem begins there–with the way you think.

Stressors of varying intensities are increasingly becoming a part of everyday life. Unfortunate events and losses occur, and they can affect you deeply. You are not *always* misjudging life events–they're very real. Self-reflection is important. You're not at fault, but you *can* contribute to your own negative experiences. It's possible that you were not that great at an interview. Or that you might have gained unhealthy weight. Or you are sarcastic and hence people are upset with you. You don't enjoy losing a job, family member, or money in the stock market either. Life is a mix of fortunate and unfortunate happenings. This becomes more important when unfortunate events occur, because eventually, your emotions are a result of how you feel about yourself, which largely depends on *how you think* when this happens.

Bad moods might convince you that they surfaced because of some negative event, and you forego the possibility that an underlying thought about the event was even involved. Like a relationship break up for example. You don't feel sad because you broke up. You feel sad when you think that you broke up because you are worthless and nobody will love you again. You could go through life, focusing on many such negative events without realising that your thinking led to the recurrent feeling of sadness. And it lingered.

You don't have to be a slave to your negative thoughts. Depression doesn't have to be your lifelong companion. There is a way to break the loop.

7

Twisted Thoughts Could Trigger Negative Emotions

"If our thinking is bogged down by distorted symbolic meanings, illogical reasoning and erroneous interpretations, we become, in truth, blind and deaf".

—Aaron Beck, American psychiatrist

You now know that thoughts generate emotions. Positive thoughts arouse happiness. Negative thoughts on the other hand, damage the mood if not investigated with mindful processing. Any thought could become adversarial if we apply inaccurate filters and see things unalike what they really are. We *all* tend to do this from time to time. Reason? Because we have gotten conditioned to it.

For a moment let's distract from depressive thoughts and listen to a story about a 1950s Japanese movie, which has given rise to the psychological term, the "Rashomon effect."

Akira Kurosawa's film *Rashomon* was set in eleventh-century Japan. Three characters in the movie took shelter from lashing rain, beneath the ruined *Rashomon* gate guarding the entrance to the capital. The gate was a shabby hangout. As the priest and the woodcutter waited for the rain to stop, they told the commoner that they'd witnessed a distressing tale.

A noblewoman was sexually molested in the forest, her samurai husband killed, and a thief arrested for the offence. The film related four distinct versions of the crime, as told by the thief, the woman, the spirit of the samurai (through a connection medium), and the woodcutter, through flashbacks. All stories spoke of crime, murder, molestation, or suicide. And each storyteller was convinced of the reality of his or her version. Ultimately, all characters appeared sloppy. Every version had inadequacies and inaccuracies.

While a fictional story like that roused the interest of behavioural researchers and called this the "Rashomon effect", it unravelled the fact that the world might run on relativism and the unknowability of truth. People rarely see eye-to-eye on the same event or incident. And we each tend to have our own versions of everything that happens to, and in our lives.

Now, back to why this story is relevant. The term "cognitive miser" coined in 1984 by psychologists Susan Fiske and Shelly Taylor, explains that we could be miserly with cognitive activity, because we want to conserve the use of our brain. Our brain could be so overloaded with large volumes of information every day, that short-cuts speed up information processing, and make our life less complicated.

As conscious and intelligent beings, we forever interpret the world around us, making sense of things. A part of this involves establishing connections between thoughts, ideas, actions, and their consequences. This is how we make attributions. We use automated reasoning techniques (also known as biases) to wade through puddles of daily existence without excess brainwork. Gilbert (1998) called such thoughts *fast track defensive algorithms*. Biases make our life convenient.

What is surprising, however, is that these connections that the brain makes, can sometimes be flawed. Such errors are known in the scientific world as cognitive (thought) distortions.

Cognitive distortions are twisted thinking styles, not grounded in logic. You tend to experience these thoughts spontaneously in response to events, and they're rooted in *your* core beliefs about yourself, other people, and the world around you. They are often convoluted versions of reality, just like the Rashomon effect. They may be inadvertently adopted by people reflexively. These thoughts are wrong and lead you to feel negative emotions.

Aaron Beck, the father of cognitive therapy, was a psychiatrist who also trained in psychoanalysis. One of the conclusions of his observations with depressed people was that *all* of their narratives of incidents in their lives seem to represent erratic and inconsistent degrees of distortion of reality. Obviously, we all have some limitations in memory and vocabulary. So, our descriptions are bound to be distinct from another's. But Beck noted that when you are depressed, there is a systematic, consistent, and unrelenting cognitive distortion—*a bias against yourself.* That is why depressed people tend to feel small, incapable, helpless, worthless, and guilty. This can also be termed in technological language as "faulty information processing" in which events, people and your own self get misinterpreted as negative.

Salient Facts About Cognitive Distortions

These:

- are consistent thinking patterns
- invariably are inaccurate or false
- are challenging to recognise
- become a regular feature in life
- are deceptively realistic or true

- colour everyday interactions
- generate negative emotions
- suck you in a negative loop
- contribute to your depression

When you are depressed or sad, your brain erroneously decodes the present, future, and the outside world negatively. As a result, the interpretations of your interactions and experiences tend to become biased. I know, willingly you don't want to think inaccurately. Also, you do not want to experience negative emotions as a result. But unless you learn how to spot these inaccuracies and decode their effect, your life and mood will most likely stay the same.

Let's play detective to identify these twisted thinking styles and understand how they deceive you.

8

Black and White Thinking: Narrowing Your Perspective of Positivity

> "More than anything she wanted the world to be uncomplicated, for right and wrong to be as easily divided as the black and white sections of an Oreo. But the world was not a cookie."
>
> —Roshani Chokshi, *Aru Shah and the Tree of Wishes*

Throughout your life you are taught, reminded, possibly even pushed to realise the divisions between opposites like right and wrong, healthy and unhealthy, polite and rude, good and bad, and so on. This categorisation makes life simpler. But when you use this dichotomy in the everyday interpretation of relationships, character traits, and future possibilities, it may limit your potential to perceive things for what they are.

You recall Jaya and Veer's discussion about considering a long-term commitment? It had been Jaya's idea, and Veer had asked for a year to sort his finances. He didn't indicate that he *did not want* to be with her. But Jaya took his statement as an absolute either/or. Just because he did not jump up and say, "Yes we should get married *right now*"; she assumed that he did not want to marry her *ever*. So, she doubted his commitment, character, and integrity. She felt miserable about it. This was the start of her negative thought cascade, possibly a result of many other cognitive factors that we're unaware of.

This is known as black or white thinking. It reframes probabilities by pushing thoughts to extreme polarities so it is also called polar thinking. Things and people then look awesome or awful, amazing or disgusting, wow or aargh. That is why it could seem that some friends are the best, until one day they appear like the worst. At one time you feel good about an achievement and on another, you're in the dumps. The day the stock market falls, you might fail to realise that it's done well in the past or could be better in the future. A negative remark from a senior or partner can throw you off the boat into the deep blue sea. You're thinking everything is great; and one day when something untoward happens, you feel that nothing about you or your life is worthwhile at all.

There is no denying that good is different from bad. Likewise, acceptable is superior to unacceptable, and beautiful is better than ugly. This dichotomy undoubtedly saves time and makes you decisive. But if your mood had to swing between a jubilant high and dismal low in response to many such inferences on a regular basis, it could get exhausting. Life does not exist in binary planes *all* the time. You're thinking on the edge when you're black or white, thereby living on it too.

Black and white thinking is also called "splitting", because everything is split into a 0-1 game where the mind seeks extreme endings. It's as if, you want it all perfect, all too fast, all the time. Such dualistic thinking works remarkably well when you're shopping for a bag, shoes, car, or a home. But in personal relationships, goal setting or establishing your self-worth, for example, this could fail.

Depression could make the "splitting" in your expectations and realities, rather inflexible.

No one is infallible. So, it's impossible for anything or anyone to stay perfect in your eyes forever (not even yourself). By expecting yourself or the world to be flawless, you assure the worst emotional outcome—of being "let down". It could also break your trust in goodness because the world and its people suddenly appear miserable and wretched to you. If they aren't *white,* then with this filter in place you tend to colour them *black*.

EXERCISE: Do You See Things in Extremes?

Do recall if you've thought this way in any specific situation or instant. Put a check mark (√) on the statements that seem to hold truth for you.

- ☐ I need to know beforehand if I am going to enjoy something.
- ☐ I see life as a game, you either win or you lose.
- ☐ I'm specific about who's good and who's bad in my life.
- ☐ There's a right or a wrong answer, there's nothing in between.
- ☐ All the world's an enemy. There are just a handful of friends.
- ☐ I see life as a series of transactions. It's a wise choice.
- ☐ According to me people who aren't on time, aren't worth it.
- ☐ I think some things just work for you or they don't. That's it.
- ☐ If people let me down, I'll never trust them again.
- ☐ Things always need to be done "absolutely right".
- ☐ Mediocrity doesn't work. It's got to be awesome always.
- ☐ I cannot bear it if I'm lesser than the best.
- ☐ People should always be nice, else it's horrible.

If you did recall feeling like this even a few times, it's possible that you are seeing life in "black and white" mode. This leads us to questions like, "Am I a good, or a bad person?", "Is he ethical, or immoral?" and "Is this world miserable or amazing?" A positive response is difficult because nothing and nobody can always be perfect. Invariably then everything appears negative, and it becomes easy to be critical of yourself, others, and the world. This negative triad is the core perceptual deficit in depression (Beck, 1976).

EXERCISE: ABSOLUTE WORDS IN YOUR VOCABULARY

Do you use these words in your vocabulary? Slight use is expected. But do recall your statements that may have utilised these, and how they had an impact on you.

absolute
adequate
all the time
always
avoidable
awful
best
black
blameless
broken
cataclysmic
certain
defeated
defective
disgusting
disparaging
enormous
entirely
eternal
every
fantastic
fascinating
fatal
faulty
favourite
flawless
foolish
fully
furious
gigantic
greatest
guilty
harmless
hideous
hopeless
horrible
huge
ideal
imperfect
impossible
just
lacking
literally
malfunctioning
married
miserable
missing
multiple
must
necessary
never
no
nobody
none
no-one
obvious
one-of-a-kind
only
overwhelmed
pathetic
sure
terrible
terrified
thrilled
true
ultimate
unavoidable
unclear
unconditional
undecided
unequal
unimportant
universal
unnecessary
unpopular
unquestionable
unsuccessful
valid
vital
void

everybody	inaccurate	preferable	vulnerable
everyday	incomplete	redundant	white
everyone	incredible	ridiculous	whole
everything	incurable	right	woeful
exhausted	inferior	substandard	wonderful
fair	infinite	superior	worst
false	irrefutable	supreme	wrong

Absolute words, phrases, and ideas denote totality, either of magnitude, or probability. Magnitude means that in the present tense, something is entirely enormous, or awfully miniscule. And probability indicates that in the future something will be faultlessly right or miserably wrong. Absolute thoughts are independent of context and unqualified by nuance. They linger, without authority, need, or permit.

If you are using these, you are telling yourself (over and above telling someone else) that it is either A or Z and there can be nothing in between. Depression modifies your vocabulary in negative ways. Besides using unhelpful words, emotions, and connotations, absolute adjectives and adverbs described above, begin to rule your syntax. Be mindful of these. They are regular words when used in normal context, but if they have a negative impact on how you feel and behave, you benefit if you placed a rain check on them.

Moderation as a doctrine is long emphasized by Aristotle, Buddha, and Confucius. Reality is not absolute, and it cannot be simplified into black and white each time. The whole spectrum of colour and experience sits in between black (absence of light) and white (blend of all seven colours of light).

EXERCISE: Analyse Your Polarised Thinking

Do you tend to think in polar extremes? If yes, have you given active thought to the outcomes of such binary thinking that divides everything into inflexible categories? These questions would help introspection.

- Do you notice absolutist thinking in everyday life on a regular basis?
- Do you feel awesome and awful about things and people, ever so often?
- If you thought this way, did it ever impact your relationship with people?
- Did black and white thinking affect your own mood negatively, ever?
- Did you discount the grey possibilities in your fixation with black or white?

Black or white thinking assures answers. It offers security, control, and power. Grey style thinking is labour-intensive and energy consuming. Yet, it is more constructive and accurate. When you allow yourself a little uncertainty, and see the many shades of grey, you realise how soothing they can be for your eyes and your mind.

9

Overgeneralising: Making Invalid Extrapolations

"The propensity to excessive simplification is indeed natural to the mind of man, since it is only by abstraction and generalization, which necessarily imply the neglect of a multitude of particulars, that he can stretch his puny faculties so as to embrace a minute portion of the illimitable vastness of the universe."

—James George Frazer, *The Magic Art and the Evolution of Kings, Part 1*

Of all cognitive distortions that filter realistic from imagined possibilities, overgeneralisation is the easiest to apply. It is rooted in principles of behavioural conditioning or what we simply call, learning from experience. Governed by the dictum, "once bitten, twice shy" you tend to believe that you will be bitten again, and again. So, you might choose to be shy forever. Overgeneralisation occurs when generalisations are made with few observations or experiences.

Has it ever happened that you ate dinner at a restaurant, and that same night you got sick? Did you decide it was an *unhygienic* place, and you'd never go there again? Or you took an alternate route to get to office, and got stuck in heavier than usual traffic? Did you discern to not take that road because it's *always too crowded*? Such generalisations are sometimes useful, and yet, frequently impractical.

Overgeneralisation in depression, however, can be more overarching. It colours the past, present, as well as future, negatively. And makes you take into account, the littlest previous adverse events, that make you believe that negativity will colour the present and future too. Then, you react and act in sync with your negative belief.

Jaya (mentioned in the earlier chapter), had been ruminating over the notion that her boyfriend Veer was not committed because he had not immediately agreed to her proposal for marriage. They had some unpleasant spats after that, and he suggested they take some time out to clear their minds and then revisit the discussion. Soon, she decided on winning him over with a special dinner. Unfortunately, Jaya's cooking attempt backfired. Also unexpectedly, Veer's mother had a medical emergency, so he could not make it in time.

That's when Jaya's mind raced. "This *eternally* has to happen. There's not *one* date he can make it to in time. He's *always* chosen his family over me. I've *never* mattered. I'm the *last* on his priority list. My luck is so *warped*. The dish turned out *awful* today–just like it happens *all the time*. I'll *never* be able to cook. Or be happy. *Nobody ever* prioritises me. I'm *always* second choice. My life is a *miserable* mess. I'm *cursed*!"

Did you notice in a few lines, how words like always, never, eternally, least, warped, awful, all the time, or cursed; were used repeatedly? It's understandable that at that time Jaya would have felt sad. *All* her allegations were *partially* true. But by overgeneralising, Jaya had used unrealistically broad language and extreme words to articulate her evaluation of events and people (in this case, her boyfriend) in her life. When she stated that this *always* happens to her (whether true or not) she reacted in a way as if this *did* continually happen. She became angry and frustrated not just with Veer, but with everything in her life at that moment. She even went on to pronounce that she is *cursed*. All because Veer was late for dinner; and her food had unfortunately flopped. Was this reasonable? She thought it was. So, Jaya genuinely became sad, and she began to cry.

When you overgeneralise, you perceive emotions deeper and stronger than they are. Negative words become predominant, and you tend to act upon what you wrongly believe. The rational part of you knows this is wrong, but your mind thinks like this, effortlessly.

EXERCISE: Overgeneralisation is a Real Thing

Overextending rules from one item to another happens with everyone. You may not have experienced these situations, but you might be able to identify with them in some way.

- When a child tells you that two of her 'tooths' broke and that 'hurted' her, she is overgeneralising language rules pertaining to singular and plural, as well as present to past tense. She wasn't taught that the plural of tooth was 'tooths' or the past tense of hurt was 'hurted'. But she extrapolated these from a few words she'd been taught before. She just didn't know that they were wrong. She assumed, based on previous experience.
- When you buy a new gadget, you often open it up, connect the wires and wait for it to work because you've done it before. But this time it has different settings. If you make wrong connections based on what you know of earlier

models, you may short circuit the wiring and damage your device, or in most situations it might simply not work. Generalisation doesn't always help.

- When you see smiling faces on few people's social media feed, it becomes easy to suppose that their lives are complete. This is really a curated version of their personal reality and does not embody the sum of their existence, struggles and complexities. Yet, this small sample from the larger universe could make you believe that your life is imperfect, and rouse feelings of insecurity, envy, or unhappiness.

Overgeneralisation thrives on incomplete information. It could occur when the pressure to gain an understanding is high. But it could happen without that gravity too. If you took things at face value and didn't overanalyse them, you'd most likely be happier.

Overgeneralisation makes reactions and outcomes extreme. You selectively observe facts and latch on to pieces of information that fit the pattern, inadvertently using all available evidence to reiterate your misfortune. You get stuck in a self-created web of negative thoughts.

EXERCISE: DO YOU OVERGENERALISE?

These statements tend to spring up when you're low, rejected, or dejected; and make you feel worse. Do check mark (√) if you've thought this way in any situation.

- ☐ I grew up thinking I'll *never* do anything in life.
- ☐ I often feel I'm good for literally *nothing*.
- ☐ My friends *constantly* put me down.
- ☐ My colleagues *always* make plans without me.
- ☐ We *never* end up watching a movie of my choice.

- ☐ My work is *never* appreciated, however hard I try.
- ☐ Everyone gets me wrong, *all* the time.
- ☐ *Nothing* has ever worked for me.
- ☐ *Nothing* will ever work out for me.
- ☐ *Nobody* cares about *anybody*.
- ☐ The world is a *miserable* place.
- ☐ I'm not capable of *anything*.
- ☐ *No one* understands.
- ☐ Everybody is selfish and self-nurturing.
- ☐ I'm unlucky with *everything*. Period.
- ☐ *Everyone* in the world is more fortunate.
- ☐ I'm *always* sad.

Do you think these statements can be *completely* true? For example, the ones about friends. It's possible that *some* friends might be *somewhat* unreasonable and reject you *some* of the time. But *all* wouldn't be *completely* unreasonable, *all* the time. This isn't about loyalty; it is about the way *you* feel. Likewise, "I am good for nothing", are plain words, but they stab self-confidence. Is it possible that you are good at *absolutely* nothing?

Overgeneralisation is nothing but "unjustified oversimplification on the basis of a single incident". Beck (1976) and a series of researchers after him, repeatedly insisted that this negative filter is the most reliable indicator of depression. When you are depressed, your reactivity to negative events becomes hyper intense, especially when negative attributions are directed towards your own self. This negativity could spill on to everything in life. You begin to feel that you are never worthy enough, are not treated well enough, and will not ever be happy enough.

Nearly everyone overgeneralises. The brain does not want to be misled. So, it seeks, memorises, and reapplies past lessons. When you are depressed, however, you tend to over apply negative learnings that bring the mood down. Taylor and Brown's research (1994) affirmed that people who are not depressed could overgeneralise positive events. They exaggerate opinions of control over random situations, skew memories in a positive fashion, and might also become overly optimistic when predicting the future. Beware of the overgeneralisation trap both ways. Though overgeneralising is evolutionally purposeful, you must use it decisively. Your outcomes will then be adaptive and functional.

10

Catastrophising: Seeing Your World End, Perpetually

"The wound with which she travelled vibrated within her. She thought, I shall never have what I desire. I shall become bitter and defeated and dim, and I shall never really paint, I am a freak, a crippled animal, something to be put down, put to sleep, put out of its misery."

—Iris Murdoch, *The Green Knight*

Alarming things happen in the world from time to time. It would be naïve to assume that nothing bad can, or will, happen in life. That would in fact, be reckless. But you have to examine your life and realise how bad things that happen in your day, catch you off guard. Catastrophising is such a kind of cognitive distortion in which your brain exaggerates the meaning, importance, or likelihood of negative life events. The smallest setback, therefore, appears like a massive disaster. When extrapolated to the past, present and future; this distortion could make you believe that everything that happened to you was miserable, what's going on right now is distressing, and whatever happens tomorrow will be despicable too.

Reacting, and sometimes overreacting a little bit, to usual and unusual situations is healthy. It's what makes you human—your retorts, expressions, and responses to life's experiences. Over time, you develop likes and dislikes, identify your strengths and weaknesses, and become aware of your coping capacities. Any event that is potentially threatening (to your life, happiness, or sanity) qualifies as a stressor. Your uncomfortable emotional response to it is what you experience as stress. A well-rationed quantity of stress is understandable, but an emotional catastrophe (disproportionate fear) in response to an overestimated threat, is not helpful. Such catastrophising does not get you positive outcomes even though the result could ultimately be negative, and some amount of your stress was genuinely merited.

Catastrophes aren't only floods, famine, or death. They do include all of these. But on an everyday basis, they're simply an agonising enormity of what your life experiences feel like to you at that point. For example, a friend not picking the phone when you really wanted to speak with him, you not getting the score you expected in an examination, or, fumbling in an office presentation which could potentially decide your promotion. Experiencing every event as earth-shattering can be daunting. It feels like your world is ending and you're watching it sink, defencelessly gasping for air.

Continuing from the previous chapter when Jaya learned that Veer was going to be late for their dinner date, she catastrophised that he didn't prioritise her. In her frustration, she picked the phone to call her childhood friend, and wept. "Veer isn't going to show up at all". But Veer said he was going to be *late*. This meant he *was* going to show up. She had to be patient. And he did, this time with a bunch of flowers. The gesture was a welcome surprise that changed Jaya's mood for the better. As they were getting into a comfortable conversation, the doorbell chimed, with a bunch of flowers yet again. The note on this bouquet read, "Your smile matters most. Keep smiling. Love, H". Harpreet (the same childhood friend) had sent flowers to cheer up his buddy. But for some reason, guilt snuck into Jaya's being. Assuming Veer would doubt her commitment, she burst into tears and began apologising. These thoughts crossed her mind.

- He left after the bouquet arrived; he was upset.
- He must think that I'm having an affair.
- He assumes I am fickle and erratic.
- He will imagine that I cheated on him.
- He thinks I am an emotional wreck.
- He thinks I am dependent and needy.
- I've made a complete fool of myself.
- I will never be able to gain his trust again.
- He's already having issues with me. He'll leave me.
- Oops I did it again. I always mess up. As usual.

Jaya seemed like she was overblowing the present situation and considering the future to once again, be very bleak. This catastrophic forecast was irrational. Veer had not mentioned anything untoward. Her guilt was stirring these catastrophic thoughts, and her subsequent crying and apologising was rather counterproductive. If anything, Veer could have wondered, "Why is she apologising if she hasn't done anything wrong?"

When you catastrophise, you overestimate the probability of a negative outcome. The truth is, no matter how well things are going they can still be fragile. Like the little piggy in the childhood tale, who was worried about the wolf going huff and puff and blowing her house down. So, she built a house with concrete and stone. Now, she needn't worry about the hungry wolf anymore. But then an earthquake could still run down her house. For no fault or deficit on her part. Should she keep worrying?

Beck (1976) as well as Ellis (1980) agreed that people with depression tend to magnify the unpleasantness of negative events and go into a negative spiral. But there isn't as much error in *estimation* of the threat. It is the miscalculation of the capacity to *deal* with it. And the heightened emotional pain perceived in response to powerlessness. Helplessness is deeply connected with catastrophising.

The likelihood of adverse outcomes of personal significance can make people sad and anxious. Humans evolved in an era where survival demanded us to put up a fight. We had to imagine the worst because it helped us stay guarded, and fight when required. But if you react to *every* change like it's catastrophic, the mind tends to opt for the "freeze" state instead of the adaptive "fight-flight response". Like a deer caught in the headlights, you halt right where you are, and find yourself unable run off the road (which would otherwise be the wise move to save yourself).

When you fear the worst and it doesn't happen, the suffering is wasted. When you fear the worst and it does happen, you suffer twice. A catastrophising thought can be useful if it motivates you to prepare, and not panic; so that you feel free, fearless, and focused in the face of crisis–big or small.

EXERCISE: Catastrophising *Can* Appear Normal

These situations may not have occurred with you but put a check mark (√) if they sound rational and realistic to any extent.

- ☐ I didn't get hired. ⇨ I'm still jobless. ⇨ I feel humiliated.
- ☐ I wasn't prepared for the meeting. ⇨ This is shameful.
- ☐ My boyfriend broke up with me. ⇨ I cannot survive alone.
- ☐ I've put on weight. ⇨ I am an embarrassment to my friends. ⇨ This is appalling.
- ☐ I broke my routine. ⇨ I always blunder up. ⇨ My life is pathetic.
- ☐ I don't focus in meetings. ⇨ I'm not performing. ⇨ It's a sorrowful state.
- ☐ I was rude to my friend. ⇨ She's not talking to me. ⇨ I can't take this.
- ☐ I'm moving abroad for work. ⇨ My parents will have no support. ⇨ It's miserable.
- ☐ My senior said my work isn't up to the mark. ⇨ I could get fired. ⇨ This is tragic.
- ☐ Mom asked to seek my brother's advice. ⇨ She doesn't trust me at all.
- ☐ My daughter isn't home. ⇨ She didn't answer my phone. ⇨ She's in trouble.
- ☐ My friend didn't respond to my message. ⇨ Nobody wants to be my friend.
- ☐ I didn't pass the test. ⇨ I won't make it to university. ⇨ It's the end of my career.
- ☐ My module wasn't approved. ⇨ My work is never showcased. ⇨ My life is miserable.

There seems to be some rationale to these statements. All the above scenario outcomes could be true. You may have had rejections on dating sites, job portals, friend groups and social networks. But there is an exaggerated dejection here. None of these occurrences hold guarantee that they *are as bad* as you imagine them to be or that you are *as helpless* as you envision yourself to be.

EXERCISE: Catastrophising Checklist

Think about something important in your life which could be worrisome. Examples include a health concern in you or someone dear to you, an examination, interview, presentation, reappraisal, promotion, maybe financial insecurity. Basically, anything of significance that could have a potentially negative outcome. Put a check mark (√) if any of these statements reflect your thoughts about that event.

- ☐ I'm repeatedly thinking about how I want this resolved.
- ☐ I'm convinced that something very bad is going to happen.
- ☐ I can't stop thinking about how awful the result could be.
- ☐ I'm wondering about how miserable I'll feel if I fail.
- ☐ All my attention is focussed on imagining the outcome.
- ☐ Sometimes I'm unsure, but mostly I worry this will be bad.
- ☐ I'm concerned that things will get worse this point forward.
- ☐ I'm reminded of all painful experiences of my life.
- ☐ I react emotionally when I think of what might happen.
- ☐ My life cannot go on like this. I can't handle this.
- ☐ It feels like nothing about this issue is getting any better.
- ☐ I just cannot take this anymore; the way things are going.
- ☐ It's so miserable to be in this situation (or state or position).
- ☐ I'm overwhelmed and frustrated thinking about this.
- ☐ I can't change the way I feel about what might happen.

These statements may be somewhat applicable to your problem, if not wholly. If you feel this way, you might be catastrophising, and this could make the problem appear more disastrous than it is. This doesn't mean that you needn't worry about it. Health, finances, achievement, security, stability, safety; are all realistic predictors of well-being. But stressing over it incessantly and seeing your situation as insurmountable can't help. This sustains a negative mood, breaks relationships, and supports a low mindset.

EXERCISE: Analyse Your Catastrophising

If you have had calamitous thoughts, have you ever pondered over the outcomes of your catastrophic thinking style?

- When you think in extremes, how does it influence your relationships?
- How does imagining the worst, impact your own mood and thoughts?
- Are you discounting positive options while fixating on imagined tragedies?
- Do you notice such calamitous thinking happening in your daily life?
- Do you feel like your world is crashing to tiny bits, ever so often?
- Are you becoming an expert at creating your own private hell?

What inflates catastrophic imagination is ambiguity, inadequate communication, incomplete facts, and impatience. If you listen to the news and radio broadcasts, or read the morning paper, you will know that misfortunes occur everywhere. Pressures, frustrations, and battles are an inseparable part of life. Enduring demanding situations has become a universal experience. Yet, the situation's demand is contingent on one's personal perception and coping. That is why gracefully juggling between partner, spouse, house, children, work, bills, parents, lovers, in-laws, death, loss, poverty, illness, injury, injustice, anger, guilt, and endless other stressors has become even more necessary. The event is not as catastrophic as your perception of its outcome.

When you catastrophise, you think negatively about your nature, character, abilities, ideas, opinions, relationships, jobs, possessions, creations, body, as well as other people and the world. The perceived lack of your personal capacities makes it difficult for you to keep your head above the water, making you feel like you are drowning. Stressors could very often *seem* uncontrollable but stressing over them *can* be controlled.

11

Mental Filtering: Losing Positivity through the Mind's Sieve

"The show doesn't go on because it's ready; it goes on because it's 11:30."
This is something Lorne [Michaels] has said often about Saturday Night Live, but I think it's a great lesson about not being too precious about your writing. You have to try your hardest to be at the top of your game and improve every joke you can until the last possible second and then; you have to let it go.

—Tina Fey, *Bossypants*

Mental filtering is a form of twisted thinking in which you focus on the negative aspect of a situation, filtering out all the positive, often in the pursuit of perfection. You of course *see* the positive, but something always seems amiss. If you had to play the optimism versus pessimism game, you'll invariably see your glass as half empty. Truth however is not a perception, it is factual. Your glass is only half filled with water. So, calling it half empty or half full are both correct. But choosing a negative view and saying "there's no point drinking the water at all, because half a glass won't quench my thirst", may be inappropriate. When you refuse to drink, you stand the chance of getting dehydrated.

Mental filtering in depression can be attributed to unreasonable longing for perfection. You begin to play the "if and then" game, a lot, with such a filter in place. The smallest positive appraisal becomes conditional on an unreasonably high average. Anything short of that gold standard appears inadequate. And if you keep seeing people, events, and your own self as incompetent, it could feel demoralising.

Jaya's mind was generally twisting reality, making it work to her disadvantage. One afternoon she made an office presentation wherein the auditor asked, "Jaya, did you consider the changes in the economic climate in developing countries? Or have you focused only on developed nations?" She clarified the query. When the meeting was done, many officials including the CEO complimented Jaya. But she was upset that the auditor had asked her such an obvious question. As if he didn't respect her competence. Statistically the response to her work had been exemplary. But Jaya saw it as a bad day. Once again, she started feeling miserable about *everything*.

Is such anger and sadness appropriate? Or valid? How many times has your apprehension stemmed from an inability to impress someone sufficiently? And pushed you into a low self-esteem black hole? A time you unreasonably felt the need to be wanted, loved, appreciated, and desired? Maybe your insecurities pushed you to feel this way? Possibly your efforts weren't fixated on aiming for success, as much as they were on running from failure. A negativity bias in depression places focus on the negative even though there is equal probability of positive outcomes.

EXERCISE: Do You Use a Negative Mental Filter?

Let's list all the good and bad that exists in your life below, with a pencil. These could include character traits, support systems, friends or foes you made and lost, accomplishments and setbacks, profits and losses, successes and failures, new and adrift relationships, as well as people alive and deceased.

Imagine each of these to be tiny invisible particles that float in air. Let's call them the good and bad life molecules. To distinguish these two different kinds of molecules from each other, you could allocate a smaller size to the goodness molecules, and larger to the calamitous misfortunes that you underwent or experience every day even now.

Good Molecules in My Life	**Bad Molecules in My Life**
....	....
....	....
....	....
....	....
....	....
....	....
....	....
....	....
....	....
....	....
....	....
....	....

Now, you've mixed all these together. You have your own personalised blend of such positive and negative elements. At most times, the wind in life seems to be blowing smoothly. You're breathing normally, despite good and bad air.

Suddenly one day, you face a rough storm. At this bumpy moment, all air is sifted through a sieve. Unfortunately, the good molecules that were smaller in size pass through your mind's filter and are lost. Only the larger negative ones remain. You're only breathing harsh and unclean air now. Undoubtedly you feel choked. You gag and gasp, finding it hard to survive.

Does this sound like your mindset, especially during difficult times? Moments when you felt or feel like everything was miserable, and that nothing good has ever happened, happens, or will ever happen to you? An instant when you used your own personalised negative filter that caused more harm, and did you little or no good?

EXERCISE: CHECK YOUR NEGATIVE MENTAL FILTER

It's not a perfect world and yet, it's all right to crave perfection. Sometimes it drives you to excellence but at others it brings down mood and motivation. Put a check mark (√) if any of these statements reflect your general style of thinking.

- ☐ Being average doesn't cut it, I need to be the best.
- ☐ I want to always be praised for a good performance.
- ☐ I want to be perfect, so nobody will be able to point fingers.
- ☐ Failing at anything is a horribly miserable feeling.
- ☐ It doesn't feel right when I am not perfect.
- ☐ If people don't like my work, I take it as a personal flaw.
- ☐ Everything should be right, for me to feel alright.
- ☐ Being satisfactory is as good as being awful.
- ☐ If I'm not the best always, I don't feel worthwhile.
- ☐ If it's not going to be perfect, what's the point?
- ☐ Mistakes aren't acceptable to me.
- ☐ "Ideal" is the way to be.
- ☐ I care too much about people's impression of me.
- ☐ I have an incessant need to excel, and grow.

- ☐ I am = my achievements.
- ☐ People and I, expect me to be perfect.
- ☐ Mistakes make me (or anybody) a lesser person.
- ☐ Talking about my faults is horrible.
- ☐ Failing at anything is disappointing.
- ☐ If people aren't happy with me, it worsens my mood.

Did you check some or many of these? If you have an eye for picking on a single negative detail in yourself or others or the world in general, then like a drop of ink in a beaker that colours the entire water black, your perception of reality can get darkened. You might develop the penchant of zooming into the problem so closely, that everything else could get blocked out. The speck on the wall would look like a massive blotch. In fact, the focus on the problem and failure could become so deep, that you fail to see any wall (or the rest of the events in your life) at all. By sieving out all the positive through a mental filter, you make it easier for yourself to feel disappointed even when you've excelled, and rightfully deserve to feel proud.

We face little and big hardships daily, all of which demand attention for resolution. There are two kinds of solutions to these—an idealised one, and a realistic one. If you focus on the ideal and dismiss the real solution sitting before your eyes, you're likely craving a perfect world or what we call an "impossible average". Striving for perfection is not the problem. But giving up on the goal because it could not be perfect, could prove wrong.

This tends to happen in depression. It hurts no one but you, when you distort perceptions and are unable to see life for what it is because the mind sifts out the good, leaving behind the bad. This way you miss out on silver linings. When you get rid of the filter, a positive reality unfolds.

12

Emotional Reasoning: Beating Sound Logic with Feelings

"I am convinced that the act of thinking logically cannot possibly be natural to the human mind. If it were, then mathematics would be everybody's easiest course at school and our species would not have taken several millennia to figure out the scientific method."

—Neil de Grasse Tyson, *The Sky Is Not the Limit: Adventures of an Urban Astrophysicist*

Emotions are often called the guiding light. Sometimes the "gut feeling" beats available evidence and is rooted in a frequently inexplicable "I just feel so" kind of explanation. Emotions contribute to everything you think and do, even if only slightly. They influence the intellect, which is otherwise geared to drive logical choices. That is why when emotions take over the mind, they could supersede rationality.

When emotional, you might think, feel, and behave unreasonably. Like when you didn't make it through an important interview, and you concluded you would be jobless forever. You know that one shortfall does not define your life, and you could give other interviews where you might succeed. But you may have been so sad and sensitive at that time, that you couldn't think differently. Emotional reasoning becomes a cognitive error when you conclude that *all* your emotional reactions represent reality. So much so that you discount evidence that contradicts it. It seems surprising that you would continue to think adversely, despite the available logic confirming that your view is faulty. Similar to how some people say, "I know it's not true, but somehow I can't help feeling like this." Like many other cognitive errors, you may have been conditioned to reason emotionally, and in time this becomes spontaneous. It could turn into your style of analysing all situations, driving you to a negative outlook.

Jaya had been emotional and begun to feel that nothing was right between her and Veer. All this when he was respectful, calm, and patient. He even decided to introduce her to his family and was doing all that he could within his capacity to support her. Jaya could see it too. But that irksome voice in the needy corner of her head cried, "He's not into me, I wish he prioritised me and agreed to do things my way." Just because Jaya felt overwhelmed all the time, she concluded that her relationship was stressful. This crushed her. Hence her reaction, "Why does this have to be so hard for me? Aren't romantic relationships supposed to be smooth and a source of happiness and contentment? Why does my relationship have so many crinkles? Here I am trying so hard to iron them out, yet some issue always comes up and knots things all over again."

Jaya's argument sounds logical. But this was an emotional response. There was very little justification for what she felt. It was going alright, she didn't have reason to complain as much as she was, and yet she perceived her life and relationship to be miserable. She discounted all evidence that negated faulty intent on Veer's part. Jaya was stuck in her negative thoughts that told her nothing was fine. So, she continued to feel depressed. All driven by (incorrect and faulty) emotional reasoning.

When you reason emotionally, you resign to defencelessness and want to hit back, or get upset with your partner, family member, child, parent, friend, storekeeper, manager, supervisor, subordinate, or anyone who opposes or abandons you, as if leaving you out there to drown in the ocean.

If only you realised that this misery emanates from faulty processing in your brain's emotional centre and isn't based on sound logic, and that you should not believe these deceptive signals. Unfortunately, robotically you react on a whim, and the world (or you) are unable to decipher why you feel *as* hurt as you do. This worsens feelings of isolation.

EXERCISE: People Reason Emotionally, Off And On

These situations may or may not have happened with you. Maybe a friend, partner, child, parent, or acquaintance spoke to you about this. All of these are real examples from lives of real people I have interacted with in my practice. They felt this way and insisted, "I know I shouldn't, yet I do." Please put a check mark (√) if these situations, thoughts, and feelings sound rational or realistic to you.

- ☐ A pimple on my face worries me even though I know it's a small thing, and nobody will judge me for it. It's not a character flaw after all. I know I look nice. Why do I sense this inadequacy, as if I am *ugly*?
- ☐ I feel bad that the presentation did not go as well as planned. I know I have no reason to feel *this* guilty about it. I was better than most others who spoke on the topic. People said I was great too. Yet, I somehow don't *feel* good.

- ☐ I'm frustrated that I'm not getting attention from a couple of friends of late. I know they're busy with their lives, and there's no real change in their behaviour. But something tells me that I want more from them. *This* isn't enough.
- ☐ I know I'm a good mom, I do my best for the kids—I cook, clean, serve, pay for school, take up studies, pretty much everything in the book. And yet I get this feeling of "being at fault" that I'm not there for them the way I should be. I feel *guilty*.
- ☐ I've done well at work, but a voice in my head says I'm silly or not good enough. Maybe my colleague got the promotion, that's why? I know he's experienced, and we all knew that he was going to get it. Am I feeling *jealous*? Why though?
- ☐ I'm angry with my wife even though she's doing everything she can for me. The other day she prepped a surprise dinner, and I blew off on her as I had a stomach ache. I know it's wrong, but I just *can't be nice* to her.
- ☐ I'm upset that my diet plan hasn't made me lose weight. I know it takes time and I must be patient but I'm not seeing results. So, I feel like bingeing. I binged the other day and felt miserable about it. I'm unable to *get a hold* over how I feel.
- ☐ I mentioned to my cousins that I'm working on weekends, so they didn't invite me to the family lunch. I saw photos on Instagram and now I feel left out. I wouldn't have been able to go anyway. But I'm *upset* because they didn't invite me.
- ☐ The person on the dating site wasn't my kind of guy. I nonetheless sent him a request. He rejected it. I know I didn't like him anyway, and it shouldn't matter. But it does, and it makes me angry that *he* did not like *me*.

A common thread in the emotions of people in these real-life scenarios is that each knows the logic, acknowledges the rationale, agrees that they should not react adversely, and yet each feels low, sad, angry, or miserable. What they're feeling in all these examples, is a maladaptive, defensive, and reactive emotion, that hasn't passed the test of reason. The superficial emotion is covering up something deeper. Anger could be a cover for hurt, frustration shells jealousy, and anxiety could be masking low self-esteem.

This is why emotional reasoning is illogical. It is an appropriate response generated by your mind to a deep-rooted negative emotion. But this emotion is unavailable for scrutiny because you've unknowingly masked it and become unaware of it. Hence, logic fails you. If you are in sync with how you *really* feel, you'll be able to connect with people and yourself better and feel more positive emotions.

So, the next time you're feeling tense, frustrated, or stuck without really knowing why, maybe it is about something different from what you perceive. There could be some other reason that you're not willing to face—maybe it's too embarrassing, shameful, and belittling to admit. Maybe in childhood your classmates ignored you and made plans without you. That is why, in the future, your cousins not calling you for the weekend lunch triggers the emotional memory unconsciously. You couldn't go for the lunch anyway, but you felt upset, because you simply *weren't invited.* You got emotional.

You can't modify emotional reasoning unless you learn what feeds into it and replace that with optimal emotional responses that shape your thoughts and behaviour to your advantage.

EXERCISE: Know When You're Emotionally Reasoning

Many people are accused of being mechanical because they don't express their emotions much. Others seem hysterical because of over expression. In effect, what matters is how you feel, and whether your emotions are working for, or against your wellness and happiness. Put a check mark (√) if any of these statements reflect your thinking, feeling and behaviour. There are no right or wrong answers.

- ☐ I get happy easily (I'm reactive).
- ☐ I get upset and sad often.
- ☐ I'm sensitive to how people treat me.
- ☐ I focus a lot on feelings.
- ☐ I tend to feel extreme emotions.
- ☐ I cannot control my reactivity.
- ☐ It takes me a long time to snap out of negative moods.
- ☐ I get more upset than others do.
- ☐ Many have said I overreact.
- ☐ I could go from negative, to neutral, to positive, quite fast.
- ☐ Bad news ruins my day way more than it does to others.
- ☐ I get disappointed easily.
- ☐ I'm an emotional person in general.
- ☐ Little things frustrate me.
- ☐ If things don't go my way, it bothers me.
- ☐ Compliments enhance my mood markedly.
- ☐ If I do something wrong, it affects my mood adversely.
- ☐ My negative emotions consume me.
- ☐ I follow my gut more than logic.
- ☐ If I'm annoyed, my entire day gets ruined.

If you checked some or many of these, it might be true that your thoughts and behaviours are driven more by emotions, than logic. "How does this work for you?" Being on an emotional roller coaster (like any roller coaster) can make you nauseous. Reality doesn't even matter anymore when you're on that bumpy ride. All that remains is *your* interpretation of *your* reality and what colours *you* use to paint *your* life's portrait at that time.

Brushes of emotion tend to paint ambiguous portraits. Your beliefs become different from reality, and you might stress over things that aren't problems at all. It's time to change the brushes as well as the paint. Then, reality will be distinct from fiction. And happiness, clarity and peace will come about easily.

13

Labelling and Mislabelling: Designing Nasty Labels That Stick

"Labels are for filing. Labels are for clothing. Labels are not for people."

—Martina Navratilova

Labelling as a cognitive error, is a way of generalising a single trait, quality, or flaw, to an entire person. It creates categories in our mind because we get conditioned to see things that way. An obvious reason why we use labels otherwise in life, is that they are convenient for categorisation. The chef who labels spice jars and places them in specific racks, can retrieve them easily while cooking. Pharmacies mark medicine cabinets alphabetically to get tablets instantly when you ask for them by name. Shoes are identified by sizes, so you pick sneakers that fit your feet just right. It's an era of labels, bar codes, hashtags, dockets, markers, tags, chips and codes—all because labelling is opportune to life and it activates responses that we have learned and know (conditioning), without forcing us to think too much. Labels make life easy.

But can you fit *people* (including yourself) into such all-encompassing pigeonholes for similar convenience? Physical labels are far more well-defined, like short, lanky, slim, obese, fair-skinned, red-haired, endomorphic, or muscular. They have valid metrics and don't appear judgmental because they are factual. But character labels? Are they precise, and more so, purposeful?

EXERCISE: Character Labelling May be Instinctive

Labelling starts early in life. It appears natural, reflexive, and normal. Consider the descriptions described in the examples below. You may have encountered experiences in life (with yourself or people you know) where you used or considered some or many of these. Can you recall or imagine such labels?

- Ms. Margaret is a *strict* teacher; don't expect leeway just because you're unwell.
- Mr John is an *easy-going* coach. He won't fuss about rescheduling the class.
- The term exam is *critical*. It will decide your future subject selection in college.
- Annabelle's store is *pricey*. You're less likely to get good deals there.
- The lady auditor is *unreasonable*. She asks for unnecessary statistics.
- Meera is *touchy* and will throw a tantrum if you forget to wish her on her birthday.
- Joe is *impulsive* and will get angry if you tell him that you're not showing up.
- Sue is a *reliable* friend. You know that no matter what happens, she'll be there.

All these labels appear to arise from logic, grounded in a previous experience that made you formulate them in the first place. Future interactions tend to get easier when these are established. Labels save time, assist decisions and predict outcomes with a reasonable degree of precision. They make you feel like you're in control because you know how much to prepare, when to react and where to exercise caution. Labelling as you can see, is natural and useful.

But what if these were wrong labels? That Mrs Margaret was kind, and you were misunderstanding her assertiveness? Also, wouldn't your party plan be in jeopardy if you realised that Mr John could in fact, not reschedule your class? And what if that exam result didn't really count, that Annabelle's store had great discounts that summer, and the auditor was not as unreasonable as you'd anticipated? Touchiness, impulsivity, and reliability in your friends could just be *your* perception and may not be grounded reality. All these labels *might* be misleading you. And you could be unaware of their plot.

Labelling divides the world into rigid categories. Stronger, fiercer, grimmer, and harsher character labels do worse. When you stick a (permanent) character label on an event, person, or yourself, a pool of binary adjectives come into play. They make you see others or yourself as good or evil, events as doable or unachievable, and the world as miserable or marvellous. Labels feed into polarised thinking. Working in sync, these two could sorrowfully cloud your perception of reality. In a world where there are equal possibilities of winning and losing, a label doesn't help in critical situations. The depressed mind tends to focus rigidly on heavy-duty negative labels.

According to the theory of linguistic relativity proposed in the 1930s, you don't label things because of what you see. You see things based on how you've labelled them. Negative labels in depression generate a self-fulfilling prophecy wherein your entire perception becomes contingent upon the tag you have attached to anything. If you label life as unfair, the failed interview seems unjust to you, and you react angrily. When you label your partner as selfish, he or she appears egoistic, and you get upset. Because you label yourself worthless, you feel inadequate and underperform. Character labels influence perceptions, emotions, and behaviour. You continue to remain oblivious to their damaging conspiracy.

If you remember, Jaya was to meet Veer's family to take their relationship forward. She was nervous but was trying to stay composed. A tiny voice in her mind kept giving her little jolts, "Jaya, Veer's mother is going to know that you lack self-confidence. She might feel that you're not good enough for Veer."

What Jaya lacked was emotional flexibility. She made all this sound like it was carved in stone. She did not have the answers. Impulsive by nature, she wasn't willing to withstand uncertainty. Labels made the outcome certain for her, even if it was adverse. This wasn't the first time she had used negative labels. In the past, she'd accused Veer of being *apathetic*, branded herself as a *bad chef*, felt *inadequate* at work, and now berated herself for *lacking self-confidence*. She perceived her future mother-in-law as *critical* without even meeting her. Strong words, without any real evidence.

EXERCISE: Mislabelling Seems Reasonable

These statements are similar to the previous exercise about catastrophising. Like before, you may not have been in these situations, but notice whether the outcome added here sounds rational and realistic to any extent. Particularly note the labels that are in italics and bold. Do put a check mark (√) where the label appears logical.

- ☐ I didn't get hired. ⇨ I'm still jobless. ⇨ I feel humiliated. ⇨ I'm ***worthless.***
- ☐ I wasn't prepared for the meeting. ⇨ This is shameful. ⇨ I'm ***incompetent.***
- ☐ My boyfriend broke up with me. ⇨ I cannot survive alone. ⇨ I'm ***unlovable.***
- ☐ I've put on weight. ⇨ I am an embarrassment to my friends. ⇨ This is appalling. ⇨ I'm ***ugly.***
- ☐ I broke my routine. ⇨ I always blunder up. ⇨ My life is pathetic. ⇨ I'm ***a loser.***
- ☐ I don't focus in meetings. ⇨ I'm not performing. ⇨ It's a sorrowful state. ⇨ I'm ***sloppy.***
- ☐ I was rude to my friend. ⇨ She's not talking to me. ⇨ I can't take this. ⇨ I'm ***awkward.***
- ☐ I'm moving abroad for work. ⇨ My parents will have no support. ⇨ It's miserable. ⇨ I'm a ***cruel*** child.
- ☐ My senior said my work isn't up to the mark. ⇨ I could get fired. ⇨ This is tragic. ⇨ I'm ***stupid.***
- ☐ Mom asked to seek my brother's advice. ⇨ She doesn't trust me at all. ⇨ She's ***partial.***
- ☐ My daughter isn't home. ⇨ She didn't answer my phone. ⇨ She's in trouble. ⇨ I'm a ***horrible*** mom.
- ☐ My friend didn't respond to my message. ⇨ Nobody wants to be my friend. ⇨ People are ***fake.***
- ☐ I didn't pass the test. ⇨ I won't make it to university. ⇨ It's the end of my career. ⇨ I'm ***retarded.***
- ☐ My module wasn't approved. ⇨ My work is never showcased. ⇨ My life is miserable. ⇨ The world is ***unfair.***

Worthless, incompetent, unlovable, ugly, loser, sloppy, awkward, cruel, stupid, partial, horrible, fake, retarded, unfair—all labels in the above examples are not unheard of. Many people in life are told, or may have called themselves at least one of these at some point in life. Have you used these labels?

Mislabelling or false tagging with an incorrect portrayal makes character traits final. Any deficit, shortcoming, inadequacy, weakness, fault, or flaw on your part, then gets carved in stone, leaving no room for second chances. You begin to measure yourself (and the world) not by your effort or commitment, but by mistakes and slip-ups that you (or others) make. Instead of changing for the better, you feel insecure, upset, and sad. Depression accentuates this bias. The mislabelling filter pushes you down the rabbit hole, shielding your vision of a broader and happier reality–one that could be founded in affirmed details, solid facts, and hard evidence. When your mind doesn't know something, the temptation to assume is natural. Negative assumptions tend to appear more realistic. Hence, negative labels follow.

It could also be that you make negative assumptions and use labels to challenge yourself, so that later you could doubly rejoice at your success. If you say, "Nah, my interview wasn't good, I was nervous" and you get the job, it's as if the reward surpassed your expectations. But calling yourself "nervous" or "loser" repeatedly, before and during the interview, will most likely lessen your chance getting the job.

Faulty vocabulary of labels makes them sticky. Instead of saying, "I am not as strong as I'd like to be" you end up saying, "I am weak." Where you could say, "I could and really need to work harder," you blurt, "I am lazy and a loser." Some labels may be true, but it does not help to engrave them. Labels are best written on sand so that they can be washed away, and you build room for self-improvement and change.

14

Should Statements: Putting Undue Pressure on Yourself and Others

> "Should is a futile word. It's about what didn't happen. It belongs in a parallel universe. It belongs in another dimension of space."
>
> —Margaret Atwood, *The Blind Assassin*

Most of us continuously work towards wellness, strive for happiness, sweat for success, and toil for prosperity. We put in our best effort and eagerly await results. But all good things that we desire, demand, or even deserve, don't always arrive. On the other hand, bad things that we didn't want, need, or ask for, often do. It's natural to want good outcomes. But the tide isn't always in our favour. When that happens, we feel bad, upset, and sad.

"Why didn't everything go as planned? It should have!"

"Musterbation" is a term coined by Albert Ellis to describe a phenomenon whereby people live by absolute and unrealistic demands that they place on themselves, others, and the world. These rules come out in a series of must and should statements that we repeat to ourselves. The "should" distortion, also described by psychologist Clayton Barbeau as "shoulding", is less about the outcome, and more about the catastrophic emotional consequence it has on you simply because it did not happen the way you desired. Oftentimes you don't even *need* what you thought you did. It isn't of much consequence that someone didn't behave the way you expected. It's about the sensation you anticipated but missed out on. If only your mind could be open to the possibility that things might be different from the way you're seeing them.

In Jaya's case, the day she was to meet her boyfriend's parents she felt that impressing his mom was important. So, the pressure was mounting. Veer's aunt, her husband and their daughter were also present. A large family, they all were soon asked to sit at the huge conference-style dinner table. It inadvertently transpired, that the only two seats left for Veer and Jaya were far apart. Jaya immediately felt awkward. She felt she should have sat next to her boyfriend. Later when food was served, more "shoulding" ensued.

Jaya was allergic to mushroom, and the highlight of the evening was delicious oyster mushrooms, a family favourite. There were plentiful other dishes, more than sufficient to satiate any hungry stomach. Yet something, many things, irked Jaya's mind. "I should've known that others were invited. They should've let Veer and me sit together. She should've realised I'm allergic to mushroom. Veer could have been sensitive to my preferences. They should have treated me better."

Reality is complex, especially when many versions of it come into play, like the Rashomon effect. Veer's mother had wanted to keep the evening casual, hence the invitation to the extended family. The informal seating was to make Jaya feel like she was part of the family. Mushrooms happened by chance, and there were many other dishes to gratify anyone. None of this was about the people, dinner seating, or mushrooms. These were Jaya's personal expectations which were unfulfilled, so she felt neglected and sad. It was a unique, one sided, personalised perception of an attack on her, which wasn't consciously intended. And yet, Jaya felt miserable. To some extent we all might agree that Jaya's despair is justifiable. But then, is it really?

EXERCISE: Are You "Shoulding" Yourself?

These statements about you or your life may have crossed your mind at some point in time. Do put a check mark (√) on any that apply.

- ☐ I should get things right.
- ☐ I mustn't get upset.
- ☐ I should know how to deal with people.
- ☐ I shouldn't have been so silly.
- ☐ I should be able to handle this on my own.
- ☐ I should snap out of this.
- ☐ I should cook meals that people rave about.
- ☐ I shouldn't fumble in presentations.
- ☐ I should be more confident.
- ☐ I should be excelling at work.
- ☐ I should've gotten the promotion by now.
- ☐ I must crack this interview.
- ☐ I should have a perfect body.
- ☐ I should be happy at all times.

These are good "should" statements. They sound encouraging. But life can be incredibly challenging, and it may not *always* be possible for you to have *all* of this. If you keep "shoulding" yourself, these turn into irrational and impractical demands. If the lack of their fulfilment arouses inadequacy and personal failure, then these statements turn out to be discouraging and self-defeating. They bring on a sense of hopelessness and low self-esteem, both of which can worsen an already sad experience of depression.

EXERCISE: Are You "Shoulding" Others?

Now look at this set of statements. It is possible that you may have thought, spoken or felt like this about *others* at some time in your life, in a specific situation. Or you may feel so in general too, about a person. Do put a check mark (√) on any that apply.

- ☐ He should know better than that.
- ☐ She should do her job, and do it well.
- ☐ He should call me, if he wants to resolve this.
- ☐ She should prove to me, that she loves me.
- ☐ People should respect me.
- ☐ My partner shouldn't dump work on me.
- ☐ My manager should notice when I do a good job.
- ☐ My subordinates should acknowledge me.
- ☐ My parents should recognise what I do for them.
- ☐ My children should appreciate my efforts.
- ☐ People should always keep their promises.
- ☐ My date shouldn't be late.
- ☐ She should've remembered my birthday.
- ☐ She should've recalled I had other plans.
- ☐ I can't believe she cut into my lane. Her driving license should be revoked.

These statements do not sound unreasonable either. It's all right to have checked each one of them too. But holding on to these, sets pace for disappointment. You can control *your* behaviour.

Other people's motivations and actions are influenced by *their* mindsets, personalities, resources, and life-situations, and may not match what you had expected. If your emotional wellness becomes contingent upon that uncertainty, you could feel resentful. Such "shoulding" places you on the edge of the emotional cliff, and you stand the chance of falling, anytime.

EXERCISE: Are You "Shoulding" The World?

This set of statements reflects beliefs in general. You may or may not have thought, spoken or felt like this *generally* in life. Do put a check mark (√) on any that apply to you.

- ☐ The world should be a fair place.
- ☐ People should get what they deserve.
- ☐ Friends shouldn't fight.
- ☐ Employers should understand.
- ☐ Teachers should be considerate.
- ☐ Couples shouldn't argue.
- ☐ Service should be better.
- ☐ Colleagues should cover up for each other.
- ☐ Each team member should work their hardest.
- ☐ Reservations should be honoured.
- ☐ The economy shouldn't be shaky.
- ☐ Healthcare should be free.
- ☐ Politicians should be trustworthy.
- ☐ People should be more accountable.
- ☐ Everyone should be honest.

These are idealistic outlooks, which are nice to have. While the world is a righteous place, it can also be occasionally unfair. If you use "shoulding" this way, then a few unmatched ideals make the universe appear unjust and uncaring. And you tend to feel bitter and defeated. This could diminish the energy to do what you want and need, to bring about the very change that can improve your mood and life. Having expectations is not the problem, the demand that they *should* be met, and feeling bad when they aren't, is.

EXERCISE: Be Mindful of Your "Shoulding"

It can be surprising to know how often you might be using the "shoulding" distortion or "musterbation" every day. Try to make a note on these lines.

- Am I "shoulding" in my daily interactions? How often?
- Do I use this when I'm already feeling down?
- Am I using it when I am stressed?
- How do I feel when I think like this?
- Does it happen with specific people?
- Does it happen in certain environments?
- Does it happen at a specific time of the day, month, or year?

"Shoulding" goes hand in hand with black and white thinking. It takes away the sense of choice and leaves little room for negotiation. It happens when you don't examine all facts and motivations before you make attributions, and that is why you feel painful emotions. Life gets better when you realise that many a time, the outcomes that you desire do not actually matter. People do.

15

Personalisation: Making Yourself the Centre of the Universe

Every time we start thinking we're the centre of the universe, the universe turns around and says with a slightly distracted air, "I'm sorry. What'd you say your name was again?"

—Margaret Maron

A unique human trait that differentiates us from animals, is our fondness as well as capability to connect, collaborate, and coordinate with others. Sociability demands that we portray our best persona, and fuss over what others think about it. This is a rather adaptive way of making it about "us". Personalisation is therefore normal, and can fuel perfection. But if you start taking things personally *all* the time, you make yourself the centre of the universe, and could attribute every negative occurrence to your own personal deficit, incapacity, or insufficiency. You could also develop negative feelings towards others, assuming that all their unconstructive words and actions are directed towards *you* alone.

This drives sadness and resentment; both of which contribute to and sustain a depressed mindset.

Beck inferred decades ago that depression possesses a knack for generating a negative self-bias. Personalisation clubbed with overgeneralisation in depression can make you believe that a defect at a single task is an all-encompassing fault in your character. Do you recall the times when Jaya personalised the statements and behaviours of Veer and his family, and felt miserable about them?

- Veer wanting time to commit to marriage, implied *she* wasn't good enough.
- Veer asking for a short break meant he didn't have feelings for *her* anymore.
- Veer being late for dinner suggested that he specifically took *her* for granted.
- Veer's mother preparing mushroom casserole implied she disregarded *her*.
- Not being able to sit next to Veer meant that his family was sidetracking *her*.

None of these were personal attacks. Yet, Jaya felt and reacted like she was struck hard each time. Her lens was focused only on *herself* and how *she* felt. None of what she experienced was incongruous to her situation and obviously none of her emotions were all-out bizarre. From her viewpoint, her reactive emotions were valid. But her lens failed to zoom out to see the bigger picture. So, she reacted adversely. She felt disrespected, rejected, and dejected.

EXERCISE: PERSONALISATION APPEARS REASONABLE

These statements cite incidents that may or may not have occurred in your life. Do the outcomes sound rational and realistic to any extent? Particularly note phrases in the end that are in italics and bold. Put a check mark (√) wherever the conclusion appears logical.

- ☐ I'm new to driving. I'm driving slowly. The person behind me starts honking. I think, ***"I am such a bad driver."***
- ☐ I call my friend thrice. She doesn't answer. I feel rejected. I think, ***"She doesn't care about me; she responds immediately to anyone else."***
- ☐ I reach office late. The manager is speaking to a client. He doesn't acknowledge me. I feel snubbed. I think, ***"Nobody respects me even though I'm the boss."***
- ☐ My wife has a bad day at work. She storms into the room and screams at me for not spending time with the kids. I think, ***"Wow, she's got no respect for me."***
- ☐ My colleague fumbles in the presentation. Boss says *this* team could have done better. I feel berated. I think, ***"Boss dislikes my performance.***"
- ☐ I make an investment. My friend says it's a bad time to invest. I feel ridiculed. I think, ***"My friend criticises anything I do."***
- ☐ My friend comes for my party but looks uninterested. He doesn't talk much. I feel disrespected. I think, ***"He's got some serious ego tussle with me."***
- ☐ My boyfriend is stressed. I want to talk to him about it. He says he doesn't want to talk. I feel incompetent. I think, ***"I don't matter to him***.
- ☐ I try to cook. I follow the recipe to a T. The dish doesn't turn out good. I feel incapable. I think, ***"If I touch it, it has to fail."***
- ☐ The economy is unstable, I know. I don't get a bonus (I do deserve it though). I feel low. I think, ***"Good things never happen to me."***

- ☐ I join a dance class. The teacher isn't paying any attention to me. I feel neglected. I think, ***"This world is unfair, only to me."***
- ☐ I buy a lottery ticket daily, for 15 years. My friend buys his first lotto and wins close to 10 lakhs. I'm envious. I think, ***"Luck has never been my companion."***
- ☐ I seek the best therapist for my depression. I don't get better after 4 sessions. I'm disappointed. I think, ***"Things work for others, just not for me."***

How did these sound to you? Any logic that you could mirror? The negative emotions felt here appear misleadingly realistic. But if you reason with them better, you'll agree that whatever happened, was not intended for the person (or you) in particular.

The initial statements and occurrences reflect the mindset of the *other* person, who was making his or her point clear through disapproving words or actions. But the truth is, they would have spoken or behaved this way with *anyone* else in that situation. It was not specifically intended, targeted, or focused on anyone (or you) in particular.

The statements towards the end reflect a chance effect. For instance, nobody can *ever* know who will win the lottery. Buying a ticket daily for 15 years is no assurance that someone stands a higher chance. Likewise, so many other instances like road accidents, someone overtaking you, a bird pooping on you or your windshield, unforeseen sickness, or a poor-quality pizza from your favourite pizza place do not, cannot and should not reflect a planned misfortune that was carefully crafted and specially delivered just for *you*. When you condition yourself to believe that it's all about you, you become powerless; and nothing about your situation can get better anymore.

EXERCISE: Do You Personalise?

The following statements cite thoughts, feelings, or behaviours. Do put a check mark (√) on those that appear true for, or about you in general.

- ☐ I'm hypersensitive to teasing, even by friends.
- ☐ I am not good with jokes on myself.
- ☐ I cannot bear the thought of slipping up in public.
- ☐ If I fumble in front of people, I'm embarrassed.
- ☐ I'm conscious about what people think about me.
- ☐ I'd be hurt if my friend doesn't wish me on my birthday.
- ☐ I'm not so good with criticism and feedback.
- ☐ If a friend doesn't show up, I feel that he doesn't care.
- ☐ I'm sensitive to being told, that I'm over sensitive.
- ☐ I feel anxious when I'm challenged or opposed.
- ☐ I often assume, that others are right and I am wrong.
- ☐ I worry about people being judgmental of me.
- ☐ I tend to take things to heart.
- ☐ I give too much importance to other's opinions.
- ☐ I cannot bear the idea of being blamed.
- ☐ I get defensive easily.
- ☐ I'm not so open to people's perspectives.
- ☐ I think people take me for granted.
- ☐ I'm uncomfortable when I don't get what I believe I deserve.

All of these, again, appear like rational expectations. Still, they are self-focused personalised ideations that are not realistically attainable. You might think that this is who *you* are and what *you* want. That's fair. But this could be bringing *you* hurt, disappointment and sadness if your demands aren't getting fulfilled. You are the centre of *your* universe, but everyone else in the world around you, lives on *their* own planet. So, they react from *their* emotional space. It becomes less productive for you alone, when you hold on rigidly to the good as well as bad opinions others have of you.

EXERCISE: Be Mindful of Personalisation

When you detach from expectations, you're not dependent on others to feel happy, sad, frustrated, elated or ecstatic. When you are depressed, a narcissistic tendency overrules. It appears that any and every thing around (especially unfortunate negative events) are all connected with you, are about you, or caused by you. Your mind needs a break from this.

These statements affirm irrational personalising.

- Any feedback seems like criticism to me.
- It's my job to make sure that people like me.
- Mishaps happen with me because I am unlucky.
- I am invariably in the wrong place at the wrong time.
- I have a heavy burden, and I alone must lug it around.
- I am the only one who has to struggle.
- Everybody I know must see me, know me, and value me.

Like grains of sand that tend to slip away when you clench your fist too hard, you lose the most, by holding on to things. We *have to* work on letting go.

16

Jumping to Conclusions: Mind Reading and Fortune Telling

"Never jump to conclusions, because you never know where you might land."

—Unknown

Ambiguity has unique effects on the human mind. People like mystery novels, and live sporting events, and many enjoy gambling too. Uncertainty in these situations brings a distinct sense of thrill and joy. On the other hand, vagueness about health, weather, traffic, or the outcome of an exam, interview, or relationship, can be nerve-wracking. This leads to the tendency to want to break out of it, know what is going to happen, and make a conclusion already.

Uncertainty isn't ignorance (lack of knowledge); it is the conscious experience of "I do not know what the outcome will be". Generally, when you don't know, you practise caution, search for facts, and ponder over the pros and cons of a decision. But depression has another game plan in times of uncertainty. When something important is at stake, you may overestimate the risk of losing it. When information is unreliable, you suffer the sting of doubt. And when there are multiple causes and outcomes to consider, you fret over the complexity. In effect, your tolerance to uncertainty gets dampened. To break insecurity, your mind tends to hurriedly jump to a conclusion which invariably is negative.

If you recall, time and again Jaya felt helpless and awkward in the face of uncertainty. She didn't want to risk losing Veer, she disliked the ambiguity she sensed from his messages, and found it hard to deal with all the complexities that personified his family. Each time a message, discussion or event was not to her liking, she jumped to a negative conclusion and reacted emotionally. Jaya needed immediate answers. Impulsivity embodied her.

EXERCISE: Are You Uncomfortable With Uncertainty

The following statements cite thoughts, feelings, or actions. Put a check mark (√) on those that appear true for, or about you.

- ☐ Risks make me uneasy and apprehensive.
- ☐ Waiting for important outcomes makes me restless.
- ☐ Surprise events upset me (good surprises, even birthdays).
- ☐ It frustrates me to not have all the information about things.
- ☐ I'm impatient when it comes to making decisions.
- ☐ My plans feel ruined if things don't happen as I envisioned.
- ☐ When I'm unsure about something, I feel inadequate.
- ☐ If I doubt the success of an outcome, I withdraw.
- ☐ If I'm not sure about what'll happen, I cannot focus.
- ☐ I have more doubts about things, than other people.
- ☐ Smallest suspicions stop me from doing things I want.
- ☐ I need to prepare for everything in advance.

- ☐ If I know everything, I'll be in better control of my life.
- ☐ Wanting to know everything doesn't let me enjoy life.

If you did check any, know that you're one of many who share a dislike for anything that's indefinite, indeterminate, problematic, unreliable, untrustworthy, doubtful, unidentified ill-defined, variable, or sporadic. What you do with your dislike for uncertainty, determines your ultimate emotional outcome. When you jump to a conclusion or assume an outcome without sufficient evidence, you're using one of two twisted predictive processes–fortune telling and mind reading. Fortune telling is general prophesising about the future while mind reading involves an assumed surety of what someone else is thinking, feeling, or implying. You invariably use both to establish a negative hypothesis. If you believe the hypothesis without testing it, catastrophising ensues.

You might wonder, why does my mind have to assume the negative every time it doesn't know something? Why can't I jump to positive conclusions? Aren't valences equal on both sides?

According to Beck's cognitive theory, the depressed mind gets associated with negative representations that include but are not limited to failure, rejection, loss, emptiness, self-blame, guilt, threat, danger, distrust, risk, and a fear of domination and manipulation. Fortune telling is like having a crystal ball inside your head, which relies on these representations, and uses them to churn out likelihoods and estimates. Given a negative internal model, how difficult is it to assume adverse outcomes when faced with risk and complexity? Therefore, the mind continually predicts sadness. But that's the whole point; this crystal ball exists only in *your* head and the miscalculations in *your* mind represent an outcome that *cannot* be genuine.

EXERCISE: ARE YOU ATTUNED TO FORTUNE TELLING?

The following statements cite thoughts that may have traversed your mind, feelings you sensed, or events that occurred in your life, sometime in the past. Do put a check mark (√) on those that appear true for, or about you.

- ☐ If someone doesn't call back, they're probably unwell.
- ☐ In examinations, I always assume that I will fare poorly.
- ☐ Before any interview, I'm convinced that I won't make it.
- ☐ I tend to think that the odds are usually against me.
- ☐ If I don't know everything, I think others will fool me.
- ☐ When faced with a challenge, I always assume I'll fail.
- ☐ When I'm worked up, I get a feeling that I will faint.
- ☐ When I am in pain, I react like it's never going away.
- ☐ When I cry, it feels like the sadness will last forever.
- ☐ If I'm rejected, I think that I won't be able to move on.

Maybe your friend *was* unwell. and you possibly *did* fare poorly in the examination or interview. Likewise, the odds may have been against you *often*, and your life *is* demanding. But there is no guarantee anywhere in all of these instances, that *what* you imagined each time *was definitely* going to happen. Even real fortune-tellers don't make predictions with that degree of inevitability. And yet, the negatively-inclined depressed mind so often makes "guaranteed negative assumptions".

EXERCISE: ARE YOU TUNED TO MIND READ?

The following statements cite thoughts and feelings you may have had in the past or could reflect present reaction to situations.

Maybe the event didn't occur exactly this way. But do put a check mark (√) on what appears true for, or about you.

- ☐ If a friend doesn't respond to my message, I gather he or she doesn't like me.
- ☐ If I eat alone at the cafe, I worry people will call me a loser who has no friends.
- ☐ If I get to office a few minutes late, everybody thinks I am a work shirker.
- ☐ If two friends meet up without me, I'm convinced they don't want me around.
- ☐ When I don't make it through a job interview, my family thinks I'm incapable.
- ☐ When the manager said I need to do better, he implied that I'm useless.
- ☐ When my client wanted a second opinion, I assumed he didn't like my idea.
- ☐ If my staff doesn't seek my advice, I assume that they don't value my opinion.
- ☐ If I tell my friends about my depression, they will consider me to be a loser.
- ☐ When my therapist said I must work harder, she actually meant I'm a hopeless case.

Did you resonate with one, some or several of these? You would agree that these aren't logically causative, do not reflect the truth and have no evidence to back them up. The mind still jumps to believe in them like they are the sworn truth, and reacts sorrowfully by feeling rejected. How devious is depression, that it convinces you to conclude the worst, each time?

It is common, sometimes appropriate, and frequently helpful to guess what others are thinking by paying heed to their gestures, body language, reactions, and words. It is only when these guesses are negative, and we continue to believe and react to them without evidence, that fortune telling and mind reading become a problem. Your emotions don't exist in a vacuum. Thoughts that fuel them sometimes hide in your subconscious mind. That is why you must apply logic by making your thinking conscious and deliberated.

If you really knew how to predict the future, wouldn't you put it to more constructive action? Don't let your mind fool you.

17

Discounting the Positive: Nullifying Every Good Experience

"Thou canst not think worse of me than I do of myself."

—Robert Burton, *The Anatomy of Melancholy*

Discounting the positive is a hard-wearing form of twisted thinking, distinct from mental filtering which focuses on the negative by sifting out the positive. This wicked thought filter acknowledges but convolutes positivity by rephrasing it adversely to convince you that all favourable occurrences in your life are by chance, or a result of pity, luck, or fluke. This is rooted in a perceived (false) belief that in principle, things are *nothing* but miserable, dismal, and wretched, and you are incompetent, pitiable, and incapable.

Self-motivation is complex. You're often hard on yourself because you've lived and learned, that survival can be difficult. So, you keep a reality check in place to attain difficult goals. When things don't work out as you hoped, it may appear normal to have negative and self-critical thoughts. But what happens when things aren't as bad? Or they're rather good? Are you appreciative and supportive of yourself then? Or do you beat yourself nonetheless, because now you are wired this way?

EXERCISE: Are You Discounting the Positive?

Think about a time when something was going well and you were praised, complimented, or admired for your effort, looks or some skill. How did you respond? These situations may not be exact representations of what happened to you, but there might be some similarity. Do checkmark (√) what might have been or is true for you.

- ☐ I am not worthy of this compliment from my manager.
- ☐ The interviewer wasn't competent, so I passed the round.
- ☐ I'm incapable, they gave me this award to motivate me.
- ☐ My friends are being nice because they know I'm sad.
- ☐ This presentation went well by fluke.
- ☐ People pity me, that is why they say my work is good.
- ☐ I may have been good, but not sure that's true anymore.
- ☐ My mistakes define me and negatively label me always.
- ☐ I have a caring family, but I'm too sad to acknowledge it.
- ☐ My partner is nice but I'm a disappointment to her.

These statements are grim and dark. They might appear passive aggressive too. It's as if you're unable to see *any* positives, count *any* blessings or put in work to make *anything* better. Do you feel like this? It's paradoxical how this distortion allows every good thing to be perceived as derogatory, and makes every compliment appear deprecating.

This style of thinking makes you unjustifiably tough on yourself and could generate as well as sustain low self-esteem. A core symptom of depression, this breeds scepticism. Feeling unworthy was bad enough. But misconstruing successes as coincidences could almost simulate a delusion where you continue to see failings, despite evidence to the contrary.

Jaya's story reflects this distortion. She could nearly *never* recognise that she looked good, cooked well, toiled hard, or that her efforts at work, home, or in the relationship ever added up. When people praised her, she assumed a pretentiousness that was intended to belittle her every move. After the dinner at Veer's house, the family had identified Jaya as a charming, friendly, and a loving, young lady. And yet, Jaya retorted to Veer, "I don't believe this is true. You're being nice because I'm upset all the time. I'm not even sure you want me anymore. I'm a dismayed, demanding, and depressed human being!"

These were fierce words. She'd discounted *everything* positive between them and warped it to a degree that challenged their basic contexts—of trust, love, and commitment. What was Jaya aiming for? It's likely that her low self-esteem was pushing her to lose faith. She'd worked herself up to a state where nothing appeased her. Jaya wasn't aware that her despair was rooted in her thinking style. Her thoughts occupied an esoteric territory in her mind, and she assumed them to be the undisputable truth.

Thinking negative thoughts does not imply that you are crazy. It just means that like everyone else, you have your individual reasoning styles which tend to get tortuous with recurring disappointments. Unfortunately, when these escape the radar of conscious awareness, they get more fixated. A depressed mind churns out negative thoughts robotically, focusing on glitches and dismissing solutions.

Are you able to see the problem?

Part - II

THOUGHTS RULE YOU, BUT WHEN TWISTED, THEY COULD FOOL YOU

(Cognitive Behavioural Model of Depression)

"When we feel bad, we often automatically decide that either we are bad, or another person is bad. Both of these moves cause damage and distort the truth; which is that we are all navigating difficult conditions the best we can, and we all have a lot to learn, and unlearn."

—Dean Spade, Mutual Aid: Building Solidarity in This Crisis

COGNITIVE ERRORS EXPLAINED IN SECTION TWO OF THE BOOK offer a grounding base for you to pinpoint inaccuracies in your thoughts and nudge you towards the freshness of positive and rational thinking. This section of the book will work on ways to identify, and then challenge twists in your thinking, which could lead you to unwanted emotions. This process is better known by technical terms like cognitive restructuring, breaking cognitive distortions or cognitive therapy.

You will realise that all thinking flaws or cognitive distortions have a woven consistency. This means that many twisted thinking styles co-exist. That is why one untwisting technique applied to a given negative thought, can break several cognitive errors in one shot. Net result? Positive thinking, and resultant positive emotions.

The examples and narratives mentioned here are those of real clients and patients who consulted me over the past years and how we worked together towards perception of a different reality from what their mind was making them believe. The reason why I have used examples of many different people in this section is to help you see how each person's story describes so many different distortions, and one single technique can combat plenty of these, all at once.

The initial chapters will help you understand common barriers in your mind to this process. Then, we will slide into an explanation of different methods that can be applied to challenge negative thoughts. This new and different path is designed to lead you to a happier and peaceful space.

18

Do I Really Have to Change? What If I Don't?

(Overcome Hurdles to Self-change in Depression)

"If you put your nose to the grindstone rough,
And keep it down there long enough,
You will soon conclude that there are no such things,
As a brook that babbles or a bird that sings.
These three things will your world compose:
Just you, the stone,
And your ground-down nose."

—Anonymous

A frequent retort by my patients and clients when I speak about cognitive therapy is, "So, this is *my* fault? I'm the one who should change my thinking, while people around me continue to be inconsiderate? Why is it okay for the world to be unfair? Why should I work so hard on myself, to obtain what is already my birth right—my *own* happiness? This idea itself makes me sadder."

Cognitive therapy is not easy. Healing takes time and patience.

If you recall the sore memories of what you've endured, the pain you've tolerated, discomfort you've stomached, and hardships you underwent, there's enough in each of those accounts to contend that depression does make sense. It seems sadness is tangled irreversibly with the very things that make you human—your imagination, weakness, vulnerability, and a basic capacity, to feel. All undesirable emotions seem like instinctive responses to negative life occurrences. From this standpoint, depression sounds profoundly natural. As if the touch of it, however unfriendly, could be a fitting reaction to life's long-suffering questions and society's inflexible shortcomings. Sadness after all, *is* one of the many primary human emotions. How then will you find the motivation to change, and not feel sad anymore?

EXERCISE: Sadness and Frustration–A Part of Life

These are some common occurrences in life. Do put a checkmark (√) on any or all that may have made you feel sad, unhappy, gloomy, glum, dejected, frustrated, or depressed.

- ☐ A friend promises, but doesn't show up.
- ☐ You're blamed for something you didn't do.
- ☐ Your parents compare you to your sibling consistently.
- ☐ Your partner cheats on you.
- ☐ Your most reliable employee picks a job with your rival.
- ☐ Your new and shiny car is scratched by an envious vandal.
- ☐ Your partner disregards your overtures of affection.
- ☐ You're doing your best but not seeing 'positive' results.
- ☐ You're faced with impossible deadlines, everyday.

Many of these happen. None of them feel good. They reiterate that the world can be unfair, life isn't perfect, and people who we know and interact with almost daily, could let us down. Emotions are good companions. Sometimes happiness, joy, pleasure, and ecstasy travel beside you. At other times sadness, anger, frustration, and misery accompany you. It is the gradation in perception of emotions (positive or negative) which decides how you eventually feel. Sadness is different from depression. Likewise, feeling fed up is distinct from feeling suicidal, and anger is separate from aggression.

Cognitive therapy helps you perceive negative emotions on the milder side of the spectrum and creates scope for applying logic to modify your thoughts and behaviour so that you can feel better. It is based on the premise that *you* have the power to control your mind. Depression will not allow you to feel good. So, no matter how unfair it seems, *you* need to initiate the battle with depression *yourself.* People around you can help, and we will discuss how to make that happen too, but the race starts with you. Your cognitive restructuring and mindfulness will play a big role in beating depression and get you to the finish line in time. Sadness *cannot* always be avoided, but depression that frequently results from it, *can*.

Beware And Be Aware Of Your Emotions

Emotions are omnipresent. We all get emotional from time to time. It's the awareness about emotions that helps you realise why you feel the way you do, so that these can be tackled better. I am reminded of my early days as a psychiatrist in practice. I had set up my office, trained my staff well in patient support, and assured practice guidelines, so that appointments were scheduled in time for optimal patient experience.

One afternoon, barely a few days into my private practice, I had an emergency request for a patient whose brother asserted she needed immediate evaluation. I agreed to wait. It was several hours late into the evening, beyond the time I allowed myself to stay at work before they arrived. A flurry of thoughts traversed my head in the interim.

- It's a waste of my time.
- This isn't professional.
- Am I being taken for granted?
- Should I see her another day?
- Can I reschedule the meeting?
- Why do I feel this is unfair?

And yet something kept telling me that none of these thoughts, and the resultant reaction of feeling upset were befitting. By emoting this way, faulty processing of information was taking place. Here are some thoughts that helped me feel calmer.

- They may be stuck in unexpected traffic.
- Maybe the patient wasn't cooperating.
- It's likely that they feel apologetic too.
- I agreed to wait; so, this is my choice.
- He respects me; hence wanted to see me.
- I'll be assertive about timings next time.

I did see the patient eventually. She and the family apologised for being late. Seeing me did give her newer perspective, and she has followed up for subsequent sessions by herself, ever since. It made me realise that not everything untoward that happens to me is because of someone's spite or arrogance towards me. It wasn't directed at me even though I briefly felt it was. It cannot, and is not, *always* about *me*.

Forgive, And Learn To Let Go

There's still the continuous dilemma—how and when do you decide to forgive, can you ever forget, and when is a good time to let go? Which feelings are okay to keep? How can you become willing for change? When will your emotional vocabulary be adept enough to choose correctly from oppression, suppression, expression, or depression?

Answers to these questions will nourish your desire to think differently. Changing isn't easy. The comfort zone is too comfortable, even if it is one of turmoil and depression. The run to the end of the tunnel is long. Even though there is light there, it's takes time and effort to navigate to it.

EXERCISE: Do I Need to Change? What? And Why?

Here are some questions, answers to which decipher the appropriateness of your negative mood state and fuel your incentive to drive self-change. They tell you whether change is required, what really needs to change, and why that change is important for you. Once this realisation is made, your job becomes easier.

- Am I suppressing how I really feel?
- Am I concerned about depression stigma?
- Do I have misconceptions about change?
- Am I in denial, thinking there's no problem?
- Am I running away from my problems?
- Am I stubborn, and resisting what is good?
- Am I doing anything to get better?
- Am I lacking skills that'll make me happy?
- Am I expecting too much out of myself?
- Am I blaming the world for my misery?

- Am I logical, or are emotions ruling me?
- Is this momentary or has it become enduring?
- Do I respect myself as much as I deserve?

Acknowledge when you're being resistant and be mindful of changing it. There's a fun part to change though. Once the wheel of wellness is rolling, it's hard to make it stop. When you learn how to be happy by thinking differently, you could keep feeling so, literally forever.

AM I SUPPRESSING HOW I REALLY FEEL?

It's normal to want to look strong, and not always reveal what you feel. Not everybody in the world is welcoming and considerate of unconstructive emotions. Many could even be quick to judge. Humans are self-preserving. In an era where we had to fight to survive, we made ourselves appear strong in the face of every fear. But you must be aware of the façade, even if you're rightfully using it to protect yourself.

I remember one of my patients repeatedly assert to me during her therapy sessions, that she wasn't *so* depressed, and things aren't *that* bad. I had to remind her that my estimation of the problem did not matter, hers did. I knew the seriousness of her distorted thinking and how much she incessantly tried to convince herself that she was fine. While this was a good defence in life, it interfered negatively with therapy. She kept hiding how she felt, and as long as she continued to do that, how was I going to be able to suggest where and how she must change? And without that, how would she? Change becomes easy when you're honest with yourself; because you are doing this for yourself, nobody else.

Am I Concerned About Depression Stigma?

We are aware of the far-reaching agony about the stigma of depression. It is logical to worry about some segments of society misconstruing depression for character weakness or a personality flaw. Societal stigma is *not* as adverse as the self-stigma you tend to carry on yourself about how you feel. Nearly two decades of my practice are proof of the scepticism people have about seeking help, not because someone else would know, but because seeking help itself means, "I am weak, and I could not manage this myself".

For every 2 patients I see in my practice, there are without exaggeration, 20 or more who will connect, book an appointment, and withdraw, because they worry about how seeking help would impact their self-image. The fact that they need to see an *outsider* to resolve something *inside* them, seems frightening and stigmatising. If you had to ask yourself, the answer lies within the question itself. When you perceive a depression stigma, then you already know that you could be depressed, and you agree that you need help. You just need to fight the taboo, reach out and seek that life-changing support, which is so readily available and obtainable today. After all, you deserve it, don't you think?

Do I Have Misconceptions About Change?

Many people are ill informed about CBT and worry that it will change their brain in mysterious ways. It has been rightfully emphasised that cognitive restructuring could change the brain circuitry and neurochemicals, and modulate the responsiveness of thinking and memory centres. All only to make you think and feel positive emotions forever. But these scientific concepts are often surprisingly misunderstood, if you don't know enough about how cognitive therapy works.

I had a patient who worried that she did not want to be metamorphosed into a submissive zombie who couldn't feel emotions—one who was complacent with everything. She assumed that with therapy she would lose control over her thoughts, feelings, and interactions. If she changed her style of thinking, she would become a puppet. When I explained how therapy works, she became eager to seek help. She brought on change effortlessly with step-by-step support and guidance. Ignorance feeds fear. When you know how this is going to help, you will accept this treatment better.

AM I IN DENIAL, THINKING THERE'S NO PROBLEM?

Nobody enjoys the diagnosis of depression, or tuberculosis, or malaria for that matter. But depression is worse because it comes with a sense of culpability. It was interesting when I was once approached by the husband of a patient, for *her* depressive symptoms. She refused to eat, speak, meet people, engage with anyone, or even care for herself or her 5-year-old child. She did not believe that anything was wrong with her. She'd lost her job and insisted that she was definitely upset. She also justified this as a reaction to her job loss. She told him *he* needed therapy as something may have been off about *him* for worrying so much about her.

I asked him to suggest family therapy to her—focusing more on their son and how the two parents could help his recently surging tantrums. Though this was a result of her low mood, she had failed to see a connection. She agreed to therapy. Through discussions, I delved deeper into the emotional climate at home. Her diagnosis did not matter, how *she* felt did. All she needed was to be convinced that she could in essence feel happier, cope more maturely, and be a better mother and wife. She just did not want to accept the idea that she herself could be depressed. She was in denial. With empathy, support, and understanding, she was willing to change. What else did we need? The mission was accomplished. She got better and the family atmosphere improved. She even got a new job within the year.

Am I Running Away From My Problems?

Some adverse emotions are so long-standing, they become part of your persona. You begin to see them as unrelated to your perceptions. So, you spend your time and energy running from real issues. You don't think of changing yourself because you lose the logical connection between your thoughts, emotions, and actions.

I remember a patient who presented to me with a steadily increasing consumption of alcohol and cigarettes. She'd been drawn to smoking cannabis joints too, on occasion. She never once acknowledged what drove her to consume these substances. When I asked about work, family or general health, she thought it was unrelated banter. It was only in passing that she mentioned the recent breakup with her boyfriend, and her inability to cope. She missed him terribly. "The pain of separation is unbearable" she said. She was running from her underlying problem into the direction of psychoactive substances. The substances *had* the power to numb her pain. But unless she realised that she was depressed after the breakup, how could she change and why would she change?

Am I Stubborn And Resisting What Is Good?

Humans are creatures of habit who recognise change as *demanding*. The hard wiring in the brain can be so rigid that even in the face of adversity, you might want to stick to the "old ways", despite the evidence that they're not functional. In practice, I observe this in clients who tell me, "This is who I am. This is how I've always been. So, I guess, this is how I'll continue to be. Is there anything else that can be done to make me feel better? I'm not sure I can change or whether I want to make the effort to."

This defensiveness to change already encompasses the cognitive distortion of fortune telling. It can be so challenging when the reason to seek therapy (cognitive distortion) itself is its deterrent. What I tell these clients is this: You can try with small steps and see how that change works for you. Every tiny step is a little drop that eventually adds to the ocean. If you can be patient and see life that way, you will become more accepting of and willing to change.

Am I Doing Anything To Get Better?

When a patient's boyfriend ghosted (vanished forever from her life without any warning) her, she was lonely and sad. In time, she lost interest in everything pleasurable and was visibly depressed. On tireless coaxing by friends, she agreed to see me. Her first question was, "Doc, are you getting me my boyfriend back? If not, then what's the point in seeing you? How are you going to help? I'm not sure which part of my life and mind, you can change. So, my golden question to myself is—why am I here?"

It was a hard question to answer immediately, knowing that little I said would convince her at the time. But I did have a counter question, "Maybe speaking with *me* will not make things better for you right away. But can you tell me what *you* have been doing for the past two months to make anything better for *yourself*?" This sparked insight in her mind about how ignorant she had been of her own state of wellness. She had done nothing to heal herself, because she believed that the *rejection* and *ghosting* was the problem. Now she realised that her *reaction* to it was, and it was time to do something that might actually help her feel better.

Am I Lacking Skills That'll Make Me Happy?

It's a fact, the very event that causes *you* to feel sad and depressed may not have the same effect on someone else. What does this other person possess, that you are missing? Stress that you experience is less dependent on the strength of the external stressor, and more contingent on your internal stress buster. Your attitude, resilience, coping style and personality are anti-depressant skill sets that protect you from stress, burnout, anxiety, and depression.

I remember the patient who decided that since she was feeling sad, she would not meet her friends. She was too embarrassed to admit her depression. She lacked the social skills to reach out, seek assistance from others, or stand up for herself. With a little nudging, in no time her engagement in harmless banter with friends made her laugh and elevated her spirit. When she realised where she was going wrong, she was keener to change, build social communication skills, and became open to therapy too. All of this widened her horizon of hope and helped her tremendously.

Am I Expecting Too Much Out Of Myself?

It's great to strive hard and be strong, to want to master and conquer. But unrealistic expectations could root failure and break your own determination. Do you beat yourself up for not being competent enough in managing your own emotions, simply because you believe you are supposed to always be perfect?

My young, depressed client insisted that her father was more severely depressed than her, and it was her duty to take care of him. When she was unable to do so, it lowered her mood to an extent that she felt unworthy. She believed it was her responsibility to assure her family's physical and emotional well-being. They believed in her and often called her the "man of the house" as she always put up a brave face to fight any adversity that befell them. This built a continuous pressure for success, excellence, and approval. When she felt out of control, she couldn't bear it, and it broke her. She couldn't match up to what she expected of herself. Seeking help wasn't even on her radar. How could she? She was supposed to be infallible.

The desire to be in control is an elemental human shortcoming. Many people refuse to accept their emotional failings – anger, frustration, envy, sadness, as well as depression. Bottling things within can prevent the primary emotion of sadness from surfacing. But it could also get replaced by worse secondary emotions like irritability, sarcasm, and passive aggression. If you accept sadness as a normative emotion and open yourself to the idea of change, you could feel more empowered than before, and your depression will be healed from its root.

Am I Blaming The World For My Misery?

There isn't anyone who hasn't been upset with the world at some point when faced with failure, disappointment, or rejection. Unforeseen natural events like a storm also frustrate us. "It wasn't supposed to rain today. The meteorological department should be more precise in their forecasts". Likewise, "The exam should have been easier," or, "The interviewer could have been lenient", or "My friend should have made it in time for my party."

I had once received an email request from an old client saying that she wished to re-instate therapy. She'd stopped barely after a couple of sessions a few years ago. Obviously, we hadn't really broken much ice, let alone bring about meaningful change. This time she said categorically, "Doctor, you must make sure that my problems are solved and that I am healed. It was not very fruitful the last time around." From what I remember, her misery was deeply ingrained in her husband's lack of involvement, insufficient care, and poor understanding of her troubles.

I suddenly remembered why she'd stopped seeing me. She was displeased with my idea that her expectations of her husband could contribute to her own emotional turmoil. She believed then, as well as now, that her troubles were the outcome of an unconcerned husband and inadequate therapy. If that stayed, how could she change?

She felt rejected and blamed the world for her pain. Any negative emotional reaction from me would reinforce that belief. I calmly assured her I would do my best but also needed her to pledge the same. As I supported her more, she became accepting of my suggestions and stopped fighting me, as well as her irrational beliefs. Change became easy.

Am I Logical Or Are Emotions Ruling Me?

I'm certain that every negative emotion anyone feels is reasonable. It hurts when things don't go the way you planned, hoped, or expected. But think of the outcome of your reactions when all of this occurs. You could follow the logical path—identify thinking errors, shift your focus on enhancing yourself, be with people who make you cheerful, openly express how you feel, sort differences that tarnish relationships, and resultantly, feel happy. Or you could choose the emotional route—feel sorry, disappointed, and upset with yourself or someone in your life who caused this pain, get cynical, and gradually grow to dislike the universe in general.

Many people I have seen in life follow the emotional route. They unknowingly, yet steadily, dig a dark hole of negativity and pessimism for themselves and get mired deeper into negative thoughts that keep them there. Depression plagues judgement. But there is a way to bring back happiness with suitable logic.

You've got to stop feeling sorry for yourself and start initiating change that will solve each of the problems that are bothering you.

Is This Momentary, Or Has It Become Enduring?

At a diagnostic level (per the DSM-5), we agree that negative mood and behaviour symptoms that persist continuously for more than two weeks, could qualify as depression. But at the thought level, there's more true-to-life logical ground to this. Holding on to memories about negative events (and the resultant painful emotion) beyond their duration of relevance does not serve any purpose. We all easily do that for more than two weeks. This way the low mood and other depressive symptoms persist.

I had a patient who presented with a long-standing history of frustration, irritability, sadness, and dejection relating to what she called a "bad marriage". She insisted that right after they'd gotten married four years ago, her husband did not give her as much love and attention as she'd expected (she was comparing herself to friends who'd been married around the similar time frame). She agreed that things were better today, but also asserted that her most important years as a newlywed wife had been "ruined". And she couldn't, maybe she didn't want to let go of that pain. It "rightfully" justified her being upset and frustrated with her husband. She felt that she needed to keep resenting him. She wasn't somehow realising what this process of holding on was doing to her today, in the present.

When you retain negative emotions beyond their point of relevance, they're useless. And only cause harm. She was rightfully upset with her husband four years before, but that did not hold weight today. If she could communicate this with him, maybe even understand the cognitive distortions that had contributed to her sadness earlier and continued to do so now, change would be attainable, and she could be happier.

Do I Respect Myself As Much As I Deserve?

It seems obvious that those who do not respect themselves enough might find it easy to seek external help, simply because they are aware of their self-esteem deficit. But human emotions could work contrary to obvious logic. A new patient repeatedly had no-shows for appointments. She wanted to test whether her therapy team cared enough to reach out to her each time to reschedule a new slot. When the support staff stopped calling her on account of endless cancellations, she appeared one day and cried relentlessly. "How I wish *someone, anyone,* on earth cared about how I feel. I guess you have also given up on me, doctor. What should I do, I have nowhere to go!"

I sat her down and explained how she first needed to respect herself for others to value her. She needed to express authority in her choices for her own care. This was true in her exchanges with friends and family as well. The constant fear of rejection dissuaded her from being her natural self. She was also now avoiding therapy that could help her. When she began to respect herself more and became autonomous, she attended sessions regularly. Of course, she got better too.

Believing you are unworthy of love, incapable of care, and undeserving of attention will only make it more so. What you need most when you're feeling depressed, is to believe in yourself and accept that you can be feeling low, but it is in your hands to make it better. That is how change will become natural and easy.

19

Identify the Kink in the Way You Think

(Learn How to Spot Your Cognitive Errors)

> "She hoped to be wise and reasonable in time; but alas! Alas! She must confess to herself that she was not wise yet."
>
> —Jane Austen, *Persuasion*

The best student isn't one with the highest IQ or sharpest memory, but one who's willing to unlearn what hasn't worked, and relearn from basics, what might. Twisted thoughts generate many layers of rational cover-ups that mask their offense. These need to be exposed and then modified. Like mould that slyly eats into solid concrete bit by bit, distorted thoughts plague everyday thinking by making it appear logical. And the prey (you) never realises what happened, or when, and why depression surfaced.

I distinctly remember my patient, Shruti, and her keen enthusiasm to do anything to feel better about herself and her life. Young, hardworking, humble, and respectful, she even made notes during therapy sessions, to discern where she was going wrong so that she could do something, anything, to set it right. However, the disenchanting truth that self-change is an effortful and demanding process irked her. She wasn't prepared for this.

There was too much going on in Shruti's life (that also makes it sound like anyone's else's life actually). So much was happening that disconcerted her and dampened her mood. There was a consistent mix of happy and frustrating moments. While she beamed with delight in the joyous ones, the lows flustered her deeply. Shruti was a living example of the thinking errors mentioned in the previous chapters, and she was finding it hard to break their vicious cycle. Her thoughts kept pulling her down.

I suggested charting Shruti's moods. Every single time she felt *any* emotion, she was to write it out. "Oh my God, so I will be recording my moods all day? Looks like that's all I will be doing!" she cried. "Yes, I'd love that," I said. She had not the slightest hint that little droplets of frustration in her day, were adding up to the ocean of misery she expressed when she saw me each week. And it was drowning her life. I needed her to see it. Thankfully, Shruti was convinced. She promised she'd do this for herself.

I gave Shruti a list of different emotions to cherry-pick from, so that she could become mindful of how she felt. Oftentimes when she concluded she was depressed, she really was disappointed, dissatisfied, disillusioned, or even disgusted. I also asked her to rate the severity of her moods, whether positive or negative, on a scale of 1 to 10. This helped her realise that all emotions exist on a spectrum and that everything is not always catastrophic.

I knew how Shruti felt. I had to evaluate what made her feel the way she did. Since she had already mastered the art of tracking emotions, the focus now shifted to events that triggered these emotions. So, together, we got on to an emotion trigger identification mission. I explained to her that any and every event, person and interaction of her day was of significance because it *did* affect her mood, whether she realised it or not.

Through her mood tracker we were recording, assessing, and soon going to be analysing every emotion she experienced within the context of when she sensed it, how intense it felt, and what may have contributed to it. She wasn't aware of her cognitive distortions yet, but I was going to enlighten her about them, to make her see things differently.

On the first day itself Shruti made a lengthy record of all events, people, conversations, and exchanges that made her feel less than optimal. On one occasion she felt a little sad (intensity 2), at another, quite distressed (intensity 8), a few times very dismayed (intensity 9), and one time, a little disheartened (intensity 4). She had expressed similar events in the past too, but now we had it in black and white, in front of us. It was more real and modifiable. Her tracker did speak out loud.

Every morning Shruti woke in her joint family home to the sound of her mother-in-law badgering the house-help. Shruti believed that this morning charade was the lady's deliberate attempt at disrupting her sleep. So, she woke to an upset mood each morning. An over perfectionist all through childhood, Shruti had excelled in studies, sports, extra-curricular activities, and more. She placed less focus on household chores, and more on career goals. She disliked how she never got credit for this. Shruti's life goals were all about excelling, growing, and achieving.

Her mother-in-law, on the other hand, had been a homemaker who took pride in managing the house. One afternoon her husband complimented his mother for cooking great food and managing their home so well, and Shruti felt dismissed. When he came late from office despite promising he'd be there to watch a movie with her that night, she felt neglected. She was convinced that she could never be happy in that joint family setting. Seven days of mood recording, and we knew all about her emotions–what she felt, how intense it was, when she felt so, and what she was thinking at that time. It was time to turn the spotlight on her thinking errors. So, we discerned the below.

Shruti's *black and white thinking* was convincing her that her own cooking was bad, and that her husband sided with his mother. She *personalised* her mother-in-law's banter with the house-help, attributing it to be particularly directed at disrupting *her* sleep. Likewise, she insinuated that her husband particularly took *her* for granted and hence didn't come home in time to watch the movie with her. She *jumped to the conclusion* that her mother-in-law doesn't respect her. She recounted that her mother-in-law *should* understand her job demands and be considerate, and finally *catastrophised* that she would never be happy living in that house.

Shruti hung her head in disbelief when I explained how her thoughts seemed convoluted and twisted. She did see the logic clearly, even though she couldn't change her thinking yet. I told her the purpose of this exercise was not to shift culpability from the world on to her, rather it was to decipher ways to crack the code to her happiness. She understood that she was *reasoning emotionally* and that had to change for her to feel differently. Knowing this itself, was a battle, half won.

Let's nudge you towards the path I guided Shruti on. Step by step.

Step 1
Monitor how you feel

I want you to record in detail how you feel, so that you become aware of your emotions. In the table, you can write what you feel in one word. This would be the most predominant emotion at that given point in time on a particular day. To assist you in pinpointing your feelings I have added a list of emotions after this table. Once you master this, we will go to the remaining columns on the right.

My Daily Emotion Tracker

Emotions you felt	Triggering Event	Contributing Thought	Cognitive Distortion

Below are the emotion lists; the first two show positive, and the other two have negative emotions. Both have been sorted into sub-categories respectively for convenience. A good start would be to record them by the hour. It could even be more often than that, if you observe that your moods tend to change frequently. All moods and their switches are worthy of mention. This exercise will make you attentive to your feelings and help expose the emotions you otherwise end up hiding.

I ask you to enlist both positive as well as negative emotions because oftentimes you do not realise that happiness is also a companion in your journey. This way you can change something when you don't feel good, alongside enhancing the moments where you do.

Once you write out what you feel, rate its intensity on a scale of 1 to 10. If it's extreme (negative or positive), mark it as 10. If it's a mild emotion then rate it as 1 or 2. Based on how you feel, you can choose from the spectrum of minimum to maximum. This way, we know the emotion quality as well as its intensity.

Look at this list of negative emotions. If you think you're feeling any of these or any other emotion, put it down in your tracker.

ANGRY	DEPRESSED	CONFUSED	HELPLESS	INERT
aggressive	alienated	argumentative	alone	bored
annoyed	ashamed	authoritative	craving	callous
bitter	bad	baffled	cut off	cold
controlled	desperate	disillusioned	distressed	dormant
critical	despicable	distrustful	doomed	dull
disgusted	diminished	doubtful	empty	indifferent
enraged	disappointed	embarrassed	fatigued	insensitive
exasperated	discouraged	hesitant	feeble	lifeless
fateful	dissatisfied	indecisive	hungry	listless

ANGRY	DEPRESSED	CONFUSED	HELPLESS	INERT
frustrated	gloomy	judgmental	incapable	preoccupied
furious	guilty	lost	incapacitated	reserved
hostile	lousy	manipulative	incompetent	robotic
hot-headed	low	perplexed	inferior	sluggish
irritated	pessimistic	puzzled	invalid	tired
malicious	powerless	shy	overwhelmed	uncaring
mean	ripped	stressed	paralysed	unconcerned
offensive	self-critical	tense	pathetic	uninterested
resentful	sulky	uncertain	shut down	unresponsive
unpleasant	terrible	uneasy	useless	untouched
upset	weepy	unsure	vulnerable	weary

Look at this list of negative emotions. If you think you're feeling any of these, or any other emotion put it down in your tracker.

AFRAID	HURT	INSECURE	ANXIOUS	BROKEN
alarmed	aching	broken	aghast	alienated
anxious	afflicated	conquered	butterflies	betrayed
apprehensive	agonised	crippled	distraught	cold
attacking	appalled	crushed	dreading	deadpan
cowardly	crushed	defeated	edgy	detached
dismayed	deprived	demoralised	fidgety	distant
fearful	humiliated	destitute	fretful	dreading
frightened	indignant	diffident	jittery	frigid
horrified	injured	disheartened	jumpy	glacial
insecure	insulted	envious	nervous	immovable
panic	mauled	jealous	nervy	impassive
restless	miffed	lost	scared	impersonal
scared	mutilated	overcome	spooked	laidback
shaky	offended	overpowered	strung out	lost
suspicious	pained	pitiful	sweaty	meaningless
terrified	rejected	resigned	tense	remote

Emotion Felt	Triggering Event	Contributing Thought	Cognitive Distortion
Frustration (8)	Traffic on the way to work	- I must be on time, always. - This happens only with me. - Things never go as I plan. - My team will disregard me. - I know it's not my fault, but… - This traffic system is useless.	Shoulding Personalising Polar thinking Fortune telling Emotional reasoning Labelling
Resentment (8)	Disagreement with a colleague about a point to be put forth in the review meeting	- He always wants his way. - He should respect me too. - He thinks I am an idiot. - He's got a problem with me. - He's just a stubborn mule. - Everyone disagrees with me.	Polar thinking Should statement Mind reading Personalisation Labelling Overgeneralisation
Anger (7)	Office politics wherein you did not get credit for your effort	- People should be fair. - This manager is the worst. - I am victimised all the time. - My organisation is corrupt. - I have to deal with so much. - My hard work goes to waste.	Should statement Polar thinking Overgeneralisation Polar thinking Personalisation Mental filtering

AFRAID	HURT	INSECURE	ANXIOUS	BROKEN
threatened	tormented	ridiculed	troubled	reserved
timid	tortured	self-hatred	uneasy	stony
uptight	victimised	small	uptight	toneless
wary	withdrawn	subdued	wired	unemotional
worried	wronged	vanquished	wrecked	untouched

Look at this list of positive emotions. If you think you're feeling any of these or any other emotion, put it down in your tracker.

OPEN	LOVING	HAPPY	FOCUSED	FUN
amicable	admiring	blissful	absorbed	active
approachable	attractive	cheerful	amazed	animated
confident	close	childlike	amused	bouncy
connected	concerned	delighted	attentive	enjoyment
easy	considerate	easy going	captivated	excited
embracing	devoted	ecstatic	courteous	exhilarated
empathetic	gentle	elated	curious	frolicky
flexible	gracious	euphoric	dedicated	funny
free	grateful	fun-loving	determined	great
friendly	humble	glad	entertained	intelligent
harmonious	indebted	glorious	enthralled	liberated
interested	kind	gratified	fascinated	lively
kind	lenient	jovial	fixated	mischievous
outgoing	loved	joyous	intent	optimistic
present	passionate	jubilant	intrigued	outgoing
receptive	patient	mellow	involved	playful
satisfied	respectful	merry	mused	thrilled
supportive	sensitive	overjoyed	observant	tickled
sympathetic	sweet	rapturous	occupied	unlimited
tolerant	tender	splendid	resolute	wonderful
welcoming	warm	thankful	thoughtful	youthful

Look at this list of positive emotions. If you think you're feeling any of these or any other emotion, put it down in your tracker.

GIVING	POSITIVE	PEACE	STRONG	RELAXED
altruistic	adaptable	adequate	affirming	aware
benevolent	approving	assured	confident	easygoing
bighearted	bold	blessed	dependable	free
bountiful	brave	bright	dynamic	grounded
caring	conscientious	calm	energised	light
charitable	constructive	carefree	excellent	loyal
compassionate	cooperative	comfortable	honest	lucid
empathic	creative	confident	mature	meditative
gallant	daring	content	perseverant	natural
generous	doing	easy	reliable	normal
giving	eager	fine	responsible	placid
good	enthusiastic	forgiving	sane	radiant
helpful	exuberant	fulfilled	secure	reflective
humane	hopeful	good	solid	refreshed
kind	inspired	grateful	stable	reposed
outgoing	keen	okay	supportive	rested
polite	motivated	pleased	sure	restored
sacrificing	productive	quiet	tenacious	revitalised
selfless	resourceful	serene	truthful	steady
sympathetic	responsive	unburdened	unfailing	sunny
virtuous	upbeat	uplifted	unswerving	trusting

Step 2
Recall the event that triggered your emotion

Events in your day invariably trigger emotions. It could be traffic on your way to work, office politics, disagreement with a colleague, quarrel with the storekeeper, squabble with the bank employee, your blood test report, or simply the evening news, stock updates, or your spouse seeming sad about something when you got back home.

Triggers can be internal too, like memories that appear out of the blue. If you're sitting with friends and recall a time you went sky diving, or when your team won the tug-of-war in high school you may break into an unexpected smile. Likewise, before th review meeting, if you recollect how your previous boss disregarde your suggestions, or when a colleague snubbed your idea and late sought credit for it as his own, you might feel agitated. Every eve or its recollection contributes to your emotions. If you really wa to take charge of your mood, you must start getting mindful what precedes it.

Step 3
Identify the thought that made you feel this way

An event (or person or conversation or memory) *is* a trig following which your emotions ensue. But events trigger thoug which then make you feel. Try and identify the thoughts al your day's events that contributed to your emotion, and write the table. Sometimes there are a series of thoughts that contri to one feeling. These consistent feelings become a mood. No these thoughts, as they traverse your mind.

Step 4
Pinpoint what could be wrong with the way you think

Your thoughts will always appear logical. In the previous cha you learned that your brain possesses the ability to distort th for convenience, causing you to feel negative emotions. Le a few of your emotions, their triggers, and contributing th into perspective to validate their logic and identify the co distortions they feed.

Emotion Felt	Triggering Event	Contributing Thought	Cognitive Distortion
Anger (6)	Quarrel with the storekeeper when he didn't keep your order ready and you were delayed	- My wife will say it's my fault. - He only does this with me. - My plan is messed up. - I know he's overworked, but, - He should be more diligent - This guy is good for nothing	Mind reading Personalisation Catastrophising Emotional reasoning Should statement Polar thinking
Bitterness (7)	Squabble with the bank employee about a bounced check	- People are so incompetent. - I will never get my money. - Mistakes happen, but why? - I shouldn't have to take this. - It has to go wrong with me. - Everybody is a fraudster.	Polar thinking Catastrophising Emotional reasoning Should statement Personalisation Overgeneralisation
Sadness (6)	Abnormal finding on your blood test report	- I am going to die. - I am plain unlucky. - I am going to be sick and die. - I know it's not that bad but… - I shouldn't have this problem. - Everything is wrong in life.	Fortune telling Personalisation Catastrophising Emotional reasoning Should statement Polar thinking

Emotion Felt	Triggering Event	Contributing Thought	Cognitive Distortion
Helplessness (5)	Evening news about all the bad things that are happening in the world	- The world is so miserable. - Politicians need to do better. - Things will never change. - I am helpless amidst all this. - I will be jobless and poor. - There's never positive news.	Labelling Should statement Fortune telling Labelling Catastrophising Mental filtering
Worry (8)	Stock market fell and you lost quite a bit of money	- I alone make bad investments. - I will be penniless and poor. - This is a miserable life to live. - This economy won't improve. - It just doesn't go well for me. - I feel like a complete loser.	Personalisation Catastrophising Polar thinking Fortune telling Mental filtering Labelling
Guilt (5)	Wife feeling sad because you haven't been spending time at home	- I am an inadequate husband. - She's just unhappy with me. - Maybe she wants to leave me. - Nothing I do will be enough. - I cannot ever keep her happy. - Only my wife is demanding.	Labelling Overgeneralisation Mind reading Mental filtering Polar thinking Personalisation

This exercise isn't that easy. But you can master it. Let me explain by making you aware of the struggle one of my patients faced.

Arun was another energised client, who wanted to better his life by challenging negative thoughts. He had mild long-standing depression with occasional bouts of anxiety about his work performance. Arun's opening remark was that his life is miserable. I asked him to explain. He alleged that office work drained sanity out of him and made his life hell. He had a hard time sleeping and felt like a harassed soul. His social network was limited and family support, poor. Motivation for anything was half-hearted, and recently, cigarettes became his best friends. Arun said he felt inferior and cursed.

Undoubtedly Arun was unhappy. I gauged he was a good copywriter (from the picturesque description of symptoms). I saw an all-out sense of displeasure but couldn't specifically understand what was wrong. Until he and I knew what was going on in his mind, it would be hard for either of us to help him set it right.

Sometimes we think we're just irritated or frustrated or depressed all day. At this time the positive and negative emotion lists can guide you. When you identify your emotions on a spectrum, you become mindful of how you feel. Here is what a spectrum looks like.

Concerned >> Nervous >> Worried >> Fearful >> Anxious >> Panicky

Bothered >> Uneasy >> Annoyed >> Irritated >> Frustrated >> Angry

Disturbed >> Dejected >> Sad >> Gloomy >> Miserable >> Depressed

Uninterested >> Slow >> Tired >> Bored >> Sluggish >> Dull >> Lifeless

When you endure a troubling event, you aren't always thrown into panic, anger, or depression instantly. In fact, all unbearable states begin with a bearable feeling. Concerned, bothered, disturbed, and uninterested are normal states of the mind and mood. When they progress on the spectrum, they become troubling. Strongly articulated vague emotional vocabulary expresses the brutality of what you feel, but it could leave the underlying problem unidentified.

Arun started noting emotional triggers. Each morning, he recorded sadness or anxiety, triggered by a calendar reminder of his daily meetings. His accompanying bothersome thought was, "My work will not be appreciated. It will be yet another unfulfilling day." While he was actually at work, there were other triggers. Someone would raise a query about a script he'd written. He would think, "This person thinks my idea isn't worthwhile". Arun was sensitive and didn't take feedback well.

Arun was mind reading, fortune telling, personalising, using black and white thinking, and catastrophising. The slightest trigger made him jump to a shattering conclusion of being rejected, overruled, and scorned, maybe even lose his job. When I enlightened him on this, he stuck to his logic of how this had happened with him before, and it would likely, happen again. "You don't know my colleagues and my work environment doctor, I do"; was his retort. He couldn't see the distortion.

Sometimes you are whole-heartedly eager to change, to feel better, but you just can't see how your thinking is distorted. Me implying you should think differently, may seem like a baseless suggestion. You need to believe it yourself.

There are ways to work with the hypothesis (postulation) that your twisted thought in fact *is* authentic. We need to put your thought to test, to assure that your assumption is foolproof. The next few chapters describe these tests. When you see for yourself that your way of thinking is twisted, you are determined to give it up and think differently.

20

Technique 1: Arrest your Negative Thought and Put It in the Witness Box

"In life, we sometimes have to place ourselves under a microscope and examine our thoughts, our heart, and our spirit."

—Jeffrey G. Duarte

The culprit always screams out loud, "I'm innocent, I didn't do anything wrong, I'm not culpable. Please believe me. I speak the truth, and nothing but the truth." Like in the previous chapter, Arun's anxiety and sadness provoking thinking was no different. It convinced him that his work would be reproached and so, he reacted in accordance with anxiety and sadness. His irrational thought seemed rational and innocent to him.

Every day, your thoughts try to mislead you this same way. To be fair, you'll have to put these thoughts to trial and examine them to assess their validity. This is hard because in such cases, you're the public prosecuting counsel as well as the counsel for defence. Also, this is your very own thought being cross-examined. The plea must be carefully sought, bringing in witnesses to make this a compelling argument. It would work best if you performed your job impartially, attentively, and calmly—weighing the evidence before you came up with a final decision. You are the chief justice too, giving the ultimate verdict.

Validating Your Worrisome Negative Thought

In Arun's case, we brought this thought to the witness box, "My work will be under-appreciated." As a simulation to the oath, I asked Arun to be fair in his presentation of evidence. As prosecuting counsel, he began to present supportive proof.

The first piece of information was a mental filter that focused on last week's fiasco in which the boss disregarded his idea and asked for evidence to back it up. This was assisted by the cognitive defence of overgeneralisation; based on his previous boss nit-picking errors in his work (he agreed that she did this to everyone). Finally, personalisation was an added witness, who insisted that the disregard was directed at Arun alone.

To sum up his argument, Arun recounted feedback, opinions, advice, and occasional recommendations, which he misperceived as an attack on his work ethics. He reiterated facts at an emotional level, using circumstantial evidence repeatedly, to argue that this *would* happen again because it *always* happened. He was honest to the best of his capacity, but the argument unfortunately seemed baseless.

Checking For Opposing Evidence

This time I decided to play defence counsel as Arun was not trained in the cognitive restructuring process yet. I began to cross examine all the evidence that was laid out. I questioned last week's blunder, requesting details about the part had gone wrong and how he had been berated. Apparently, Arun had incorporated some content that could potentially be disrespectful to some audiences, given the cultural context of the story he was creating. He had been respectfully asked to modify it. In the editing process, some information wasn't saved owing to a technical glitch. And the boss had been upset, but later realised that it wasn't Arun's fault. Arun had mistakenly assumed that his basic script was declared as flawed, and his subsequent suggestions had been ignored. So, he had become upset. Arun unknowingly focused on the negative aspects of the incident and exaggerated them, only retaining the part where his boss was upset and dissatisfied with him.

Digging Harder For Evidence Around The Thought

Continuing as defence counsel, I next interrogated Arun's disparaging incidents at the previous job. His earlier boss was a 49-year-old woman who had unfortunately been in an emotionally tumultuous situation herself. Her 21-year-old daughter was diagnosed with a personality disorder, and her behaviour at home was disruptive. As boss, she was emotionally charged up and was insensitive with her expectations (of everyone). She set harsh deadlines and was intolerant of slip-ups. I demanded prosecution counsel's views on how this reflected on Arun's performance, what affirmed that every boss would be like her, why this was not construed as a passing unfortunate phase, rather, what fed the misapprehension about this being a permanent occurrence. Witness Arun was quiet. There was no explanation. In fact, he agreed that through this process, some positive traits like tolerance, patience, and forbearance had been inculcated in him. I rested my argument.

Making A Rational And Fair Judgment

Now I asked Arun to be the judge and offer his verdict. I insisted he must be fair, reasonable, and impartial. He could see the value in the defence counsel's (my) argument. He agreed that even though he felt he was a disappointment to previous bosses, he accepted that it wasn't destructive criticism that they offered. He had performed to the best of his capacity, needed to learn how to take feedback constructively, and was already on the path to self-improvement. Arun finally decided that his performance was more likely to be within normal expectations and that things were going reasonably well, so he needn't worry as much. He was going to try and be calm, and not react as strongly to events that transpired in his office henceforth.

NOTES: 7 Probes to Cross Examine a Negative Thought

To think differently, you have to play an effective defence counsel role when you challenge your negative thought. Else, the prosecuting counsel in you will obliviously believe the false evidence, and the judge (who is also you) will side with the negative thought. Here are seven cross-examination statements. If you have a negative or worrisome thought bothering you, put a check mark (√) on any, many or all the below to gauge whether your thought is factual in reality.

- ☐ I have all the possible information about my thought, out on the table.
- ☐ All evidence unquestionably insists that my thought is truly, factual.
- ☐ There is no missing information to suggest that my thought is deceiving.

- ☐ I am not being biased when it comes to my reaction about this thought.
- ☐ I am certain there are no other probabilities that could come out of this.
- ☐ I have been objective and detached when I have formed a verdict as this.
- ☐ I can bet my life on it, that this thought is the absolute and whole truth.

If your thought meets all of the above criteria, then the hypothesis is true, your defence counsel has failed, and your thought is actually not twisted. But if any of the above are missed, then there's a strong chance that your thought is deceiving you. You should be motivated to give it up by challenging it in a structured way as described above.

21

Technique 2: Break Perfection If You Want to Beat Dejection

"...you can pretend that bad things will never happen. But life's a lot easier if you realize and admit that sometimes they do."

—Lois Lowry, *A Summer to Die*

Your inner perfectionist can be a forerunner of excellence, but if extreme, it can also paralyse survival. Unhealthy perfectionism feeds the cognitive distortions of black and white thinking, "shoulding", personalisation, as well as negative mental filtering. Perfection has rightly been labelled as not just the enemy of the good, but also, the rival of creativity, productivity, and sanity.

If you look at the first example in the table on page X, the desire to not be late for the office meeting is rational but the resultant frustration about the traffic stems from unhealthy perfectionism. An absolutist mind however, will rationalise, "I must give up on my personal standards and accept inferiority? I should become ordinary. That's the recipe for happiness?" It's not so unassuming, but there are ways to approach the fixity on excessive perfectionism.

Spot-Check On Competitiveness

Being trivial is never the goal. You do not want to mess up or fall short. But staying handcuffed to the fear that you might falter, doesn't help. Question your competitiveness, to see what it's costing you. When you are over competitive, you engage more with others who are so too, and together, you may disrupt each other's peace by bringing comparisons into every situation. This way, life becomes a perennial race, every space a battle ground, and everybody, a contender.

The first sign of unhealthy competition is a shooting heart rate when you're allotted any task, even a mundane one. You will have to set yourself free of the "I need to be the best" chains, because they become the very hindrance to you hitting your target. You would do better if you reached a meeting ten minutes late in a jovial mood than making it in time, but being anxious, fearful, and sad about the fact that you were just a little late and missed out on being voted the best employee in the boardroom. When the goal is wrongly set, you gain little pleasure even when you meet it.

Spot-Check On Insecurity

Insecurity is a perceived incapacity on account of a real or imagined deficiency. Feeling awesome about who you are and what you do, ought to be independent of how others think or what they say. I remember a patient who felt inadequate, incomplete, and insufficient each time he visited a colleague's home. This co-worker, his counterpart in office, had recently bought an expensive vintage car that had become an object of envy for many. Always somewhat unsure about his competence, he now felt even more insecure and wondered if he was performing well enough at work.

"If I was, I'd get a promotion and I'd be able to buy such a car too," he assumed. He was reasoning emotionally and reaching vague inferences. Why was he torturing himself simply because someone else was beaming in prosperity? He agreed that the car was unreasonably expensive, he didn't need it, and that his current car served him well. What he was missing, was a sense of self-worth, not a vintage car.

Self-sufficiency will help you realise that you don't need or want what you think you do. When your cup is already full, you are less likely to cry for more and feel miserable about not having the thing that you most likely could not even accommodate.

Spot-Check On Reality

Happy, clean, and all-impressive lives are a mirage. When you lose your capacity to accept the ordinary (in yourself, others, or the world), the focus shifts on expecting as well as delivering more than average, every single time. That is a harsh demand to fulfil, setting you up for disappointment. Imagine having an expectation of perfect—from your partner, parent, child, boss, colleagues, subordinates, cab driver, grocery vendor, tax consultant, governments, political systems, and more—all the time. How realistic is that?

In the mission to escape unhealthy perfectionism, you would benefit from letting go of expectations, living in the moment and building the psychological flexibility to glide between mood states. The universe is different from you; and you might have to accept that "real" is not always "ideal". It is a beautiful world, even though it may not be as picturesque as you had imagined with your mind's eye. When you stop chasing the impossible dream, you'll start realising the more attainable one, and happiness will become easier to attain.

NOTE: 7 Blows on an Unhealthy Perfectionistic Thought

Every time you feel a deficit, look out for the unhealthy component of your over perfectionism. This will keep you braced to perform better and prevent any self-bashing that saps your positivism to keep you depressed. These statements help validating your perfectionistic thought. Put a check mark (√) to know whether your distorted thought is an outcome of over perfectionism.

- ☐ I don't fear failure. I am open to any new learning here.
- ☐ I'm not comparing myself to a standard. It's no competition.
- ☐ My thought is not linked to my self-confidence.
- ☐ I'm focusing on my performance, not on results.
- ☐ I'm not demanding 100% performance, 100% of the time.
- ☐ I'm not holding on to things that are not in my control.
- ☐ I'm not self-critical, or seeking external validation.

If the thought (stemming from your expectation) meets all the above criteria, then it's probably accurate. But if any of the above are missed, then your thought is tricking you, and you should know that reality could be something different. Focus on *your* game and compete with *yourself*. Accept *your* inadequacies and keep learning. When you acknowledge that life can be hard and often less than perfect, things will start to appear easier.

22

Technique 3: Quit Blame and Shame, Play the "What If?" Game

"So many things are possible, as long as you don't know that they are impossible."

—Mildred D. Taylor, *The Land*

Cognitive distortions leave little scope for negotiation. They could prompt two painful mood states–shame (associated with guilt) and blame (imagined external attack). Consider the example on page X about feeling guilty on account of not being able to spend enough time with your family. Or a commitment which you were obligated to but could not fulfil. A sense of inadequacy can get generated if you focus exclusively on your own shortcomings. Nobody expresses your deficit to you in as many words, but you feel sad because you tend to think you're worthy of shame and blame.

Unlike the cross-examining method (like a qualified attorney), the "what if" technique is a simple challenge that sows a seed of doubt about your negative thought and opens up room for alternate possibilities. These might not be as self-defeating.

Let's go back to Shruti's thoughts. Shruti believed that her mother-in-law disliked her because she didn't help with chores or take charge of household responsibilities. That is why she orchestrated a dramatic display every morning, *only* to trouble Shruti. I asked Shruti, "What if your assumption is true. What can, or should you do about it?" I suggested, "Let's test it by you waking earlier on some mornings, helping with basic chores (just as an experiment), making yourself more visible around the house, and watching out for the spectacle." She agreed.

To her surprise, the drama occurred, nonetheless. Shruti was not the protagonist. Nobody was shaming or blaming her. Then we tried a different game. Now that we'd shaken the belief somewhat, I said, "What if you disregard this thought completely? How will you behave with your mother-in-law?" With this thought in place, Shruti started acknowledging her mother-in-law more, and their communication improved. She, in turn, returned the favour. The banter subsided. Shruti had either felt guilt (when she shamed herself) or resentment (when she blamed her husband's mother). The "what if" game added new perspective to her thoughts, and she became relaxed. Her frustration and sadness lifted.

Scenario Switch

The mind is adept at establishing worst-case scenarios. Place those aside for a while and imagine some best-case scenarios for a change. A negative mindset gets mired (unknowingly) in imagining catastrophes. In such a state, creating fictional success or fantasy positivism can be simulated to a laughing club in which one laughs even without feeling happy. In the process, however, one begins to actually laugh naturally. Best-case scenarios allow the mind to break rumination and help see reality in a less polarised and personalised manner. They convince you that *if* you thought differently, *then* your reality would change.

Seek Clarity

Assumptions are cunning. They push you into a deep ravine, where there is endless scope for accusation, guilt, and resentment. At the same time, asking for clarification isn't easy as people get defensive or are simply unable to express. You can only control what you say or do. So before reacting, step back and seek that clarity in your own mind. Search for cooperative options and workable solutions. When the matter gets clearer, solutions spring up effortlessly.

NOTE: 7 What Ifs to Apply to Your Negative Thought

Negative thoughts can be tested with the "what if" game. You must play with possibilities. If you think differently, there might be a different outcome. Think deeply about that (assumed) alternate outcome and see where the new idea takes you.

- What if I keep believing this thought and go on with life? What will happen?
- What if I gave up on this thought? Just as a trial, what if I don't believe it?
- What if this thought of mine is not real? What would the other person think?
- What if this thought was a result of my touchy nature? What does it mean?
- What if this thought is a trick and I've been falling prey to a mind prank?

- What if all this is fake and reality is something very contrary to my beliefs?
- What if I am actually missing out on opportunities because of this thought?

The "what if" game works well when your thoughts are single-mindedly fixated on a possibility that is direly negative. Just as your imagined outcome has no guarantee, likewise there's no assurance of what would happen if you played this game. It indeed opens up room for negotiation though. With that in place, pessimism could transform to neutrality or positivity, someday.

23

Technique 4: Use Adjectives That Define, Not Labels That Malign

"We fail to say the right words because we choose to say the wrong words. We choose to say the wrong words because we fail to think about the right words."

—Ernest Agyemang Yeboah

According to *cognitive theory*, all thoughts (even the most twisted ones) have logic feeding them. Long-standing conditioning process fixates it–be it authentic or faulty. An offshoot of this philosophy is the *labelling theory*, which describes how words that you call yourself, make you live up to those tags. You *become* who you *think* you are. To make you who you *really* are, you must break the conditioning that your mind is accustomed to.

We cannot survive without labels. In language use, every adjective is a label based on how you use it. During exam time and before an interview, you could be *hardworking* and on weekends and summer break its normal to be *lazy*. When meeting someone on a first date, you could be *jittery* and while defending your idea in the office meeting you might get a bit *aggressive*. Using labels to describe mood and mind states is alright. Like "I acted really *stupid* at that party because I had a little too much to drink", or "I was *nervous* at the interview and so I fumbled a bit". When you make the label permanent, it defines your personality in entirety. That might be inappropriate and false.

My patient said that she came to see me because she was a loser and was hoping I could change that. I asked whether she wanted me to help her with a different label grammatically or analyse whether she was a loser, or suggest ways in which she could become a winner in life. I wanted her to contemplate on some of these questions:

- Was she really a loser?
- Why did she call herself a loser?
- Could it be possible she's not a loser?
- Could she do something to not be a loser?

Listen Carefully To Your Own Voice

The fact is straight—you think, feel, behave like, and become who you *think* you are. A character label is like a coat you wear *over* your skin; but oftentimes you believe it to *be your skin*. You must make this process mindful, and then test its validity. It starts with catching yourself each time you use a label reflexively. Before you know it, you've called yourself fat, silly, useless, incapable, ugly, dull, dumb, worthless, or the worst. And you behave like you really are. You make it happen the way you anticipate it. Say the right thing to yourself.

Use Factual Descriptions

Simple adjectives state facts. Colourful labels express intensity of emotion, without saying what can be done to change it. For example, "I am the worst mother", does not describe what you're doing wrong, or why you are a bad mother at all. It shows agony, guilt, sadness, misery, self-reproach, and pain. But it does not give any hope of what can be done to change. You are restricted within the limited potential of your label. You get frustrated and feel unhappy and you also cannot engage in tasks that could help your child's cause. You continue to believe and behave like the worst mother. Nothing changes.

Instead, you could tell yourself, "I've been too busy with work of late, and haven't had the time to help my daughter with her schoolwork or cook good, nutritious food for her. It's heartbreaking to see her grades fall, especially when I know she's a smart kid. I need to make time for her. I'll speak to my boss about sparing my evenings."

Worst mother is a harsh label. *Busy, overworked, disorganised, distracted* are more action-arousing words describing how you perceive yourself in that moment. Every negative label can be rephrased to sound more true-to-life and can be transformed to gain a better outcome.

Know That The Label Is Not Stuck On Your Forehead

Harsh labels stick and arouse hard-wearing emotions. Milder labels seem momentary and less cruel. No label is carved in stone, tattooed on your forehead, or imprinted in the minds of people you know. When you stop seeing yourself as a *loser*, you act like a frontrunner, work harder, seize every chance that comes your way, and give yourself the opportunity to be a winner. Labels can change. So can your mood.

NOTE: 7 Checks on Your Self-Label to Make it Not Stick

Imagine having a permanent label on you. It might appear authentic but what if an alternate tag fits you better? Do this analysis before you stick *any* label on your forehead. Checkmark (√) wherever your answer is yes. If it is not, your label isn't factual.

- ☐ This label is a known fact, not a personal interpretation.
- ☐ All people who know me would offer me this very label.
- ☐ I have always been this label. Nothing has triggered it.
- ☐ I've never done anything that proves this label wrong.
- ☐ I gain nothing from giving up this label. It defines me.
- ☐ I am not placing myself in a category where I don't fit.
- ☐ I'm not missing out on good things because of this label.

If you answered yes to many, your label is factual. If not, you've mislabelled yourself. When you have an unending desire for perfection, you feel like you're always lacking. So, you sneak into a restricted box with labels like inadequate, incomplete, or incompetent, stuck on it. One word doesn't and cannot define your being. Challenge your negative labels with a sound reality check. This will change your mind and mood forever.

24

Technique 5: Change Your Locus to Gain Better Focus

"If you think bad things happen to you because of external circumstances, other people, or some supernatural force–you are giving your power away."

—Jocko Willink, Commander SEAL Team 3, Battle of Ramadi, Iraq war.

Locus of control is your belief about what creates and causes things to happen in your life. When you're operating from an external locus, you tend to think that situations and events (good as well as bad) occur because of other, more powerful people, chance, fate, or luck. At other times, you might perceive an internal locus where you suppose that your own behaviour, authority, and ability, caused something to happen to, or with you. It is an accepted fact that your expectations of whether your life is in your control or influenced by outside forces will vary in different situations. But the truth is, when you are depressed, you adopt a biased locus whilst interpreting positive and negative events. Let's understand how this can change the mood in the short and long run, for better or worse.

Harshita was pursuing her PhD from a renowned university, away from home. Previously accustomed to a secure home environment, she was struggling with hostel life. She scuffled with confronting picky professors, tight deadlines, extensive reading, and a completely new style of writing. Each time she received critical feedback, she seemed to get discouraged. It made her feel attacked. She took all remarks personally, filtered out the positive, used black or white thinking and labelling to conclude she was worthless, and was catastrophising that her thesis was not going to ever get approved. She sensed that she had little autonomy over her work, and that real control lay with others in the department (professors and advisors who seemed strict and authoritative). She felt distressed and became passive. She felt she did not have a hold over literally anything in her life, at that moment. This caused her to feel helpless, hopeless, worthless, and depressed.

Her cognitive distortions were rooted in an external locus of control. Her professors were stalwarts, and she could have benefitted from their experience. But she was unable to assert her views and could not take meaningful feedback. She reflected negatively about herself, her work, and her future. If she had perceived an internal locus and felt in control, she could welcome these challenges as opportunities for growth instead of making them triggers for stress and depression. Everything could not be in her *full* control, but how she perceived things, determined whether she could do anything about them.

This example asserts that to solve problems (even if externally generated), one must first *feel* in charge, and then use that impetus to *take* charge. An internal locus that pushes you to such profitable action can be constructive.

In some situations, this inner locus however, could assume over-accountability and enhance feelings of self-blame for events that are not your personal doing. In this light, I am reminded of a young entrepreneur who left his steady (albeit mundane) job to trail the career of his dreams. His food delivery app idea was immaculate and the business did well for a few months until a setback in the stock market crashed some of his investments. He immediately cashed out his stocks. He'd also promised his clients more than he could realistically deliver, and had begun to lose money in the bargain. Soon, he couldn't sustain salaries, rents, loan paybacks and other expenses, and eventually shut down the venture to cut further losses. At the same time, his mother fell terribly sick and her medical expenses drained the family's finances. He staggered with guilt for days before gathering the courage to see me to discuss how he felt. He felt culpable for everything happening around him. His internal locus of control was generalising his assumed incapacity to such an extent that his polarised thinking, fortune telling, and self-labelling confirmed his incapability of making *any* sensible decision in his life, *ever* again.

This way, sometimes an external locus of control reinforces incapacity (helplessness), while at other times, an internal locus might exaggerate self-blame (worthlessness). How does one realise when to exercise the right control and not feel negative emotions as a result?

Identify The Real Problem

Einstein said, "If I were given one hour to save the planet, I would spend 59 minutes defining the problem and one minute resolving it." Blaming the world (external locus error) or blaming the self (internal locus error) steers focus away from the actual problem.

You lose precious time and energy fighting the resultant emotional outcomes, and squander away motivation in the bargain. In the case of the PhD student, the feedback from a fussy advisor wasn't the real problem. It was shyness, inhibition, diffidence, and possibly arrogance and a large ego on her part, which interfered with responding to her advisor's queries. She misinterpreted things to be out of her hands. The young entrepreneur on the other hand failed to realise that the market situation and his mother's health weren't in his control. Maybe nobody offered him the idea or courage to hold on to the invested assets, curb his business expenses, or pitch to fresh investors. Him being insensible and blameworthy wasn't the real problem, being unaware was. But if he kept blaming himself, he couldn't help feeling continuously guilty.

Gauge What Is In Your Hands

As card playing experts would rightly advise, "Know when it's good to hold them, and when it's best to fold them." And even though one might argue that gambling isn't great inspiration, life can be quite uncertain, just like a game of cards. If you realise your strengths and limitations, you can make a conscious decision to not feel upset or worked up when things don't go as intended. You don't have to plan failure, but it makes sense to prepare for it nonetheless. It's not possible to win each race, ace all interviews, or please every boss. When it comes to putting in effort, use the internal locus to give your best. But as far as results are concerned, centre on the external locus, and let go of the rest. Sometimes you're just not cut out for business, your crush may not love you back, you may never become a famous pianist, or end up writing a book. But none of these define your worth in the long run. Depression is not a justifiable outcome. You've got to find a way to feel good about your life.

Play A Fair Game With The Real You

Rules of the game tend to change when you feel depressed. You begin to see successes as a chance effect (external locus of control), and attribute failures to your personal doing (internal locus of control). A resultant cascade of self-loathing nurtures critical labels like, "I am no good" and "I can do nothing to make it better." Be aware of the tricks your mind is playing and let your assessment be reasonable. When you zoom out and see yourself from a distance, the reflection you observe is more realistic. You can then think objectively and feel freer to experience yourself and your situation from a non-prejudiced perspective. If you play a fair game with yourself without using a faulty locus of control, you'll most likely win.

NOTE: 7 Checks on Your Defective Locus of Control

It feels miserable to be in a lose-lose scenario where no matter what you do or say, it always seems like you're not good enough. According to this fallacy, if it goes well, it was too easy, and if it doesn't, you were too incompetent. Here are ways to check the appropriateness of your belief and test if your locus of control is erroneous.

- I'm calculating risks, not misinterpreting threats.
- I'm calling these choices, not compromises.
- I'm accountable for my actions and their consequences.
- I'm minding labels and not using rigid definitions.
- I'm not unnecessarily blaming myself for what I didn't do.
- I'm mindful of what I control and where I need to let go.
- I'm being as fair to myself as I would be to anyone else.

Theoretically, an internal locus of control keeps you in charge. Accountability isn't about taking blame for the past and punishing yourself for it, it's about accepting responsibility to shape a better future because you've learned to rise each time you fall. When you replace "compromise" with "choice", nothing will be out of your control. Not even happiness.

25

Technique 6: Stop Shoulding Around and Stand on Buoyant Ground

"'Shoulds' come only from leftover thinking. If we are truly in this moment (the only one there really is), we don't should on ourselves. It's a great freedom."

—Kelly Corbet, *BIG: The Practice of Joy*

"Should" is a strong word in everyday vocabulary. People are afraid to give up "shoulding" simply because they worry it would push them to inertia and sloth. "If it's not a must for me to succeed, doesn't that mean it's okay for me to fail?" If you really lack self-restraint, giving up "shoulding" could unfortunately push you to become ungrateful, unkind, unproductive, and unpleasant. The world runs on rules, laws, and directives. That is why it appears that "shoulds and musts" keep you in alignment with righteousness and commitment, pushing you to be an achiever. This however fails when it becomes a thinking error.

"Shoulding" as a cognitive distortion, is self-enforced obligation. According to the *regulatory theory* of human behaviour, the pressure to perform emerges from a desire to promote gain or prevent loss. This means, in life you're wired to either run towards success or sprint away from failure. "I should win" and "I should not lose" hence, become leading should or must statements in "musterbation". "Always winning" and "never losing" are ultimate illusions. Undue pressure on yourself could make you vulnerable to negative emotional reactions (in the rare chance that you don't succeed). You need to stop unreasonable "shoulding".

Should statements go hand in glove with polarised thinking and a generalised desire for perfection. They are rooted in the perpetual longing for a sense of control over things that aren't in your hands. Yet, their logic is hard to challenge because it seems sound. Would it be imprudent to say, "I should perform well", "I should pass the interview I prepared so hard for", or "I should be treated with respect?" Should statements, are rarely unreasonable in isolation. It's the epilogue that follows them, which leads to catastrophic panic, and negative labelling, if by chance, the "should" isn't fulfilled. So, to paraphrase it, "shoulding" is alright, but the aftermath of an unfulfilled should, could and should be adaptive, not dysfunctional. "Shoulding" must not strengthen the belief that without all accomplishment, "I am worthless". Here is how you can fight it.

Recognise Your Motivation

"Shoulds" and "musts" are rooted in achievement motivation. All your behaviour, action, thoughts, and beliefs could be rightfully influenced by a burning desire to succeed. This is precisely why you set standards and feel you "should" meet them. All logical. The incentives inherent to your desire however could be dual. Are you seeking an outcome, (and is that all that matters to you)? Or is there an aspect of your self-image that you hold contingent *upon* that outcome?

For instance, the consequence of finding a life partner on a matrimonial app, or let's say a new job from a career portal could matter for obvious reasons – one of these primarily offers emotional security while the other assists financial security. Your self-image that you attach to this outcome might be external: "What will people think about me after a failed interview or unsuccessful date? I will appear worthless, incompetent, or unlovable." Or on the other hand, it could be perceived as an internal flaw, "I possess no skill, talent, or quality to impress anyone. Everything I do is meaningless." If your motivation is focused on the outcome, you wouldn't be so demotivated. Your "shoulds" would then be fixated on trying harder, and some day you would indeed succeed. But if you've placed the spotlight on your self-image, it might get shattered and then you are likely to feel depressed.

The kind of motivation you hold, decides everything. Let your expectations centre on your performance, and not your self-image because of it. "Shoulds" will then cease to be your enemies.

Welcome Uncertainty

Unmet personal standards threaten *your* estimate of *your* self-competence. To start with, your expectation may already be unreasonably high. If you fail to match this, your confidence breaks further, and you fear uncertainty even more. Thoughts like, "Will I be good enough?" or "Will I ever match up?" all begin to play with your mind. Without a "should" in place, you would simply give your best and not worry about the rest. The "should" builds up a fear of ambiguity about the future, and with even more of your self-esteem at stake, the overbearing urge to fulfil it, rises. All put together, this becomes a fatal combination likely to end in avoidance, sadness, and low self-worth, which contributes to, and worsens depression.

You would do so much better if you welcomed uncertainty and told yourself, "I don't know what will come out of this, but I am here for the joy of it, and I will do my best because that's what I *can* control". This would not leave room for "shoulds" or the resultant turmoil. Your thoughts would then sound like, "Of course I'd like to win but if I don't, I'll just try harder the next time around".

Failing Is Not The Same As Failure

Winning is when you take action and meet your goal. *Failing* is when you hit your shot, but miss the target. Both offer you chance for evolution. *Failure* is when you perform no action, don't try, and resultantly don't evolve at all. Not accomplishing a goal does seem like you *failed* at what you had set out for, but it does not define you as a *failure*. Treat it as a verb, not an adjective. A content life is a balance between endeavour and achievement. Even if you haven't reached the summit, you've gotten somewhere. The good part is, somewhere is always better than nowhere.

NOTE: 7 Checks on "Should" and "Must" Statements

The moment you find yourself using a should statement, notice whether you're "shoulding" yourself for the past, or about the future. An unfulfilled "should" of the past could make you sad and depressed by beating your self-esteem, while that of the future could incite apprehension and anxiety. Try using these checks to monitor "should" statements that make you sad and uncomfortable.

- This consequence is like a matter of life and death.
- I am not linking my self-esteem or mood to this outcome.

- I don't care about what people think about this outcome.
- I'm not being emotional about this issue, I'm logical.
- I will not change my belief because my logic is sound.
- My "should" is targeting my effort and not the result.
- Shoulding pushes me towards higher goals.

If you checked most or all, it means that the "should" statement is valid and useful. If you missed many or most, then this "shoulding" seems maladaptive and is hurting you, your esteem, and your mood.

"Shoulding" as a cognitive distortion is commoner in competitive people like sportsmen and businessmen. They invest heavily and place high stakes on outcomes. It's always cut-throat for them, and they feel crushed when they fail because they never left room for uncertainty or change. Failing is not an option in their book, because they believe failing is the same as failure. If you're thinking like this, you need to realise the difference. Then if you fall, you will roll over, stand up and continue to perform. You won't give up.

26

Technique 7: Think Before You Leap, the Waters Might Be Deep

"Jumping to conclusions is a safer sport in the world of our imagination than it is in reality."

—Daniel Kahneman, *Statistics*

For the inquisitive human mind, being left in the dark is intolerable. It makes you anticipate the worst. So, you rightly seek to learn and know. In general, learning is gradual and happens by making connections between events and their outcomes. However, in times of uncertainty, when available information is limited, your brain switches from "gradual" to "one shot learning". According to neuroscience research, this "one shot" learning makes you jump to conclusions to fill up knowledge gaps. You may be aware that there is no real proof to validate your inference. But you can't help making your own assumptions.

Jumping to negative conclusions involves mind reading and fortune telling. It tends to walk hand in hand with the faulty defences of generalisation, personalisation, and catastrophising.

For some reason, you constantly believe that physical or emotional harm will befall you, and react negatively. Breaking this fallacy is not so easy because hard facts are not always readily available. Also, you don't have the patience or time to wait for reality to sluggishly unfold. You jump, without realising how deep the waters are.

It's an interesting riddle though why the mind fails to anticipate the *aftermath* of a faulty inference. Filling a mind-gap when information is missing sounds justifiable (even if you fill it with a false idea). But the emotional and behavioural reaction following such mind reading or fortune telling could damage reputation, break relationships, and lower the mood hopelessly. And yet, people use this defence so often.

One of my patients requested an emergency telephonic consultation as she was having a panic attack after she accepted the delivery of a "Divorce for Dummies" handbook (seemingly ordered by her husband). The couple had recently been on a vacation, bought a new vintage car, and made investments together. Now he was away on a four-day office retreat, unreachable, even by phone. Her mind took her to the darkest alleys where negativity was hounding her well-being and peace. "Was he away with someone else?" She couldn't work, eat, or exercise for the next four days. She also hurriedly consulted a divorce attorney to know her legal rights in case of an imminent divorce. She had sunk so low that when her husband returned, he was shocked to see her gloomy state. He immediately clarified that he had ordered the book online, for a distant cousin who was in a tumultuous marriage. She couldn't order it herself, as she didn't want her husband to know. All the emotional turmoil, pain, and misery of those four days could have been avoided by seeking facts, being patient, and not taking such a blind leap. If only her mind knew better. Here's how you can avoid jumping to conclusions.

Seek Facts

A bias that facilitates "one-shot thinking" is the inference-observation confusion in which a small piece of information (observation) is immediately followed by jumping to conclusions (inference) without a fact search. Like in the example above, the physical *observation* of a divorce handbook led the lady to bank on the *inference* that her husband who always surprised her with vacations and gifts, was now going to alarm her with a divorce plea. Without facts in place, she inferred an upcoming divorce by applying logic to what she merely *saw*. This happens often in life—friends don't return phone calls, promotions get delayed, the storekeeper seems rude, and your spouse doesn't spend enough time with you. All of these are physical observations and experiences. But they lead to negative mental inferences of disrespect, disregard, disappointment, and distress. If you gather facts by asking questions, seeking clarity, assessing deficits, and overcoming your own shortcomings (if any), you'll be surprised to see how reality can be so different from what you had assumed. Nothing challenges misrepresentation better than reality checks.

Beware Of The Gut Feeling

Intuition or gut feeling is a flash of insight that invites you to examine your own emotions. Indeed, the gut feeling comes into play when uncertainty is at its peak and there's no logic available to work with. It may also simulate an inner voice which reminds you of previous experiences that would support its argument at the given time. Like constant chatter in the background, it prepares you to automatically respond to ambiguity. Such intuitive insight can be logical if it engages both sides of the dispute. That is how some people's gut feelings are nearly right and lead them to positive outcomes.

But when the chatter leans towards negativity, you might imagine and believe in unrealistic adverse possibilities. Human experiments have shown that the amount of existing knowledge you have about something influences your gut feeling related to it. So, a deficit in that familiarity can drive negative intuitions. The trick is to remember to study both sides fairly. Try and gather facts, give yourself time, and separate fantasy from reality. Time and practice will hone your intuition to perfection. The more you get used to relying on facts, the more your gut will develop an automated style to see alternate, multiple positive possibilities. This won't misguide you.

Thicken Your Skin, Just A Little

If you are thin-skinned, you tend to get hurt easily because the gentlest opposition, minutest joke, tiniest rejection, and slightest conflict could make you feel attacked. A deep-rooted insecurity takes over and could steer focus away from the real problem. You can prevent this by taking a pause before you speak or act, because you may have not gotten the story right. This way you would have perceived offence where none was intended.

You can delay instant emotional reactions by being neutral to perplexing feelings or provocations. This way you can pick yourself up easily even when you fall. For example, people may occasionally reject your ideas, viewpoints, and concepts, or fail to give you the deserved attention or consideration. But they don't actively reject *you*. If you can acknowledge that, nothing can touch you. You're less likely to get emotional or jump to catastrophic conclusions that are highly likely to be false.

NOTE: 7 Spot-Checks Before You Jump to a Conclusion

If you find yourself imagining a tragedy and reacting like its already happened, you've most likely jumped to a conclusion by mind reading someone, or fortune telling the future. Use this analysis to cross check the validity of your conclusion. Check mark (√) statements that are true about your conclusion.

- ☐ I seek facts before forming impressions.
- ☐ My view of my situation is not illusionary, it's logical.
- ☐ I'm attentive to facts in any situation.
- ☐ My conclusion is not personal, I see the whole picture.
- ☐ This isn't an illusion, each fact is self-explanatory.
- ☐ Anyone would react likewise in such a situation.
- ☐ I've covered all bases and have all clarity needed.

Your conclusion is probably valid if it meets these reality checks. But if it fails even one or two, you could be jumping into deep imaginative waters without definitive proof and drown in the process. Oftentimes you realise that your conclusion is faulty, and you get back in sync with reality. But the damage to your mind, mood, and relationships is devastating, even irreversible. Look before you leap into the deep waters of assumption and use reality checks as your life jacket. You'll always be safe then.

27

Technique 8: Quit Black And White Because Gray Might Be Right

"If you continue with black-and-white thinking, you'll never get to see the rainbow."

—Omar Cherif

The tendency to think in extremes (black and white) becomes exaggerated when you are in a tumultuous emotional mode. A relaxed mindset realises the transient nature of events, intentions, and emotions. Depression being a sustained state of sadness that has lasted over a long time, unfortunately has the power to darkly tint your world view. That is why, one mishap tends to become a predictor of more, and you believe in the omnipresence of negativism. As is obvious, black, and white thinking strolls hand in hand with catastrophising, personalising, and jumping to conclusions. Breaking the pervasiveness of negativism is key to crushing polarised thinking.

A hold-up in arguing the absoluteness of events or intentions is that even though the evidence for black (or negative) outcomes may be sketchy, that for white (positive) results is equally unclear. Challenging a troublesome and absolutist thought is difficult without solid proof. But change can only be brought about by allowing yourself the possibility that you *may* be wrong, and that there *might* be a thousand shades of grey in between black and white extremes. Unfortunately, extreme polarities stand out more when you're worked up, anxious, or depressed. One of the grey shades could reflect real facts. The trick is to get to that shade in time, before the black arrow of negativity is inadvertently shot, causing damage no matter where it lands.

Park Your Mood, Start Driving Your Thoughts

This literally means momentarily lifting the accelerator from emotions and reflecting on your thoughts. Evolutionally, emotions defend the present and logic safeguards the future. That is why we react fast in the heat of the moment (emotional reaction) when it comes to immediate decisions and spend time contemplating (logical reaction) when the impact is going to be visible sometime later.

Emotional reasoning, however, is easier than logical analysis because the latter consumes time and energy. So, we see only a part of the problem and want to react fast. That is how a perfectly good mood translates into a penetrating storm. When this happens, your willingness to look at alternate possibilities, diminishes. Use logic. Think about what would and could happen in the future if you continued to think and behave the way you do. This analysis will break rigidity and make your thoughts and ideas agreeable to change.

Correct The Grey Colour Blindness

Surviving in a black and white world is nerve-wracking because when the universe exists in binary opposites, the slightest misfortune could make it appear cold, miserable, and unliveable. Dialectical thinking corrects the grey colour blindness and opens your eyes to shades of grey. The use of logic in extreme situations dials down anxiety and sadness which usually transpire because of black and white extreme responses.

While thinking "grey", you may have to acknowledge the difference between "I wish" and "this is". When things don't go the way you wanted or expected, appreciate that the situation can be viewed differently. All coins have two sides and so do most problems. Ambiguity is bad, but restrictively categorising people and ideas impulsively, is worse.

Life isn't "either-or". There are more options than your mind envisions. The world is actually vaster than your fractional awareness of it. Embrace the confusion and ponder over options instead of getting stuck on the first negative outcome. Enlarge the image so that every pixel becomes visible. When you see the bigger picture, little options and alternatives pop up instinctively. The gradual transition from black to white seems more apparent and the shades of grey become clearer. That is the start of your road from being an extremist to becoming more open-minded. And soon enough, the negative mood will lift.

Allow For Vulnerability

For a moment, tell yourself, "Things happen, and I can't *always* regulate them," and see how it feels. By overanalysing, prying, judging, questioning, and obsessing, you won't get all answers exactly the way *you* wanted them. Try to stop misjudging and preconceiving that *everything* is miserable just because it isn't *perfect*. Vulnerability is your measure of courage and your tool to foster authenticity. When you are vulnerable, you accept yourself and people around you realistically, and accept the elementary proverb, "To err is human."

You can do this by taking one or many chances that involve uncertainty like a game or challenge. Welcome more trials that hold possibilities of rejection and be prepared for the worst. Perhaps you could participate in a race with someone who you know is already faster than you, or attempt to lift weights beyond your capacity in the gym. When you place the "I am invincible" tag on your forehead, you leave no room for human error. Respect your humaneness and be more honest with the most important human in your life—you.

Get Comfortable With Imperfection

Defect doesn't equate with deficiency. *Kintsugi*, meaning to "join with gold", is a fifteenth century practice in Japan, which involves sticking back together broken ceramic pieces with lacquer mixed with powdered gold. This 500-year-old tradition highlights imperfections instead of hiding them. The new mended pot always looks stunning. Every time a beautiful piece of pottery breaks, it is a reminder of the beauty of human fragility as well.

We live in a world that highlights success, prizes youth, and features excellence. So, we tend to get pessimistic when things fall apart. Nobody celebrates flaws or shortcomings. But when you become comfortable with a little imperfection, the worst mishap doesn't *seem* as worrisome anymore. This fuels the search for change, improvement, and growth. At a more realistic level, perfect is a mirage. Place yourself in uncomfortable situations ever so often, so that you get accustomed to slight discomfort. This endurance will make you comfortable later when you need it even more.

NOTE: 7 SPOT-CHECKS ON POLARISED THINKING

Outcomes rarely justify the painful emotions perceived in their bargain. Despondency that extreme thinking tends to arouse, is damaging. Put a check mark (√) on what feels true about your worry. You'll be able to spot and challenge the black and white thought accordingly.

- ☐ There are no other possibilities here, no alternatives.
- ☐ There is no other "best-case scenario".
- ☐ My thought is logical, I am not getting emotional.
- ☐ Handling this is definitely beyond my capacity.
- ☐ I have full clarity from all involved.
- ☐ This is documented, it's not my *own* point of view.
- ☐ I am not extrapolating any other event to this scenario.

A polarised negative thought will rarely meet all reality checks. There always *are* alternatives. You fail to see them, only because you reason emotionally and are blinded to logical alternatives. Maybe you lack psychological flexibility. If you work with calmness and clarity, your own life experiences will guide you. Then shades of grey as well as every other colour become apparent and your mood and life will cease to appear black.

Part - IV

TO START MAKING IT BETTER, STOP MAKING IT WORSE

(Lifestyle and Behavioural Contributors to Depression)

"I craft most of my own tragedies without ever having even the remotest understanding that it is I myself who have done the crafting."

—Craig D. Lounsbrough

MOTIVATION THEORIES EMPHASISE THE ANIMAL KINGDOM'S determination to make life easier for themselves. Ants accumulate grains, bees gather honey, and squirrels stack up nuts. It's hard work, but they realise that it pays off when they eat comfortably through winter. Still, grasshoppers stroll about, all through summer singing "que sera, sera; what will be, will be," and live in the moment. That's a good mentality to have, but it doesn't help the grasshopper during winter when the air is cold, and food scarce.

This grasshopper mourns for himself. Helpless and pitiful, he most likely starves to death. Other grasshoppers see this. Some fortunate ones survive and make it to next summer. Still, they don't even try to be different. Many humans especially in calamitous emotional situations act likewise. We cannot survive crises if we've not stocked up on psychological reserves and coping capacities. As in the case of the grasshopper, winter cannot be prevented. But preparing for it by doing what is right, can prove useful.

In this section I introduce lifestyle choices and behaviours that promote, trigger, and sustain depression. Interestingly, this relationship works both ways. These behaviours are a cause as well as consequence of depression. That is why indulging in them gets you stuck in a vicious loop. I've used real-life experiences of a patient called Suman, who consistently reached out for help to heal her depression. Through her example, I have explained how she made faulty choices, and how they worsened her life and her mood. Each chapter gives you suggestions, which can be applied every day to avoid such negative habits and inculcate positive ones, to sustain a happier existence.

28

How to Not Get Stuck in a Vicious Loop

"The problem is not that I was invited to the hole I'm standing in. It's that I accepted the invitation."

—Craig D. Lounsbrough

Why humans in difficult situations fail to undertake action that would potentially improve their negative mood state has remained a dilemma. More so, why do they engage in behaviours that worsen the difficulties they're already facing? How do people trap themselves in a loop of pessimism such that one action after the other worsens their mood, and the degraded temperament further enhances unhealthy self-defeating choices? Why the vicious emotional cycle, and the inability to break out of it by using sense and logic?

Imagine having a migraine—a sharp, pricking, deeply throbbing headache that is accompanied by nausea, restlessness, and sensitivity to sound, light, smell, as well as touch. This headache doesn't let you bring yourself to do what you must, even though you know you have to, and really want to. You want to hide and be alone in a dark, quiet, and comfortable room. The migraine makes you freeze in pain and steals everything from you when it strikes.

The emotional pain of depression is similar. Depression is not always about sadness, hopelessness, and discouragement. Often, it's such a "blah" or "meh" emptiness that you want to fill it with *anything*. Whatever brings in a little enjoyment, rush, or kick in this situation becomes salient enough to gear you into action even if it is risky or harmful. This is how you fall into the trap and get mired deeper in it.

EXERCISE: If It's Not Getting Better, It's Okay to Make it Worse

How many of these situations sound familiar? They may not have occurred in *your* life, but they could stir a sense of familiarity. Do check mark (√) what you might resonate with.

- ☐ You're on a diet plan. Today you crossed your daily limit of 1200 calories because you couldn't resist dessert at the office buffet. You say, "Oh dear, today is a messed-up cheat day. Let's eat all day and I can go back to the diet from tomorrow".
- ☐ Your room is a mess and you've just taken off your office clothes. You put them in the laundry basket every day, but today you decide to leave them by the bed because you think, "The room is shabby anyway, these clothes won't make a difference".
- ☐ The drawer is overflowing with unsorted papers and mail. It only takes a few minutes daily to segregate them and trash what you don't need (90% of mail is junk). But you let it be and the drawer overflows to the point that papers occupy your whole space.

- ☐ You have several presentations to make for the annual review. Three major ones are done, two are pending. Suddenly you fall sick and realise there's no time for the two. You won't be able to do them perfectly, so you decide there's no point doing the remaining ones at all. "I've lost my promotion already," is how you begin to think.
- ☐ When your kids are addicted to the phone and you're trying to set screen time limits, they're not obeying you, and are putting up a fight. You say, "Never mind, they're going to find ways to cheat even if I set a limit. Let them just do what they like. They're beyond my control. Nothing is going to make this better."
- ☐ You believe people in office are sidetracking you. There are however three members on the board, who always love your work. You gather that three against six is not a good score. So, you stay quiet and don't put forth your suggestion in the next meeting. Now, these three also begin to think that you're disinterested in work.

It's true, majority wins. When things are going well, a single hurdle seems easy to overpower. But if things are already bleak, you don't care about them getting a bit, or a lot worse. "After all, how much low can one go below zero, right?"

Emotional problem solving is scientific, almost like astrophysics. It involves a stepwise approach–defining the problem, generating resolution options, selecting from alternatives, implementing the chosen solution, and evaluating its effectiveness. This way you regulate emotions well and cope optimally.

Depression, however, makes you think minutely about *every little thing* in your life. When you see many *little things* going wrong, you sense that *everything* is wrong. The brain says, "Everything is so bad, what's the point in improving one little thing?" Defensive pessimism sets in, and you lower your expectations of your own self. You think so much about your problem that you have no room to consider solutions—leading to a "self-absorption paradox". So, everything continues to be and feel wrong. You're driven to *stay stuck* or rather less motivated to *unstick* yourself. You become indifferent or apathetic (different from feeling depressed and pathetic). That is when you're driven towards self-defeating, groundless, and irrational choices.

You're still a reasonable person when you're depressed. You just begin to reason with the wrong logic.

NOTE: Don't Get Stuck in the Depression Loop

You think A leads to B, which is a better place. But you must keep track of times when B has led back to A, or worse. This way, you stay exactly where you were–stuck in a never-ending loop that sucks you deeper and deeper into depression. Use these tips to maintain a vision of your goal which is to feel better about yourself and beat depression.

- Accept that depression is an illness, which *will* get better if *you* work on it.
- Know that you can reach out to seek help. Help is nearly always available.
- Know that seeking help is a sign of inner strength, not one of weakness.
- Remember, investment in therapy is the best investment you'll ever make.
- When you hear a voice in your head that says you're weak, fight it fiercely.

- Do things that you were always afraid to do, to know that you *can* do them.
- When you face big or small failures, remember your little and big successes.
- Remember that doing something, makes you feel better than doing *nothing*.
- Recall when people said you can't do it and despite that you really did it.
- Remember–motivation doesn't initiate action. Action feeds your motivation.

29

Isolation Does Not Help, Connection Does

"There is a difference between solitude and isolation. One is connected and one isn't. Solitude replenishes, isolation diminishes."

—Henry Cloud

I'd mentioned to Suman that suppressing her emotions would do no good. So, she acknowledged and agreed that it was okay to cry if she felt low, and not bottle it within. I realised after a week, how she had only partly understood my words.

Suman had consulted me for the first time several weeks ago, and seemed to display many signs of depression—increasing sadness as well as irritability, frustration, laziness and the rest of the textbook picture of the atypical variety of depression. When I met her after a week, I realised she had stayed home for the last seven days. She'd announced to friends and family that she was overworked and needed extra time to get ahead in her game. Hence, the disappearing act was justified. Suman didn't want to cry in front of people because she thought that would make her appear weak.

To which I responded, "But Suman, these are friends and family. They will understand. They won't judge you". She retorted, "I couldn't take that chance, doctor. I already feel miserable about the way they see me. I cannot risk making it worse. So, I decided that I would stay in by myself and cry it out. You said I could cry."

"Do you feel better now, Suman?"
"No, I feel a lot worse."

On my recommendation prior to the week before, Suman had attended an after-office party. That hadn't gone very well either. It is a fact that depression stimulates *social anhedonia* or an inability to enjoy social interactions. Hence the preference for solitude and the "need to be alone" overrides the normal and well-accepted "need to belong". We all like, need, and want to be around people who make us feel better. But Suman wasn't enjoying interacting with people, and couldn't help getting annoyed when colleagues and friends asked her how she was doing. She did not want to tell them how she felt. She appeared slightly different from who she was earlier to people. She had become socially awkward and was visibly dysfunctional. This was causing more harm than good to her mood as well as professional image.

It's true, Suman had been more irritable than before, through this atypical depressive episode. She not only failed to get a hold over how sad she felt, but also couldn't help feeling upset with herself for not being nice to people who mattered, and were trying to be there for her. She insisted that if she tried to meet people, her revolting attitude would disgust others and lower her already shattered self-confidence at work.

Suman's depression made it hard for her to express *how* she expressed *what* she felt. To some extent, her concerns were valid—

people didn't completely understand her misery as her depressive symptoms were atypical. She was more irritable than sad, more frustrated than gloomy, and was also snappy in conversation. While she realised this, she could not regulate it. Her vanity enabled this whole state of hiding her feelings. Cutting down on her social interactions reinforced her desire for solitude. How could she fight it? She chose what *she* thought was the best way out. Which was, to stay out.

And so, we discussed her day, mood, routine, and life, in the past week.

"Did you leave the house at all Suman?"
"Yes, for groceries, alcohol, and cigarettes."
"Did you speak on the phone last week?"
"I ordered pizza, almost every single day."
"Did you respond to messages and texts?"
"Yes, work emails—at bare minimum, though."
"Did you smile much in this past week?"
"Of course, when I thanked the cigarette vendor."
"Did you lie Suman, about you not feeling well?"
"Not at all. I am depressed so I am unwell right?"
"Did you say things you did not mean or want to?"
"In fact, I did good. I did not speak at all. See?"

Suman had isolated herself for the most part—she stayed away from people, did not leave home, avoided calls and messages, and minimised human contact. This is an obvious form of seclusion. But there are ways to withdraw socially despite stepping into the world outside. Like Suman was responding to emails, heading out for groceries (as well as alcohol and cigarettes), and she did smile at the cigarette vendor. But she did not *engage* with anybody. You could pretty much go to work, attend yoga class, the gymnasium, office, or a wedding too, and still not connect with people. It's still social isolation.

From an evolutionary perspective, Darwin might call this an adaptive choice. If Suman was going to worsen her social standing with her own hostile remarks and behaviour and mess up her work image on account of distractibility and confusion, she actually gained from staying away. She wouldn't be attacked (or judged), her isolation would reduce chances of conflict, and she'd be saving her energy and vitality to put it to use later, when she felt more capable. She would not have to repeatedly lie about how she felt because she wouldn't be talking to anyone at all. By avoiding the pain (which she uniquely perceived) of interaction, she felt she was winning the game. But this kind of isolation wasn't for self-enhancement. It was destroying her.

Humans are fundamentally motivated to connect and interact with others. And yet, on a micro level, spending time alone is healthy. Time you spend with yourself–*solitude*, is ideal for creativity, insight, spirituality, self-growth, self-realisation, self-development, and if nothing else, relaxation. This is also called the theory of social balance and social recovery. I say, we all need compulsory "me time" for meaningful self-talk and winding down. But this is distinct from the isolation of depression. You cannot originate sanguine or hopeful ideas in an alone and unhappy state. When you are drowning, a friendly hand is what you really need to lift you up and pull you out to safety so that you can breathe again.

But Suman chose to ignore it because even reaching out to the helping hand seemed like too much effort. She actively snubbed the people she loved as well as those who cared about her. Since she was talking to no one, she had no opinions, suggestions, perspectives, feedback, or inputs coming in from anywhere but her own mind (which we can see, had become quite dysfunctional). When Suman stayed alone, she felt sadder, lonelier, weaker, lesser, and smaller. She was bored and was convinced that she is boring too. The more time she spent alone, the more toxic, nauseous, and suffocating it became. She was locked in a paradoxical prison of misery not realising that she alone possessed the key to her freedom.

EXERCISE: Do You Choose Isolation or Connection?

How many of these statements sound true or relevant? There are no right or wrong answers. It's just who you are, and how you may have been conditioned to think, feel, and react. Do check mark (√) any that you might seem to relate with.

- ☐ If I feel low, I'd rather deal with it on my own.
- ☐ If I spend time alone, I will find my answers.
- ☐ If I'm not socially perfect, I'd rather just hide.
- ☐ Nobody understands, so it's okay not to share.
- ☐ It's not okay to appear sad in front of others.
- ☐ It's not alright to cry in front of an outsider.
- ☐ I am supposed to manage myself on my own.
- ☐ I always need to be emotionally self-sufficient.
- ☐ My problems don't mean anything to others.
- ☐ Showing my weakness to the world is awful.

If a few or many of these reflect how you think, it's likely that you are prone to isolating yourself when you feel low. In general, a healthy blend of solitude and social interaction regulates the mind and mood. Interaction rouses context, engagement, learning, and exchange while solitude facilitates introspection, reflection, soul searching and self-regulation. The solitude inertia of depression, however, is troubling because it promotes loneliness, rumination, maladaptive coping, and isolation.

The isolation trap is a nasty one. It feels like an introspective solitary phase–a time to hide the dark story you don't want the world to know. You feel you're still going out for chores, exercise, and daily needs. You're possibly meeting friends for lunch and a movie too. You don't realise this could be maladaptive and dysfunctional. It eventually becomes a newer problem, even if it did not start out as one.

Pick your phone and look at the message folder. Have you ignored communications from people, including those who truly care about you? Or responded blandly without engaging? Have you not returned calls to friends and family? Do you see yourself creating an emotional distance that you don't really want to craft but are unable to bridge? The truth is, after a while, people will give up and back off. That is when the isolation could get deeper, concretising the bubble around you and making you feel stuck.

Unstick yourself.

At some point, you'll have to stop justifying that isolation is what you really want or need, and more importantly, break the assumption that it is right for you. You must delve deeper to tap the real fear that's keeping you distanced from the world. Are you running from people, or from their ignorance about depression? Are you escaping the conversation, or trying to minimise interrogation? Are you protecting your self-respect or safeguarding your vanity? Is this self-preserving or self-destructive? Are you getting better or worse?

Find a way to communicate with your loved ones. Tell them that you're feeling low, and that you are insulating yourself from judgment. You could even say that you don't feel up to meeting, even though you really want to. Initially, pick someone, anyone who you believe is more understanding and empathic than others. Someone you can comfortably confide in. You could start with briefer interactions, like a walk in the park, a short chat at the bookstore, over office lunch, or while you get your morning coffee. A movie might be good too, as you don't have to talk, you just watch. When you break the inertia, you become more comfortable with company. If you've pushed your friends and family away, it's time to win them back. If they ever cared for you, they will be back in your life in no time.

Depression initiates its game with two deceptive moves. It makes you feel like you're alone and also makes you want to be alone. Isolation isn't a good counsellor. Don't let depression fool you into believing that.

NOTE: Choose Connection Over Isolation

You may be self-sufficient and feel that you're fine by yourself. Even when you're not, you might contemplate that it's emotionally exhausting or painstakingly effortful to keep in touch. You tend to assume people won't care to understand or empathise. A negative mindset reinforces such beliefs. And the longer you've isolated yourself the harder it becomes to get into connection mode. People may not always understand how you feel, yet social associations *can* elevate your mood. Here are some suggestions that could help you ease into, and gradually re-establish your lost connection with the world around you.

- Engage in an activity that you enjoy, which cannot be done solo, like playing badminton.
- Sign up for group exercises instead of doing them over video and mobile apps.

- Walk in a park or a mall (alone too) to feel the presence of people around you.
- Watch a movie (solo is okay) in a movie hall, so you get comfortable with people.
- Go to the store to shop instead of shopping online, just to slowly add social contact to your life.
- Join a social, altruistic, or charitable cause to focus on something other than yourself.
- Send letters, cards, emails, or online messages to loved ones saying that you care.
- Play online games with friends and family, even if you don't want to meet them.
- Step out anywhere for fresh air. It might give you a fresher perspective of the world.
- Take care of an animal or a plant. They are not people, but they connect you to life.

30

Alcohol: Not a Good Solvent for Sorrows

"First you take a drink, then the drink takes a drink, then the drink takes you."

—F. Scott Fitzgerald, *The Great Gatsby*

I realised that I was meeting Suman after a gap of three weeks. I had reached out in between but hadn't heard from her. I was surprised to see she had gained a reasonable amount of weight in this time, seemed to have puffy eyes, and also appeared slightly uncoordinated and incoherent.

"I've been drinking again."

Suman wasn't embarrassed to admit it. Her empty life became full, often oversaturated, she described, with alcohol. She laughingly called it "liquid courage". She insisted that alcohol helped her unwind, take the edge off, and numbed her emotional pain. She swore it elevated her mood. Indulging gave Suman a sense of control, as if she could now achieve anything. This was her quick fix. Unfortunately, she didn't know it came with long-lasting damage. I told her this wasn't a good idea.

"Doc, you don't understand, alcohol calms my nerves!"

Of course I knew how alcohol worked, Suman didn't. That is why she saw it as her magic potion. I was not going to sanction it to alleviate her sadness. She argued otherwise. Probably, because the "high" offered by alcohol (and occasional cigarette smoking) made her feel transiently happier. How could I dispute her reality? Alcohol did lower her inhibitions and allowed her to feel less caged. The moment it hit her bloodstream, she felt relaxed. She didn't like what came after, especially the next morning—hangover, worse mood, interrupted sleep, and above all, guilt. But she still thought alcohol helped her. Alcohol was everywhere—in her cabinet, the workplace café, at the office party, and if not at all of these, it was easy to acquire from any store. She was constantly tempted and she consistently gave in. After the first few times she drank, alcohol consumption became her reset button. It was her signal to uncoil, reconnect with herself and forget the worries of the world. She did not want to quit. Not because she was addicted, but because she believed it helped her feel *less* miserable. And that was good enough for the moment, she thought. Nothing else was helping her anyway.

Suman was giving her depression what it wanted. Short-lived liberation with an inebriating substance—alcohol. Depression being a smart player, was luring her towards wrong choices as easy fixes. Her sharp brain (at least initially) allowed her to recognise what her choices were doing. A flickering lightbulb in the corner of her mind said, "this is all wrong". But that didn't make her give it up. Soon enough, depression and alcohol were together beginning to consume Suman's mind. The result? She slipped deeper into depression , and her judgment also began to fail.

Suman was not ready to give up her candy. She was developing an unhealthy relationship with alcohol. It cost money, affected her sleep, gave her a headache the next day, didn't let her wake up in time for work or exercise, made her gain weight, and definitely wasn't giving her liver a break either. She had started feeling physically weak too. Stopping alcohol consumption wasn't going to cure her depression. But it would prevent her overall physical and emotional health from getting worse.

Even then, Suman avoided confronting the truth. She couldn't acknowledge what it was in her life that needed to be dealt with and healed. She hid from the world as well as herself. She withdrew, so that nobody would know, not even me, her doctor. The influence of alcohol was strong enough to make her skip appointments. The anxiety about hiding her new-found fantasy nagged her over and above depression, which had now gotten clubbed with another problem—alcohol addiction. Suman had created double, triple, and quadruple trouble for herself. She had depression, which she didn't want to discuss with the world. She'd just topped the problematic emotional icing with the cherry of alcohol. Now she had to deal with both demons.

It took three weeks for Suman to suppress the voice of alcohol and show up for therapy. Suman's ultimate survival instincts had kicked in. No matter how deep her depression took her, at some vital point she sprung to the surface and sought help. She didn't drown, even though she struggled and gagged for a bit. I was glad Suman was committed to seeking help. Are you?

As much as it provides momentary enjoyment, most would agree that alcohol is not a solution for life's problems. And yet, so many people turn to alcohol or abuse other drugs for respite, especially when depressed. Are you one of them?

EXERCISE: Does Alcohol Dissolve Your Woes?

How many of these statements sound true or relevant? This could be about alcohol or other addictive drugs too. They reflect what you believe and how you may have been conditioned to think, feel, and react. Put a check mark (√) against what you seem to relate to.

- ☐ Alcohol makes one a more fun person.
- ☐ Alcohol widens the emotional horizon.
- ☐ Alcohol uplifts mood like nothing can.
- ☐ It's okay to drink to ward off a low mood.
- ☐ Alcohol should be labelled as "a friend in need".
- ☐ People are less sad when they have an alcoholic drink.
- ☐ Alcohol can offer a good night's sleep.
- ☐ Alcohol can dissolve some of life's sorrows.
- ☐ It is alright to drink alcohol to lift the mood.
- ☐ If drinking alcohol is the only way to feel better, why not?

If a few or many of these statements echo how you think, there is a possibility that you are prone to using (or misusing) alcohol (or other recreational drugs) when your mood is low.

People wonder, "Do I drink because I am depressed, or am I depressed because I drink?" Depression arising due to alcohol use is scientifically explainable. Alcohol diminishes tryptophan, which is a precursor of serotonin (reduction of which is causative of depression as explained before). The stress of hiding alcohol addiction from loved ones, associated guilt, embarrassment, and reduced self-worth–all add to the emotional damage. Heavy use can also cloud judgment and prevents you from seeking help that could potentially benefit you. Often enough even if you do reach out, reduced cognitive understanding due to alcohol use could hamper the efficacy of the otherwise life changing therapeutic approaches.

On the other hand, alcohol use by those already depressed is even more complex. Consumption is an unfortunate and yet frequent self-medication attempt, oftentimes by people who never even drank before. This could culminate in alcohol addiction if uncontrolled. The love affair between all addictions associated with depression almost always starts with an aching low mood that you're unable to shake off. The smart culprits (most commonly alcohol, nicotine, and cannabis) masquerade as allies. When you first start to use them, the grey abyss of the world gets infused with instant joyful colour. Drinking or smoking with friends, or by yourself at a pub, and eventually alone at home arouses a sense of connection in otherwise all-encompassing emotional isolation. Soon you might believe that a drink or maybe two, possibly a drag of nicotine, or chewing tobacco, or smoking up a joint of weed, take off the nervous edge providing tranquillity. It seems logical to you because you feel noticeably lighter, brighter, and more confident. How does alcohol play this treacherous game so well?

Alcohol slows down the memory centre, and momentarily makes painful emotions go away. The best antidepressant pills need a minimum of four to six weeks to show any restorative effect. And therapy? Well, that is the marathon which could take weeks, months, or years, based on how you absorb the perspective offered. No matter who sprints the race with alcohol to fight depression, alcohol tends to win in the shorter term, of course. Unfortunately, few can think long term when depressed.

The human brain is wired for learning. It quickly adapts to patterns. When you notice that alcohol or drug "fixes" work well for you, you rely less on yourself, and more on these "remedies", to keep your emotions at bay. You might reject friends, family, and professional help, and gravitate towards what *you* believe is making you feel better. This way you become dependent on the "wrong" stuff, because it actually seems "right" to your body and mind.

"Why not?" you think. "This makes me feel good, like nothing else right now can".

Alcohol is the commonest "quick fix" for depression because it makes you express, relate, and connect—all of which is inherently lost when you're depressed. And then one day, you realise that it has become the only thing you really connect with. Because it has such a strong grip on you, you're actively disconnected from the rest of existence. In time your tolerance levels increase leading to an increase in consumption. Soon, no amount of alcohol can drown your sorrows. Instead, it aggravates them. You fail to understand the difference between the low that comes from missing your drink, or the pre-existing depression itself. Emotions, mood, behaviour—all get entangled with alcohol. In a rare moment of realisation it may dawn on you that you have lost complete control. But the loss of rational judgment could make you cover up this reality too.

That is why you might continue to believe that you are drinking moderately, not engaging in unsafe behaviours, and that you can quit anytime. So, you justify that alcohol isn't all that bad an influence. Innately a chemical depressant, alcohol immediately suppresses bad memories and negative beliefs that aggravate sadness and worsen the mood. But in the long term, it recycles them. Momentarily it cons you into feeling *less depressed,* but it makes sure that you *stay* depressed for the long haul.

All of this happens simply because depression is such a lowly and painful state, that you're willing to do *anything* to make it go away. Emotional pain which is so hard to pacify otherwise, magically seems to ease away when doused with beer, vodka, whiskey, or any other recreational drug. You experience withdrawal symptoms when you are unable to access it. And then the emotional pain comes back with a vengeance. You are forced to wear your sadness like a heavy coat in summer. It becomes so unbearable that you go back to the chemical substance, reinforcing the lie that it is your best, rather only friend. You seem to not realise or care, that it is not beneficial.

When a child cries for candy and you do not give it to him, he will be insolent and angry, and it will be troublesome *for some time*. But eventually, he will stop crying. If you try hard enough and get the right help, you can quit and engage in more meaningful and fulfilling tasks that would enhance the mood in productive ways.

It's not easy to live with depression. If you rely on alcohol or other substances of abuse, the thought about consuming them haunts your mind, *even more* when you are low. The real problem is that this *appears* to be a solution while it's cunningly the bigger problem itself. Realising that alcohol isn't the right antidepressant, is a start. Alcohol is a schemer. When you resist the urge to give in to temptation, your will power to abstain will build on itself.

NOTE: Don't Let Alcohol Dissolve Your Judgment

You may or may not hold the belief that alcohol offers relief from depression. You may simply indulge because you want to blend in. You might do it because it's been a long-standing habit, all along. Yet, your readiness to change is influenced by your personal expectation from alcohol and what you believe it might do to your depression symptoms. Here are some statements that could help you realise that alcohol may not be the best antidepressant for you.

Remember that alcohol

- masquerades as a friend, then takes over your brain
- raises the severity, duration and intensity of depression
- makes you guilty, embarrassed, helpless and worthless
- causes inattention, distractibility and memory loss

- distances you from people who dissuade you from drinking
- induces sleep but also worsens sleep quality
- misleads you to think that it's helping you feel better
- enslaves you, taking focus away from everything else
- adds "addiction" to your existing troubles
- dulls you, negating the impact of treatment

31

Know Your Food and Mood Connection

"We have it in our head that if we fill our stomachs, we'll fill our hearts."

—Kate Wicker, *Weightless: Making Peace with Your Body*

Nearly half of all depressed individuals experience a loss of appetite while a third of them overeat or have increased hunger. This could lead to unwanted and unintentional weight loss or gain, which could further influence your mood negatively. Appetite and weight changes in depression are also called "vegetative symptoms". These broadly distinguish the typical from atypical depression subtypes, wherein one eats less or more than usual, respectively. Food and mood have been interesting subjects of research. Specific brain areas responsible for hunger and satiety (fullness) have shown alteration in their electrical connectivity with the amygdala (the emotion modulator which is so strongly implicated in depression). Emotions do impact food intake.

Research in 2006 affirmed that enhanced levels of serotonin and noradrenaline (lack of which causes depression) in the brain heighten the sensitivity to sweet, bitter, and sour tastes. This suggests that a decrease in the same could lower taste responsiveness and hence make people less interested in food. It is intriguing to note that these changes could occur at the tongue itself, not just the brain. Also, it's now concluded, that 95% of the body's serotonin is produced in the gut. The biological connection between food and mood is strong. That is why the other can get easily affected, when one becomes deranged or dysfunctional.

Depression sets diverse food traps. Overeating has drawn great attention to the agitated atypically depressed people, while the significantly larger population with "typical major depression" tend to lose their appetite. You may wonder, "Why the discrepancy?". Depression has many faces. So, contrastingly opposing behaviours like overeating and decreased appetite both, could reflect illness subtype based on the region of the brain involved. The low, sad, melancholic type of major depression lowers the desire to eat, while the atypical variety of depression promotes filling the emotional void with food.

For those who lose their desire to eat, initially, it isn't even noticeable. You might start by eating less and find it impossible to "clean" your plate as you did before. This may gradually progress to skipping entire meals in the day or avoiding eating for days together. You may find yourself saying, "Oh, I just forgot to eat." Exactly the way depression takes away happiness from all activities, it also sucks out flavour from food, makes eating repulsive, and kills the motivation to ingest pretty much anything.

EXERCISE: Is Your Emotional Void Not Letting You Eat?

Food is everybody's fuel. Your body needs to eat for energy, besides pleasure. An emotional void can influence appetite. These statements reflect thoughts, feelings and behaviours that contribute to reduced food intake. There are no right or wrong answers. It's about how you have recently or consistently been conditioned to think, feel, and react towards your food. Put a check mark (√) against statements that might be true for you.

- ☐ I'm definitely (unintentionally) eating less than before.
- ☐ I feel full after barely eating a mouthful, this is unusual.
- ☐ I don't feel hungry even if my stomach is empty.
- ☐ I don't enjoy my favourite food anymore.
- ☐ All food seems to lack flavour and taste.
- ☐ I get irritated when people force me to eat.
- ☐ I'm not bothered about my health anymore.
- ☐ I don't eat because I have no taste anyway.
- ☐ I don't have the energy to cook, order in, or step out to eat.
- ☐ The thought about eating makes my mood worse.

If you answered yes to some or many of these, with a background of low mood, you may have lost your appetite as well as the ability to seek gustatory pleasure, most likely on account of *typical* or major depression. Food is not an antidepressant, but it provides energy and vitality, and is also the source of precursors to neurotransmitters that antagonise sadness. Food eaten in healthy limits can momentarily enhance the mood. But when the depression is deep, guilt intense, and mood low, you may inadvertently choose subtle and subconscious self-harm through chronic starvation.

Suman's case was the opposite. Her weight gain (classic of *atypical* depression) was apparent in her last visit itself. In the initial days she had been eating less, but lately she had been indulging in chocolates, cheese, ice creams, aerated drinks, and her very own personal "comfort foods" that included increasingly large portions of pasta, pizza, and white rice. She said it herself, "I'm consuming food to fill the hollowness in my heart, not really my stomach." She admitted that *eating* had nothing to do with *hunger* anymore. She'd been a fitness enthusiast at one time—exercising, cooking healthy and yet occasionally pampering herself with her favourite foods. Stuffing herself like this, when food didn't serve the purpose of nourishment or the joy of eating anymore, was new to her. She couldn't join the dots accurately between her food consumption and mood. But she did realise they were both deranged. Just like alcohol made her feel guilty, overeating did the same, if not more. Her increasing weight made her resent herself, developing a dislike towards her body. She was beginning to love herself lesser than ever before and was getting sucked into an infinite loop of unconscious eating, drinking alcohol, and self-isolation.

Consciousness about food is reflected in correct food choices, healthy portions, balancing nutrients, working with food varieties, regularising meal timings, and taking feedback from your body on how it reacts to different foods. It is similar to how a diabetic is conscious about the sugar content and would adjust the insulin dose to match the need, or a person with high cholesterol might avoid fried foods but still consume other delicious, albeit low-fat dietary options. People are conscious and mindful about things they care about. Your body deserves your care.

Depression (both varieties) brings about food unconsciousness, which is a loss of attentiveness on the "what, why, when, and how" about food, challenging the purpose of eating (for nutrition or pleasure). A painfully low mood of typical depression detracts from the awareness that food is essential for survival, such that even a loud and growling stomach does not arouse any food motivation. On the other hand, the agitation and frustration of atypical depression fosters aimless eating accompanied by an often malfunctioning pattern of food conditioning.

Do you recall a time when you may have been at a movie theatre, munching on a huge bucket of popcorn? A lot of people I know agree to having done this at least once, at some point. Popcorn is not the best food choice. A bucket is unquestionably a wrong portion, it really isn't a balanced meal, and it could be boring to eat so much of the same thing all at once. The body doesn't even feel good after eating so much of it. None of this comes to mind at that time because it was all happening in a state of food unconsciousness. This is not toxic though, if it happens occasionally. But a consistent pattern of such food oblivion in depression could result in unplanned and unnecessary binge eating, like an addiction. Like all addictions, nothing is this gripping at the outset. What makes any behaviour or choice addictive is the reinforcement effect you perceive when you indulge in it repeatedly, turning it into your feel-good factor.

Food is recognised to offer comfort, and it is indeed gratifying. From the moment one is born, the mother's milk appeases and satiates. Be it hurt, pain, illness, or the cold, milk is reassuring for the infant. As you grow older and enjoy the food you eat, you attune your brain to the burst of dopamine (the brain's innate reward chemical) whenever you eat your favourite food item. Dopamine offers a sense of well-being. This feeling coupled with your preferred food convinces you that *food equals to gratification*. Therefore, you turn to your unique comfort foods when you're low or upset or stressed. Each to their own, you eat what *you* like because it helps *you* feel better. Not everyone may binge on pizza or chocolate. All bank on their personal favourite foods in their distinctive emotional emergencies. But all of this could result in unwanted stress eating. The outcome of this can never be functional or rewarding.

EXERCISE: Are You Overeating to Fill an Emotional Void?

We all love to eat what satiates us. But if you have been overeating lately and not feeling good about it, check the following statements. There are no right or wrong answers. It's just how you may have recently or consistently been conditioned to think, feel, and react regarding your food. Do check mark (√) any that might be true for you.

- ☐ I notice I'm eating even when I'm not actually hungry.
- ☐ I am preoccupied with thoughts about food all the time.
- ☐ I keep eating even though I feel very full.
- ☐ On many occasions I eat uncontrollably (bingeing).
- ☐ I turn to food especially when I want to elevate my mood.
- ☐ I have become reliant on food to ward off my frustration.
- ☐ I am hiding my overeating behaviour from people I love.
- ☐ I am very upset with my weight gain (due to overeating).
- ☐ I am using food to fill up a deep hollowness inside me.
- ☐ I have become touchy and emotional about my eating.

If you answered yes to some or many of these with a background of a low mood, you may be on an emotional food binge, common in *atypical* depression. This cannot and does not resolve the primary emotional conflict. Food is energising but isn't an antidepressant. If you love eating, enjoy your food, feel satiated, and exercise regularly to keep your weight and health in check, it's great. Unfortunately, in depression none of this typically happens. Food becomes a powerless pawn in the equation. The emotional void stays, you feel guilty about the binge, and get upset about being overweight. Emotional dependency on food becomes disruptive, and the low mood of depression remains unaddressed. In fact, the mood in the long-term could get way worse.

NOTE: Mind Your Food, to Feed Your Mind

How you cognise (think), emote (feel) and perform (behave) around food, is one hundred percent affected by a sad mood. At the same time, over and under eating both independently worsen the experience of depression. If you are mindful of this reality, your feelings and behaviour around food will become more meaningful. And your food habits will result in better physical and emotional well-being. Here are some thoughts on healthy eating that can inspire healthier choices and coax you to eat right even when you may not always feel like it.

- Food can be your friend or enemy. Remember to make healthy food your best friend.
- Food can be healthy or unhealthy, but your food choices don't make *you* good or bad.
- Good physical and emotional health calls for healthy food.
- Overweight and underweight are not character adjectives.
- When food has lost its connection with hunger, you still need to eat enough to survive.
- Chemicals responsible for your emotions are largely produced inside your gut.
- Food is fuel, but over-fuelling yourself could worsen your mood.
- When you absolutely don't feel like eating, is when you need it most.
- Depression sets food traps, make sure to not get caught.
- Give your body what it needs. It will give you what you want.

32

Sleep Matters—Don't Disrupt Already Disturbed Sleep

"The best bridge between despair and hope, is a good night's sleep."

—E. Joseph Cossman, entrepreneur and author

Breakthrough research at the Johns Hopkins Institute, Baltimore alleged that insomnia (inadequate or insufficient sleep) results in difficulty in emotional regulation, and lowers stress resilience, which could leave you vulnerable to depression for many years, even after sleep has been restored. It even implied that how much you sleep can decide how serious your depression will be, and whether you will recover or not. Healthy women and men whose sleep was interrupted through the night had a thirty-one percent reduction in positive moods the next day. This confirms that sleep deficit is a big risk factor for causing sadness, frustration, anxiety, and depression.

At the same time, anyone who's experienced even the slightest pang of sadness without any prior sleep problems would agree, that low mood interferes with slumber–they either sleep too much or too little, have disturbed or broken sleep, and do not feel adequately rested the next day despite sleeping sufficient hours. Sleep and depression are a two-way street. If not managed tactfully, the underlying sleep problem and mood, both continue to worsen.

Suman was finding it increasingly hard to make it in time for her morning appointments. She started seeing me early evening, as "her sun would rise only around then". The combination of inaction and disturbed sleep was making her get out of bed at noon and easing her into the groove of her day only by 3 or 4 in the afternoon, a time when everyone else in the ordinary world was preparing to get back home from work to relax. She had ongoing stressors with colleagues at work and felt hated by her boss. She was somehow managing to get by in her job though she wasn't sure it would remain as smooth if things continued this way.

I believed Suman when she swore that she was unable to sleep. Falling or staying asleep isn't easy when you're depressed. Negative thoughts seem to surface even more when your brain is freer, and you're trying to relax or disconnect. Suman used to get into bed at midnight, take just a little while to fall asleep and then be up by 3.00 or 4.00 am on most days. She'd toss and turn; her mind, awake as an owl. As most would, she started scrolling through the phone to engage herself, until dawn. It became increasingly normal for her to not even try and go back to sleep at that time. She didn't feel awake enough to work or do her daily chores. She waited to feel drained by the usual 6.00 am, and then would doze off again. This became her *new* normal. After this, she stayed in bed till noon as she didn't "feel like" getting out. She told me at each visit, "I don't *get* sleep". What seemed truer for her was, "I don't *plan* my sleep or *let* myself sleep". But she hadn't realised that, yet.

Straight Facts: Depression And Sleep *Are* Related

Sleep and depression are connected. Not as simple as a cause-effect relationship where one triggers another, but a two-way circular association, where one had the power to benefit as well as worsen the other. These facts reflect this correlation.

- 90% of depressed individuals complain about their sleep.
- Depressed people either sleep too little or too much.
- Insomnia is the most frequent complaint in depression.
- Sleep EEG (an electroencephalogram which measures electrical activity of the brain) is abnormal in depression.
- Sleep disturbances appear before depressive symptoms.
- Depression with sleep problems is more severe.
- Depression with sleep problems is harder to treat.
- Improving sleep uplifts the mood and eases depression.
- Sleep medication alleviates depression symptoms (even without antidepressants).
- Sleep deprivation can trigger depression in anyone.
- Insomnia often persists even after depression lifts.
- Depressed people with insomnia have recurrent depression.

Isn't the connection between sleep and depression rather obvious? While depression seems like the bigger devil to fight; sleeping well and sleeping right can go a long way in beating depression to a small but significant extent.

Sleep is not merely a passive, restorative, energy-conserving function. It *is* all of that but isn't *only* that. Sleeping, like breathing, has specific goals, targets and objectives for the human body and mind. You might think that if you haven't done too much in the day, you don't need much sleep, unlike someone else who's probably worked harder. But that's not true.

The body and brain follow a sleep rhythm. Just like the natural pacemaker in your heart that signals it to beat 72 times a minute, a specialised set of brain cells (supra chiasmatic nuclei or SCN in the hypothalamus) work with an oscillating flexible pattern to set the daily sleep rhythm or the body clock, to 24 hours. This fixes the sleep-wake cycle, or circadian rhythm. The body clock is innate and self-sustaining. It promotes sleep by around 11 pm and stimulates wakefulness 4 am onwards. The brain is also programmed to desire sleep approximately 16 hours after the last waking. A deliberate or unwanted change in this pattern could generate a sleep debt and disrupt your body's homeostasis (steady state).

Structurally, sleep is understood to have several stages or cycles through a given night. The REM or Rapid Eye Movement sleep is the active and alert phase, while the Slow Wave or deep sleep is associated with relaxation and restoration. Depression is known lengthen REM sleep cycles and reduce slow wave sleep. So, when you are depressed, sleep doesn't offer relaxation and rejuvenation as expected. That is why you feel like you didn't sleep much, even though you appear to be fast asleep all night, or even through the day.

"Clock genes" that regulate the body clock, coincidentally are implicated in depression too. Monoamines like serotonin, noradrenaline, and acetylcholine (deficient in depressed brains) are known upholders of the circadian rhythm and are influenced by these genes. That is why clock gene dysfunction could cause both insomnia as well as other symptoms of depression. When you don't sleep, the circadian rhythm is broken, a sleep debt is generated, and the general recuperative upkeep of the body gets deranged.

Heightened emotions, particularly sadness and anxiety are common threads in the weaving of the fabric of depression. They make it difficult for a depressed person to fall or stay asleep. At times you feel you don't have a choice and you can't control this yourself. Like in Suman's case, you give in, and unconsciously reset your body clock altogether. You sleep late, are up in the middle of the night, probably read, eat or stare at some screen, and finally wake up at odd hours of noon or evening. Erroneous, but this seems like a solution. You tend to think, "I'm at least maintaining the required hours of sleep, so my life is closer to normal." But the body clock is acting up, REM sleep is getting prolonged, deep sleep condensed, and the mood keeps getting worse.

EXERCISE: A Malfunctioning Clock is Troublesome

Imagine an era without smartwatches and smartphones. If your house clock and wristwatch both had to malfunction in such a time space, would there not be mayhem about your day? You'd most likely miss the 8.05 am bus that led to the 8.17 am train, which made sure you walked the last 4 minutes to punch in to work by swiping your card at 9.00 am. You'd probably miss out on the lunch break at 12.30 pm too, and the prefixed meal at office is only served till 1.00 pm. And what about the 3.00 pm board meeting? The one that counted towards your promotion. How would you ever get back in time for your daughter's football game?

We are normally blessed with more comfortable lives than those that include deranged clocks and rhythms. We have cues, clues, and support systems in place that compensate for the little and big slip ups. But the body clock doesn't have smart external communication systems. Visualise your internal clock crashing and disrupting your body mechanics in more ways than an altered simple sleep–wake pattern. Thyroid and cortisol hormones, as well as substances responsible for immunity, wound healing, muscle repair, pain control, memories, emotions, thinking, impulsivity, and behaviour—all get wired to a different tune when you don't sleep right. This is how abnormal sleep patterns and choices continue to worsen your depression.

The same argument might spring up in your mind, as did Suman's during my discussion the other day. "Doc, I don't watch Netflix at night with the motivation to see movies and just stay up. I really don't get sleep, so I have to do *something*, Hence I watch action thrillers, as that's all I've ever liked." Depression and sleeplessness, both continued to trouble Suman because of her choices. The problem is, you're fighting two devils in a dark room, and you don't know whether you're striking either of them, or just getting beaten up yourself.

EXERCISE: Are You Facing Trouble With Your Sleep?

These questions assess the appropriateness of the quality and quantity of your sleep. They may exist in the presence or absence of sadness or depression (as measured on previous checklists). Please put a check mark (√) on items that seem true about you, keeping the past few weeks in mind.

- ☐ I sleep more (or less) than I ideally should.
- ☐ I have difficulty falling asleep.
- ☐ Sad thoughts come to mind when I try to sleep.
- ☐ I wake up repeatedly at night (for no valid reason).
- ☐ Once I wake up, I cannot go to sleep again.
- ☐ I don't seem to fall into deep sleep whenever I sleep.
- ☐ I toss and turn a lot at night (I am aware of this in bed).
- ☐ I wake up suddenly at night with sad and negative thoughts.
- ☐ I'm hardly ever refreshed when I wake up.
- ☐ I feel I haven't slept at all (no matter how much I've slept).
- ☐ I don't look forward to waking up.
- ☐ When I wake up, I feel upset that it's yet another day.

- ☐ I don't feel energised or boosted when I wake up.
- ☐ I'm fatigued right after waking up.
- ☐ My head isn't clear after I wake up.
- ☐ I'm not satisfied with my sleep.
- ☐ I am beginning to get concerned about my sleep.
- ☐ I don't want to get out of bed in the morning.
- ☐ I'm convinced there's something wrong.

Answering yes to a few or many of these questions indicates that you're unable to sleep satisfactorily. This could be associated with depression, or if independent, it may be a forerunner of depression. Likely, this could simply be an independent sleep condition called insomnia (too little sleep) or hypersomnia (too much sleep), both of which might have no connection to depression whatsoever.

Whatever be the case, remember that sleep is vital for your body. Just like a thermometer reading of 103° F alarms you of high fever, a blood pressure of 140/90 mmHg alerts for hypertension, pulse-oximeter reading of 90% oxygen saturation denotes a lung disease, likewise, not sleeping well enough is a forewarning for something bigger that deserves your attention.

NOTE: Sleep Hygiene Tips to Sleep Better

Healthy sleep habits are called "sleep hygiene". These are non-medicinal, lifestyle choices that you make to ensure sound sleep. They help correct the disrupted sleep architecture of depression by reducing REM sleep, resetting the circadian rhythm, and correcting your sleep debt, if any.

- ➢ Keep a consistent bedtime, your mind responds to a routine.
- ➢ Save the bed for sleep and rest only, to condition the mind.
- ➢ Maintain a pre-sleep ritual to unwind before you sleep.

- Use a pre-sleep meditation audio to relax your mind.
- Get morning sunlight to reboot the body clock.
- Exercise pre-noon to boost your daytime adrenaline level.
- No naps>20 minutes. No naps after 4 pm (REM tuning).
- No alcohol, nicotine or drugs of abuse 3 hours pre-sleep.
- If you haven't slept, stay awake all day. Sleep at night.
- Try banana or milk (banana milkshake) before sleep.

33

Instead of Inaction, Choose to Be in Action

"Inaction breeds doubt and fear. Action breeds confidence and courage. If you want to conquer fear, do not sit home, and think about it. Go out and get busy."

—Dale Carnegie

Newton's first law of motion describes physical inertia. It postulates that if a body is at rest or moving at a constant speed in a straight line, it will remain at rest or keep moving in a straight line at constant speed unless it is acted upon by a force. In a similar way, depression builds up a tendency to perseverate, and you continue to stay in the negative mood state building up an *emotional inertia*. This could affect your behaviour, giving rise to procrastination and inactivity. Action, even though good for you, could seem effortful. You might decide that you don't want to pay so heavily for happiness. This way, the estimation of costs and benefits of whatever you do can become deranged, and you might select inaction. This makes you stay in a negative and inactive mood and mode. This is how depression wears you out physically, depletes you emotionally, and keeps you stuck —in a low and dark dump.

Suman had promised to be regular with therapy, so I saw her weekly. This time, as soon as she walked into my room, she insisted I see some pictures on her phone. I wasn't curious but I obliged. The pictures of her home took me aback. Suman had a nice job and lived in a lovely apartment in the heart of town. It seemed freshly painted and overlooked the sea (I gauged from the corner of one of the photos). She'd recently moved here from her hometown, and the sheer independence had been liberating. No parents to question her on why her socks were on the dining table or remind her that the jacket had a designated spot in the closet. Like her, the jacket, as well as shoes, dresses, jeans and belts were free to lounge where they liked. Earlier on, this freedom of solitude had been blissful, sometime before her depression had struck.

Suman mentioned that the previous night, she was making dinner, and realised she had completely run out of dishes. All the plates, glasses, bowls, and cutlery were in the kitchen sink, haphazardly piled up. They needed to be washed but Suman didn't feel motivated. To add to the mystery, this was a state-of-the-art condominium, with a dishwasher at the bare basics. Suman's company housed their contract employees well. She had been offered this luxurious space for twenty-four months at minimum, until her project was completed. Her future career plans would unravel soon after. Yet, she couldn't get herself to do anything.

Another photograph on Suman's phone was of the trash can, or as she now called it, the trash *zone*, because all the trash had made its way to the floor spanning a two feet radius around the can. As glass dishes could not wash themselves, paper plates, disposable glasses, and plastic spoons had made their way home via online orders. Since they could not endlessly fit the can, they were placed outside it. Along with pizza delivery boxes, plastic bags and bottles of soda, alcohol (yes, she was still drinking, though lesser), and more. Being obsessive about cleanliness and order, a cockroach or two around the boxes caught my eye. This much had transpired in just one week.

To me, none of this seemed Herculean to set right. It didn't demand an exceptional contribution of time, intellect, analytical reasoning, complex problem-solving, physical prowess, or any computational mathematical skill, for that matter. No explanation would have been sufficient to justify this boundless mess. And yet Suman had an excellent one.

"I don't feel like doing anything."

Irrespective of mood, our everyday behaviour is a continuum of some or the other activity. Where we put in effort is called action, and restful states count as inaction. Typically, we choose action or inaction based on the assumed outcome. If we know something will do us good, we tend to engage and get it done. If we see no positive outcome, we are drawn to select inaction. Based on this theory, one would assume that the estimated happiness of an action will drive our choices around it. Why then was Suman alright with the mess and cockroaches? Did she not want a clean home, a healthy body, meaningful friendships, positive relationships, career success, and a good life?

As I handed her phone back, Suman thought I was about to lecture, blame, or berate her. Before I could say anything, she burst into tears. "I'm not lazy. I'm just tired from pretending to be stronger than I am. I am lifting all the weight that seems fluffy light to everybody else, including my family and friends. But they are normal people with normal strength, endurance, and capability. If I had a fractured arm, people would empathise with me and even lift this weight for me. Unfortunately, I'm depressed and they don't see it. Even if I say it, they won't realise because my depression is invisible to them. And yet so excruciatingly painful for me."

Suman felt "stuck". In her own words, her hands and legs felt heavy and weighed down—like she couldn't move. And even though originally a hygiene enthusiast, in these states she was unable to perform any of her daily chores, shopping, cooking, or cleaning. Let's not even mention the bathing or brushing her hair or her daily hygiene routine, that she managed to accomplish only every other day. The common-sense asymmetry in her choices was too obvious. She was choosing procrastination. But don't we all have those asymmetries in some form or magnitude, and procrastinate from time to time? How was this different?

Procrastination, or putting off intended action is a universal phenomenon. People voluntarily delay necessary and personally important tasks, pushing them to a later time, because they miscalculate that it'll burden or stress them right now. What they don't realise is that the harm this causes, outweighs the stress they were trying to avoid. This is outright self-regulated failure, eventually leading to low mood and reduced well-being in the long run.

Take for example, exercise. It always calls for effort, energy, time, and often money if you spend on a gym, exercise gear, or equipment. If you have the time, you make it a point to exercise. When you have the motivation, you sign up for the marathon. When there's energy you wake at dawn to finish your workout before you head to work. And when finances aren't so much of a concern, you appoint a personal trainer or coach too, to guide you to your fitness goals. This is a well-functioning accounting system.

But when you're depressed, suddenly this system shuts down, and the cost-benefit analysis goes out of the window. The positive emotional investment in exercise gets toned down and the negative system gets jacked up. You choose inertia. And this invades all other actions and choices too. Steel (2007), explained in his research that procrastination is rampant in those who believe less of themselves, feel over conscientious and guilty, and in whom impulsiveness and distractibility are high. All of this is often the case when you are depressed.

Depression inertia is real. So many people recount staying home, skipping work, avoiding people, missing meals, failing to throw out the garbage, and not doing dishes, of course. You could spend hours on the phone, browsing videos or watching shows that offer nothing, and still take away so much from you. You lie all day in pyjamas, perhaps don't bathe because it's easier not to, and care little about makeup and hairdos. You may continue to be physically fitter than most around you, but psychologically you are paralysed by sloth and lethargy. It gets you to no good place. And yet, the reality is that nobody can threaten or bully you into taking action. It has to come from within. Intimidation doesn't improve your relationship with the most important person in the equation here–you.

"You're going to get fat and ugly, Suman. You will be a depressed alcoholic, a loser who's wasting her time watching TV, eating pizza, gaining weight, missing work, and letting her family down. Is this what your folks expected of you when they toiled so hard to raise you right, get you educated, and sent you here to live *the better life* in the city?" These aren't my words. Suman was replaying such and other ideas in her head, on her own. She was beating herself up in the hope that it would wake her up and break the pattern of wrong choices. She was whipping herself like one would motivate a horse, but unfortunately it didn't make her gallop. She felt beaten and crushed, inching closer to giving up.

Depression saps energy required even for the most mundane tasks. Unfortunately, your "feel good button" is broken. You're left out there—lonely and miserable, unable to find pleasure in any pursuits. Hence, you see sense in avoidance. "If it does not make me feel good, why do it?" is what Suman thought too. Where she was wrong, however, was that she wanted to feel good about these tasks without challenging her secondary feelings of perhaps boredom, frustration, anger, resentment, weariness, and annoyance. She insisted she needed to "feel good" and only then would she do what she thought was "right". Which ironically means, she knew what was right all along, but simply wasn't doing it. If she engaged in action, she would know how good it made her feel.

Procrastination needs to be challenged. You need to combat inaction by gauging the effect of action. There will be some discomfort, that is why you're choosing inaction in the first place. But over time you will realise that inaction is uneasy too. It worsens your mood. Alongside collateral damage like poor personal hygiene, ill-health, a spoiled reputation, tarnished relationships, or loss at work, for instance. What if you had to accept the bad feelings and allow yourself to feel them just for a little bit? All of them—boredom, frustration, anger, resentment, weariness, and annoyance altogether? Figure out why these interfere with your everyday responsibilities and things you always wanted or liked to do? Then you could break the inaction accordingly.

Like all negative behaviours that feed on themselves, procrastination is a cause as well as consequence of depression. What matters is, when you know "why", you are in a better position to figure "why not" as well as "how to". For example, consider your incapacity to clean up your room, throw trash out, keep clothes in order, or exercise. The weariness could be fuelled by an assumption that "nobody's coming home", or "no one cares how I, or my kitchen or closet really look". Maybe some of this is true, maybe most of it is supposition. Depression is known to cloud logical reasoning and make you see and assume the worst. But even though lethargy has taken over, there may still be some lurking motivation to engage in action. "I want a clean home, I aspire for a great career, I crave a good body, I'm seeking a loving partner, and I don't want to be sick." You do not have to do this for someone else (my wife will be happy), for praise (I'd like to impress my boss) or compliance (this seems like the right thing according to everybody). Exercise your free will. For your own good. And get into action.

EXERCISE: Figure Out Why You're Procrastinating

When you're depressed, everything seems difficult, and the path tiring. The point is, you don't need to have everything figured out. You must try new things, experiment, mess up, and then start over. Why not start now? These questions are short and simple, but their answers aren't. Think about them.

- *Where* is my *mind* these days?
- *What* do I really *want* to do?
- *Why* do I *want* to do it at all?
- *What* makes me want to *not* do it?
- *Am* I keeping *focus* on the task?
- *Who's responsible* for this task?
- *How* do I suppose I'll *get to it*?
- *When* do I plan to make a *start*?
- *What* do I need, to *just* start off?
- *How* do I *push* myself to keep at it?

A good motivating strategy to kickstart, is to club an unwanted task with one that is slightly less annoying. Like cleaning up while listening to music or watching a funny video, or fixing a fitness routine with an exercise buddy online for instance. You might stop disliking the first task, simply because you enjoy the second.

Another technique that could work is to toil harder when you know your energy level is at its peak. For instance, in keeping with the thyroid, cortisol as well as melatonin hormone release, moods tend to swing with the time of day, and motivation sinks at specific hours in accordance. So, it makes sense to "make hay while the sun shines" by working more when your mental energy is higher, to get ahead in your game.

The eternally common proposition of the to-do list can be double-edged. Long lists could crush motivation when you just *look* at them. But here's the twist. You could start with just one or two items on your list: maybe the easily accomplishable ones. And break bigger tasks into smaller ones to make them appear less overwhelming. If there are one hundred emails to respond to, you can start with checking five: all a step towards a larger and meaningful goal. Or clear up one shelf in your closet. Keep the bigger picture in mind, but when you're focusing on the littlest task, it's okay to get myopic, and not look too far. You can focus on the tiniest achievements and celebrate them with little prizes to gradually build up your motivation for more. You could add one item to your to-do list every day and build it up little by little, to accomplish more, over time.

Acknowledging the inertia of depression means that you can actually give in to the need to give up action for the time being. But you must discern what's feeding your inactivity. Not keeping up with your obligations does not make you lazy or a lesser human being. Your inability to function optimally isn't a character flaw. If people can't put your symptoms together and therefore, judge you, the stigma they impose mustn't be internalised. Be patient, compassionate, and kind to yourself. Take baby steps towards your goals. You'll get there in time if you keep moving.

NOTE: GET *IN ACTION* BY BREAKING *INACTION* DISTORTIONS

It's interesting how everyone who procrastinates knows that it does them no good. You may get approach and avoidance thoughts that take you closer to, and then away from the goal of completing any task you set out for. Here are some thoughts that could push you to action when you feel like it the least. You may often believe thoughts contrary to these. But these statements can challenge your false beliefs and reverse your procrastination. Try and check (√) most of them.

- ☐ This task is most likely not as difficult as I imagine.
- ☐ I am not as incompetent as I am labelling myself to be.
- ☐ I am underestimating the time I have to complete the task.
- ☐ I am overestimating the time that's needed to get this done.
- ☐ It makes more sense to get it out of the way now, than later.
- ☐ I don't need to wait for the right mood for this to get done.
- ☐ If I have to do it well, I don't need to always *want* to do it.
- ☐ Doing the job builds motivation, not the other way round.
- ☐ I might surprise myself by how quickly I can get this done.
- ☐ I need to test it, to decide if procrastination is the right call.

34

"Help Negation": When You Want to Give Up

"You may be the only person left who believes in you, but it's enough. It takes just one star to pierce a universe of darkness. Never give up."

—Richelle E. Goodrich, *Smile Anyway: Quotes, Verse, and Grumblings for Every Day of the Year*

Behavioural researchers are intrigued when they observe that patients who are at the lowest low of the depression spectrum sometimes reach such a state of utter futility concerning treatment that they quietly abandon, politely terminate, or angrily reject *any* help that is being offered to them (Clark and Fawcett, 1992). This idea brings on the concept of "help negation" wherein ironically, people who desperately need support actively avoid seeking it, and even outright reject it. Common sense would deem this to be a lack of optimism, or a hopelessness that disallows you to believe that anything could, or will ever get better. So you give up trying. But "help negation" behaviour is only partly linked with hope.

In the initial stages, very few people recognise that they might be depressed. They mistake clinical depression to be ordinary sadness that emerges from life's everyday lows, and that it will pass when the situation changes. So they don't seek help at this stage. Such people are hopeful that they'll get better by themselves. As symptoms worsen, they often get motivated to reach out. Hope is still alive at this stage. But if the depression is left untreated, it can worsen the mood, and cause deep agony and incapacity for decades together. With time, as the mood keeps waning, the intention to seek help from friends, parents, or other family members who would otherwise be a good source of support, decreases. This is when helplessness sets in, and hope begins to die.

Hopelessness is when you really value an outcome but sense a very low likelihood of attaining it. Hopelessness thrives on three beliefs–that positive *will not* occur, negative *will* occur, and you are *powerless* to change anything about it. So, you choose to exit the battlefield. Just because you see no chance of winning, you make the decision to not even try.

Hopefulness on the other hand, foresees positive outcomes irrespective of guarantees. It looks at a brighter future and a belief that things could work out well. Hope is distinct from happiness, delight, or joy—all of which are momentary reactionary emotions to something positive in the present. Hope focuses on the future. That is why hope requires waiting, anticipating, and persisting, making it hard to bring on. Somehow in depression, hope is easy to lose because you seem to become unable to see beyond the existing darkness and fail to believe that there could be light at the end of the tunnel. Hence, hopelessness prevails.

EXERCISE: Watch for Signs of "Help Negation"

Hopelessness is a negative emotion which focuses on and emphasises impossibilities. Logic says that seeking help for depression will make things better, but negative anticipation leads to "help negation". These statements represent false beliefs about help and can resultantly negate it. Check (√) any or all that you feel might apply to you.

If I ask for help for my depression

- ☐ nobody will really understand me.
- ☐ I will become anxious and stressed.
- ☐ I'll feel like I'm weak or vulnerable.
- ☐ I will feel ashamed or embarrassed.
- ☐ I will feel judged and discriminated.
- ☐ unpleasant memories will surface.
- ☐ I'll experience unpleasant emotions.
- ☐ my shortcomings will be exposed.
- ☐ my weaknesses will be endorsed.
- ☐ I will feel worse than I already do.

If you checked some or many, you are likely to negate help. People's decision to seek help for the distress they feel is the focal point of their personal experience of depression, and how they express it to those around them. Often enough, one may not be aware that this is a real medical problem, and that it has a documented solution. People tend to think this is normative and that they must just deal with it. There is also the universal worry about being judged, leading to the conclusion that discussing depression is risky, and that seeking treatment will be stigmatising. Destructive beliefs about seeking help, the desire for perfection, struggle for autonomy, and envisioning oneself as weak for reaching out—all impact the intention to get the much-needed support.

If you've ever been unfortunate enough to endure a negative response when you shared your suffering, especially from someone you trusted, it could break your faith deeply. Stigma is the biggest enemy in depression management. It significantly feeds "help negation".

A façade of strength is not what the world wants or needs from you. You're not burdening your loved ones with your stress, you're just unburdening yourself by sharing your pain with those who can and want to help. Some people are even qualified for doing so (for example a mental health professional such as a psychiatrist, psychologist, or psychotherapist). Your decision to seek help is a rational and logical choice. But then, rationality and logic are exhausted in depression. A sense of apathy or indifference could set in, and you might stop feeling emotions altogether. When you lose track of how bad things have gotten, your awareness for the need to seek help gets compromised.

Speaking to a professional can seem intimidating because you may have internalised a self-stigma as we discussed earlier. That is why, reading a book like this is safe, private, and yet, very effective. There will always be times when you may need more. That is why you ought to connect with others and speak to them. My patient Suman, whom we discussed in previous chapters in this section, had a range of trouble behaviours that were sapping her energy, weakening enthusiasm, and nourishing depression, but she still pulled through because she *never* negated help.

NOTE: Fight "Help Negating" Distortions

Friends, family, loved ones, even therapists, psychologists, psychiatrists, and other mental health professionals are human. They can falter from time to time in helping you. The world can often be ignorant and biased. Some people might be narrow-minded and effectively, unsupportive. Yet, your rational mind must learn to listen to your own personal logic. You *can* get out of the rut. Whether you use external help or not, you mustn't ever stop helping and healing yourself. Giving up should not be an option. These statements can help you combat cognitive distortions about seeking help and fight "help negation".

- If I keep hiding my problem, it will not go away.
- If I don't feel motivated, I could try being open-minded.
- People with a different viewpoint are not adversaries.
- Feeling a little vulnerable is okay. I can't be strong always.
- What other people think about me is not my problem.
- Unpleasant memories may surface, but I can process them.
- There is no contest about being strong or weak.
- Seeking will make me stronger. It can't hurt.
- I'm just overwhelmed. Depression does have a cure.
- If I don't try, how will I know if this is useful or not?

35

Don't Hurt Yourself—You Don't Deserve It

"The world is full of wonderful things you haven't seen yet. Don't ever give up on the chance of seeing them."

—J. K. Rowling, author, *Harry Potter Series.*

According to the WHO, approximately 7,03,000 people die by suicide annually. This is roughly one person every 45 seconds. But the number of people who attempt suicide is 20 times this number. Suicide ranks as one of the top four causes of death among 15-to 29-year-olds worldwide. With the way the world is moving, lives can be lost for many reasons. But suicide is a matter of choice. It is preventable.

In my experience, almost all depressed people who have attempted suicide openly admit that they did not really want to die. Of these, 7% do end their life, but the rest do not intend to. They want their suffering and pain to end. A sense of defeat, entrapment, burden, isolation, disconnection, or impulsiveness is often identified as a persuader for suicidal behaviour. Yet, there are plentiful variables which interplay with each other before one might get the gruesome thought of ending one's own life.

Consider a theoretical model here. When you feel you don't belong, or that you are a burden to others, the emotional pain or "psychache" is so harsh that your threshold to tolerate it is crossed, and you wish you didn't exist. You feel trapped internally by discomforting negative thoughts and externally by inescapable agonising life events. But pain alone does not make you want to end it all. Many people endure pain, and if they believe that it can be reduced and that they will have a good life ahead, they do not consider suicide. It is only when you react to the assumption that there is no hope to flee from the pain that you begin to think that your problems will never be solved. So, you focus on dire actions to escape it.

Hurting yourself physically (with or without the intention to die) seems to have an idiosyncratic power to immediately relieve tension. In a 2017 research, depressed interviewees reported that a slight degree of self-harm tended to improve their low mood because they perceived it as well-deserved (albeit twisted) self-punishment for wrongdoings or shortcomings. The truth is, when you indulge in self-harm repeatedly, it might become associated with a sense of urgency and craving whenever the mood is dipping, almost resembling an addiction. This is not logical though. Your desire to punish yourself could be rooted in inaccurate thinking. Hence, hurting yourself is not going to make it better.

Cognitive distortions, emotional inertia and negative behaviour states—all contribute to distorted pain perception and tend to equate life with suffering. This could decrease the desire to live and pinpoint the focus on self-extermination. The fear of enduring physical pain, as well as the universally pervasive fear of dying could deter one from this move. But what if that appears insignificant in comparison to the "psychache"? One could be driven to believe that the only way out is to end their life.

Distressing mood states ebb and flow with time. A suicidal wish could be maximal when "psychache" and hopelessness are peaking. The truth is, someone who battles the most negative mood state and manages to stay alive through it, typically never attempts suicide again because they learn that they survived their lowest low and feel more motivated to empower themselves to stay positive in the future.

NOTE: Fight Self-Harm Thoughts

When it comes to self-harm, there could be many reasons in your mind that justify the "why" but here are some reasons to convince you "why not". These statements are designed to challenge your self-harm thoughts.

- Suicide is not a natural response to adversity. There are means to cope.
- Maybe you are miscalculating the severity and permanence of the problem?
- Maybe you are misjudging your capability and capacity to fight the problem?
- Bad thoughts, bad feeling, and bad situations pass. Suicide is permanent.
- If the problem is temporary, why choose suicide as a permanent solution?
- Even when you think that people don't care, so many of them actually do.
- It will not be the same without you. There are people who want you here.
- You are not a burden, even though for some reason you may feel and think so.

- Besides heroic duties, there's not much worth dying for. You're valuable.
- Surviving difficult times only makes you stronger. There's gain in this pain.
- You're not alone, you're not abandoned, help is always available. Take it.

PART - V

THIS IS THE BEGINNING OF YOUR NEW LIFE

"Sometimes it's the smallest decisions that can change your life forever."

—Keri Russell

A SELF-HELP HANDBOOK HAS A UNIQUE OBJECTIVE THAT starts fulfilling itself as soon as you decide to read it, but gets completed only when you apply what it teaches. If you implement the advice in this book to challenge your cognitive distortions, you won't be the same person anymore. Here is how it could work. It will first sink into your subconscious mind and sit there for a while. When you absorb it into your being, you will finally see it from your perspective as "true-to-life" and "relevant". That is when you will begin to take accountability for your thoughts, emotions, actions, and life.

In this section I have discussed the doctrines of "free will" and "determinism", which reflect the role of choice and chance respectively, in the causality and treatment of depression. I also assess the link between flexibility, gratitude, and compassion, and how they intertwine with each other to work to your emotional advantage. I add a final word on antidepressant medication, which according to me is a breakthrough in treating a low mood. But I still describe cognitive therapy as the emotional vaccine that can prevent low moods from arising in the first place.

36

You Are Responsible for Your Wellness

"I find it impossible not to think that I can choose to do what I so conceive, however strong may be my inclination to act unreasonably, and however uniformly I may have yielded to such inclinations in the past."

—Henry Sidgwick

If you want to believe that everything happening to you is your destiny, and you're helpless in controlling it, there's probably some logic you might be using to justify your thought. This doctrine of "determinism" radically contends that everything in life, all reality, is predetermined. Genetic "determinism" talks of genes influencing your mood, while environmental "determinism" insists that your surroundings impact your mind.

For example, consider research that asserts, "If your parents get divorced in your childhood, it *can* instigate and sustain lifelong depression in you" (Sands et al., 2017). But this suggests relative risk, not 100% attribution. If it was absolute, then every depressed individual would give birth to distressed children, and each negative life experience could culminate in depression. In effect, going with this hypothesis, you would never be able to heal from depression because your genes are programmed for it, and events that have transpired in life would leave their negative mark on your mind, forever. It doesn't work like this.

The truth is, even the human genome project that is indexing the genetic composition of humanity cannot categorically predict how you will behave when faced with a difficult interview, relationship breakup, job loss, sexual assault, medical illness, or a calamity like a pandemic for that matter. Human behaviour is more complex than most multifaceted algorithms developed till date. That is precisely why the doctrine that opposes such "determinism" can offer an unconstrained and more realistic perspective of your mind and mood. This is the principle of "free will," which elucidates that even in the most painful emotional states of anger, frustration, sadness, anxiety, or panic, you can consciously choose the logical path, which exercises attention, consideration, reflection, and transformation. You can change how you feel, even if you have behaved contrastingly before.

Depression is still rampant, because even though "free will" asserts your power of choice, the way your brain is hardwired, everyday stressors, and a negative outlook towards life could orchestrate an ultimate predetermined hostile dialogue. As if nothing was or will ever be in your hands.

You are a self-directing and autonomous being, liable and answerable for your choices, which in turn determine your mental wellness, or for that matter illness. Yet, you live in a society that perpetually thrusts its views, opinions, and demands on you so strongly that whether you like it or not, you are influenced. That is why personal responsibility is not a cut and dried, protocol-driven outcome. Human behaviour choices are intricately complicated. But this should not validate living with depression or justify submitting to blind paternalism for your emotional wellness. "I am like this, I have been like this, so, I will stay like this," will not work. It shouldn't.

Happiness is your personal right. Conserving it amounts to your own duty. You are ill when you're depressed, yes. But the sick-role theory shouldn't change your expectation of responsibility under conditions of illness. You may get accommodations for time away from school or work, household chores, social roles, and family engagement when you're "sick". But you are still responsible for attempting recovery, by engaging in the right treatment, and attempting better life choices.

Your mental health is a state of ongoing well-being, contentment, and satisfaction, not merely an absence of the diagnosis of mental illness. The zone between illness and wellness will always encompass states of stress, worry, apprehension, sadness, and frustration, which also need attention. When you are frequently faced with recurring stressors that exhaust your psychological armour, you become vulnerable to depression.

Circumstances in the environment (nurture) as well as genetic coding (nature), both create a milieu of distress, which can push you to regress to a childlike state where rationality is lost. This multiplicative gene-by-environment interaction affects the ultimate depression risk. If life situations get so derelict, then your autonomy, right to self-determination, and making personal choices gets overridden. It may seem like your mental health is not in your own hands. Relinquishing responsibility is not helping your cause.

Recovery today is about fashioning a new mindset—a process of engendering hope, taking charge, and going on with life, regardless of depression. You must take action and do what needs to be done to stay well as well as get well, if depression strikes. Greater the responsibility you assume, likelier will be your possibility of enjoying optimal mental health for longer.

37

Putting It Together: Flexibility, Gratitude and Compassion

> "To have depression is to have no motivation; No motivation to wake up, no motivation to socialize, no motivation to live. It is a crushing weight that you just need some support to lift."
>
> —Anonymous

Psychological flexibility as a concept in emotional wellness is often taken for granted. This emotional treasure is the capacity to respond to demanding life situations dynamically by not perceiving them as stressful and adapting to them instead of becoming fixated on how troubling they are. This incorporates a cognitive (thinking), emotional (feeling) as well as behavioural (action) response. Flexibility is famed as a core tenet of mindfulness. Its significance becomes even more apparent when it is lacking. That is when you realise that you're stuck in your emotional woes and cannot seem to set yourself free.

From the cognitive perspective, flexibility means not thinking in extremes (black and white thinking), not perceiving outcomes as disastrous (catastrophising), not making assumptions (jumping to conclusions) as well as not attributing it all to yourself (personalisation). All cognitive distortions reflect stiffness in thinking. Such consistent and rigid negative *ruminations* lead to a pessimistic loop of negative, abstract, and self-focused thoughts like "Why did this happen to me and why can't I handle it better?" Brooding like this maintains and worsens depression.

Rumination is said to be the case when you keep thinking about a problem theme on a loop. Whether this is helping or hindering the resolution of your problem depends on how rationally you process it. Good emotional processing helps you figure what you're exactly feeling and make adjustments to feel better. But if you are not able to process it well enough and generate solutions, rumination enhances distress.

From the emotional angle, inflexibility in feelings is reflected in the degree to which your mood in the present moment is influenced by how you were feeling at some point previously. Allowing any mood to persist is called *emotional inertia*. You tend to feel sad, upset, angry, disappointed, and dismayed for way longer than the situation may warrant. Your sadness loses its connectivity with what really happened to make you sad in the first place. This could also be simulated with characterological depression in which depression engulfs your persona because your mind begins to identify with it and it becomes who you are. "Depressed" becomes the only way you know how to feel.

From the behavioural standpoint, inflexibility isn't *as much* about making wrong choices as it is about being so consumed by them that the rationality to see them as faulty gets diluted. That is when you get mired in behaviours that sustain and worsen a dysfunctional mood state like smoking, drinking, recreational drug use, an erratic routine, poor sleep-wake cycle, emotional eating, toxic relationships, social isolation, and more. You may detach from people who care for and encourage you and miss out on the very support that could and would make you feel better. These faulty choices could become the only way of living, and you see no way out of them.

You fight every symptom in the battle, but you tire yourself and still lose the war. The integrated system of your negative attitudes, emotions, and behaviours becomes your own worst enemy. When you're habituated to ruminate, you resist change. The more you brood, the worse you feel, and the more flawed your life choices become. A smart key to unlock negative ruminations is to build the ability to be warm, encouraging, and kind to yourself.

Gratitude is understood to be a feeling that stems from noticing and appreciating a benefit that you receive from someone and then feel thankful for it. Like economic reciprocity following the simple logic of *quid pro quo*. But gratitude really spans more than an interpersonal framework of give and take. It need not always be sensed for something given *by someone to you*. It could simply be an appreciation of something good that happened to you or in your life—like sunlight after many days of rain and thunder. This was not intended specially for you, but you could still feel grateful for it. From a psychological viewpoint, when you perceive generosity, you feel valued and esteemed. This sense of deservingness reduces self-criticism and worthlessness that are innate to depression. You will have to remove your mind's negative filters in the first place to even be able to recognise this.

Gratitude, like most positive traits, is self-perpetuating. If you are a grateful person, your world view becomes focused on the good things in life, including your own good qualities, skills, and resources. This way you see yourself as "enough" and you tend to become flexible and open to changing what "isn't good enough".

You accept that "it is okay" to not always be self-reliant, and that you could need help. Such acknowledgement also makes you compassionate and human, importantly towards your own self. This makes brooding, anger, and self-disappointment reduce, and you start encouraging instead of berating yourself.

EXERCISE: What is Your Self Compassion Quotient?

Self-compassion (a selective component of self-gratitude) assesses how you treat yourself when things go wrong. These statements describe ways in which you think, feel, or behave. Please check mark (√) any statement that is true for you with regards to your reaction when things haven't gone as you anticipated.

- ☐ I feel utterly disappointed in myself.
- ☐ I get disgusted by my incapability.
- ☐ I am irritated and put off with myself.
- ☐ I want to hurt myself to learn a lesson.
- ☐ I don't deserve to be forgiven for this.
- ☐ I keep thinking about how bad I am.
- ☐ I tend to disregard the positives in me.
- ☐ I feel small, dumb, and insignificant.
- ☐ I think I'm not gentle with myself.
- ☐ I'm like a punitive teacher to myself.

If you checked any or many of these, you could be unyielding with yourself about personal setbacks, and are unable to practise self-compassion. By reacting this way, you're criticising and attacking instead of reassuring and consoling yourself when you need it the most. The calm and peaceful feelings when someone cares for, reassures, and supports you, are linked to the release of the connectivity neurohormone oxytocin. It works exactly the same way when you show warmth and reassurance to yourself (Gilbert, 2014). Research affirms that gratefulness negates self-denigration and escalates self-empathy. Just like a humble "letting go" feeling wherein you don't hold a grudge against your own self. To feel better, you've got to show yourself kindness, comprehension, and support when setbacks and frustrations occur.

Complaining about little and big things has promoted what is called a culture of "micro-complaints" (Wayne, 2015). Small acts like maintaining a diary to list down the things you are thankful for can elevate your mood, facilitate healthy coping behaviours, and also improve physical health. We live in a world where stress is fast proliferating. So, it is even more important to protect yourself from a pessimistic attribution style, so you always sustain hope.

38

Antidepressants or Cognitive Therapy: Care? Crutch? Cure?

"The problem with taking your happy pills and puttering along as before, is that it's no better than sweeping dirt under the carpet. I want you to take that rug out back and beat the hell out of it."

—Julie Holland, *Moody Bitches*

Without doubt, antidepressant medicines (ADMs) are a standard treatment in depression management worldwide. Their efficacy has been confirmed by thousands of clinical trials. All such medicines, although famed to act in diverse ways and representing unique mechanics of action, primarily enhance the quantity of specific neurochemicals in the synapses (space between nerve cells) inside the brain. These chiefly include serotonin, norepinephrine, and dopamine. By reducing their reuptake or reabsorption from the synapses, most medicines increase the levels of the corresponding chemicals, so that more of it is available in the nerve terminals to pronounce its action.

Selective Serotonin Reuptake Inhibitors (SSRIs) prevent the reabsorption of serotonin, while Noradrenaline Reuptake

Inhibitors (NRIs) purely prevent reuptake of norepinephrine. Correspondingly Serotonin and Norepinephrine Reuptake Inhibitors (SNRIs) block reuptake of both. Some medicines could elevate levels of dopamine, while others escalate melatonin. Few could act as modulators instead of inhibitors, and alter the functioning of receptors of these neurotransmitters, instead of affecting the transmitter levels themselves. Some other medicines block enzymes that destroy these chemicals. In short, all these medicines increase the levels, and activity of specific neurotransmitters, a deficit of which is repeatedly proven to be responsible for depression. That is why such medicines help alleviate depression.

Besides core antidepressants, symptom-relieving medicines like those for sleep, appetite, anxiety, and nervousness are also frequently used to offer short-term or immediate relief to someone who is depressed. Depression that is atypical (bipolar depression) calls for mood stabilisers which prevent the swings in mood, and that which is accompanied by psychosis may require antipsychotic medication. Herbal remedies or even homeopathy is used by many, but there is insufficient evidence to support the efficacy or value, though many claim they do perceive some benefit.

Antidepressant use could come at a cost. It might result in a mild to moderate degree of side effects like sexual problems, drowsiness, weight gain, insomnia, anxiety, dizziness, headache, dry mouth, blurred vision, nausea, rash, or tremors. In some rare cases, patients develop hormone abnormalities, heart problems, or seizures, but these are typically uncommon. Any medicine can arouse hypersensitivity (like an allergy). So, it becomes important to watch out for these signs when you start taking them. Monitoring the level of your antidepressant medicine in the blood is called Therapeutic Drug Monitoring or TDM. This makes sure that the medicine is present in the bloodstream in an amount that will offer the best clinical benefit. This is more prevalent in research settings though and may not be customarily practised in everyday care of depression.

Antidepressants as well as supportive sleep and anxiety pills do tackle surface symptoms, which could be seriously debilitating in severe depression. But they do not promise to confront the core problem. Just like diabetes and hypertension, where tablets correct a chemical (in depression this is a neurotransmitter) deficit in your system, medication in depression is prescribed for at least six months, if not more, to start with, to ensure that symptoms do not return. So, they are famed to be supportive and not curative and may not guarantee that the deficit, and effectively the illness, will not recur.

If you're prone to side effects while you use medicines, it could get a little rough. The truth is, with no other intervention offered simultaneously, someone with depression who has responded well to antidepressants, still holds a five-time likelihood of being depressed after stopping medicines because no causal mechanism has been addressed. Not everyone will have a recurrence. But knowing this vulnerability, any life stress that is beyond your coping capacity can push you down the depression hole, yet again.

In general, all other factors remaining constant, one out of two depressed individuals feel better with any antidepressant, while a small percentage of the remainder respond to a very specific one, or a combination of a few. The success ratio with antidepressants rises to a maximum of two out of three people, no matter what medicine you use. The remaining one third still need something more. What do you fathom that might be?

Cognitive Therapy (CT) and Cognitive Behaviour Therapy (CBT) have been the strongest contenders alongside medicines, in the battle against depression besides other modalities like electroconvulsive therapy (ECT), repetitive transcranial magnetic stimulation (rTMS), vagal nerve stimulation, and brain surgery in rare and unique conditions. It is true, everyone could have a very specific causality and hence respond uniquely to different approaches. Yet, it has often been upheld that medicines alter the symptoms and experience, while therapy modifies the course and end outcome of depression.

None of these claims are anecdotal. The short-term similarities and long-term differences between Antidepressant Medication (ADM) and CT are explained by specialised functional neuroimaging studies like functional Magnetic Resonance Imaging (fMRI) and Positron Emission Tomography (PET) scans that we discussed before. As an immediate effect, ADM, and CT both reduce emotional reactivity which reflects exaggerated amygdala function (implicated in depression); hence the emotional turmoil lessens almost at once. Consistent therapy, however, could change the way in which you process your thoughts and emotions in the frontal lobe of the brain (responsible for reappraisal of life experiences), and this could alter the neural circuits between emotion controlling regions of the brain altogether. In Siegel's research (2007), when depressed people treated with CT modified their negative expectations, their brain structure changed. This was not the case in those treated with ADM. Change in emotion and behaviour is an outward consequence of these changes in the brain. All brought about by cognitive therapy.

That is why the cognitive model of Beck posits that when maladaptive thinking is corrected, the acute anguish as well as the risk of recurrence of depression, diminishes. Nothing good comes *that* easy, and so cognitive therapies call for commitment, introspection, and self-work. Cognitive techniques, as taught in this book, coax you to identify the thoughts that precede your painful emotions, distance yourself from the emotional responses to these thoughts, and finally question the validity of these, to replace them with constructive styles of thinking. The light at the end of this arduous tunnel is bright and promising.

ADMs from the outset have and continue to revolutionise depression management. But over the decades, the number of cases of depression in every part of the world has not significantly shrunk. Also, suicide rates, which are an indicator of depression severity, are still high. It cannot be challenged that ADMs do work faster in symptom relief by improving sleep, lessening anxiety, and preventing emotional outbursts. Biological treatments are strongly advocated in severe depression and suicidal states. Also, in its defence, treatment with ADM is less expensive and much easier than therapy. But in the longer term, reliance on medicine alone could lower the utilisation of your own internal prowess. You might get drawn to believe that depression is so biological, that your own thinking style and coping mechanism are irrelevant. If you imbibed this incorrect view, you would miss the psychotherapeutic experience that could otherwise help you cope better with subsequent depression episodes, abort a likely emergent depression, or even prevent it altogether.

CT is like an emotional vaccine that builds your immunity against depression. It changes your attitude towards your past and present experiences and coaxes you to identify the distorted beliefs that led to them in the first place. You cannot practise CT without knowing its theory. So, you often blame yourself or someone else for negative outcomes and fail to take and give credit for positive ones. Practising CT regularly on yourself will get you out of this "thoughtless thinking" mode as Beck likes to put it, and nudge you towards a mindful approach with greater self-awareness. Now that you are more equipped to identify, test and challenge your distorted conceptualisations, your good life is only about to begin.

CONCLUSION

I know that getting rid of depression is daunting. But living with depression is way worse.

The Times of India in 2021 stated, "We live in a country where depression is still considered a fancy term for feeling a *little* down and out." The same newspaper in 2020 had narrated results of a population-based survey during the pandemic, which concluded that 43% Indians are depressed. This emphasises how long and far we still must travel, to destigmatise the causality and treatment of this devilish illness and realise that the gap between knowing that one is ill and seeking help for it is wide.

When someone is asked, "How are you?" the response usually sounds like, "I'm fine", "I'm good", "I'm terribly busy with work" or "I'm okay". One rarely says, "I'm so lonely, it makes me cry," or "I'm so sad that it makes me cringe." Discussions like this, if at all, are faced with a nervousness so debilitating that the sound of sadness is buried even before it can surface. Silence becomes the most preferred language for the depressed.

Things will change when you start listening to the sound of your own voice and speaking up. Often enough it's not as much about telling someone else, as it is about first saying it to yourself. If your instant thought when you're sad is that you must deal with it yourself, your strategy may backfire. It's not *always* easy to overcome sadness alone. Emotional wounds, old and new, tend to gnaw at you consistently and the devil of depression attacks secretly, to consume you.

Depression doesn't differentiate based on race, ethnicity, education, accomplishment, age, or socioeconomic group. Depression is seen in every country on the globe. Yet, of the one in fifteen humans who have it, half are diagnosed properly and half of those diagnosed get treated, if at all. Everyone wants to be normal. Nobody wants to be labelled weak. But the curve of normal distribution will only widen when sadness and depression are normalised and speaking about feelings is encouraged. Remember, you're not alone—not in the suffering or the healing.

Hippocrates, the Greek father of medicine, described depression two thousand five hundred years before Christ. Even today, looking at the alarming numbers of its prevalence, it continues to haunt humanity. Depressed people are constantly tussling psychological pain, ill physical health, and the irking desire to give up. Stressors are worsening depression, prompting stress and unhealthy lifestyles that are worsening health. The quality of human life is declining. The right time to do something about it is right now. You have the tool right here. All you need is to make a start and see the light at the end of the cognitive therapy road.

Use the ideas and strategies in this book if you are feeling sad or depressed, as well as once you have recovered. Travel the road from illness to wellness, knowing that if by chance you slide back into darkness, there *is* a way out. All chapters are inspired by cognitive neuroscience and summated in easy-to-use self-strategies. You will surely find useful insights that will enable you to change your life. What is most important is making sure that you have all the smart thinking tools that help combat sadness and depression, and consistently nurture hope.

References

Preface

1. Arvind, Banavaram Anniappan et al. "Prevalence and Socioeconomic Impact of Depressive Disorders in India: Multisite Population-based Cross-sectional Study." *BMJ open,* vol. 9, 6 (2019) e027250. 27 Jun.
2. COVID-19 Mental Disorders Collaborators. "Global Prevalence and Burden of Depressive and Anxiety Disorders in 204 Countries and Territories in 2020 due to the COVID-19 pandemic" *The Lancet (London, England)* vol. 398, 10312 (2021): 1700-1712.
3. Evans-Lacko S, Aguilar-Gaxiola S., Al-Hamzawi A., et al. "Socio-economic Variations in the Mental Health Treatment Gap for People with Anxiety, Mood, and Substance Use Disorders: Results from the WHO World Mental Health (WMH) Surveys." *Psychological Medicine* 48, 9 (2018):1560-1571.
4. GBD 2017 Disease and Injury Incidence and Prevalence Collaborators. "Global, Regional, and National Incidence, Prevalence, and Years Lived with Disability for 354 Diseases and Injuries for 195 Countries and Territories,

1990-2017: A Systematic Analysis for the Global Burden of Disease Study 2017." *The Lancet (London, England)* vol. 392, 10159 (2018): 1789-1858.

5. India State-Level Disease Burden Initiative Suicide Collaborators. "Gender Differentials and State Variations in Suicide Deaths in India: The Global Burden of Disease Study 1990-2016." *The Lancet. Public Health* vol. 3, 10 (2018).
6. Institute of Health Metrics and Evaluation. Global Health Data Exchange (GHDx). http://ghdx.healthdata.org/gbd-results-tool?params=gbd-api-2019-permalink/d780dffbe8a381b25e1416884959e88b
7. Wang, Philip S. et al. "Use of Mental Health Services for Anxiety, Mood, and Substance Disorders in 17 countries in the WHO World Mental Health Surveys." *The Lancet (London, England)* vol. 370, 9590 (2007): 841-50.
8. World Health Organization. *Front Matter*. World Health Organization, 2017, pp. 2-2, *Depression and Other Common Mental Disorders: Global Health Estimates.*

Introduction

1. American Psychiatric Association. *Diagnostic and Statistical Manual of Mental Disorders, 3rd, ed. DSM-III,* American Psychiatric Publishing, 1980.
2. Beck, Aaron T. "Cognitive Therapy: Nature and Relation to Behavior Therapy-Republished Article." *Behavior Therapy* vol. 47, 6 (2016): 776-784.
3. Beck, Aaron T. *Depression: Causes and Treatment.* Philadelphia, PA, USA: University of Pennsylvania Press, 1967.

4. Bockting, Claudi L. H. et al. "Preventing Relapse/ Recurrence in Recurrent Depression with Cognitive Therapy: A Randomized Controlled Trial." *Journal of Consulting and Clinical Psychology* vol. 73, 4 (2005): 647-57.
5. Bolwig, Tom G., and Max Fink. "Electrotherapy for Melancholia: The Pioneering Contributions of Benjamin Franklin and Giovanni Aldini." *The Journal of ECT* vol. 25, 1 (2009): 15-8.
6. Chalah, Moussa A., and Samar S. Ayache. "Disentangling the Neural Basis of Cognitive Behavioral Therapy in Psychiatric Disorders: A Focus on Depression." *Brain Sciences* vol. 8, 8 150 (2018). 9 August.
7. Chan, Eric K. H. *Efficacy of Cognitive-Behavioral, Pharmacological and Combined Treatments of Depression: A Meta-Analysis* (Unpublished doctoral thesis). University of Calgary, Calgary, AB, 2006.
8. Chen, Li-Ping et al. "Anterior Cingulate Cortex and Cerebellar Hemisphere Neurometabolite Changes in Depression Treatment: A 1H Magnetic Resonance Spectroscopy Study." *Psychiatry and Clinical Neurosciences* vol. 68, 5 (2014): 357-64.
9. Clark, David A., and Aaron T. Beck. "Cognitive Theory and Therapy of Anxiety and Depression: Convergence with Neurobiological Findings." *Trends in Cognitive Sciences* vol. 14, 9 (2010): 418-24.
10. Cuijpers, Pim et al. "Psychotherapy for Depression in Adults: A Meta-Analysis of Comparative Outcome Studies." *Journal of Consulting and Clinical Psychology* vol. 76, 6 (2008): 909-22.
11. Ellis, Albert. *Reason and Emotion in Psychotherapy*. New York: Lyle Stuart, 1962.

12. Engel, G. L. "The Need for a New Medical Model: A Challenge for Biomedicine." *Science (New York, N.Y.)* vol. 196, 4286 (1977).

13. Freud Sigmund. "An Outline of Psychoanalysis". Standard Edition. Translated by James Strachey. London: Hogarth Press, 1938.

14. Fu, Cynthia H. Y. et al. "Neural Responses to Sad Facial Expressions in Major Depression Following Cognitive Behavioral Therapy." *Biological Psychiatry* vol. 64, 6 (2008): 505-12.

15. Gaudiano, Brandon A. "Cognitive Behavioural Therapies: Achievements and Challenges." *Evidence-based Mental Health* vol. 11, 1 (2008): 5-7.

16. Giulio, G. D. "Therapist, Client Factors, and Efficacy in Cognitive Behavioural Therapy: A Meta-analytic Exploration of Factors that Contribute to Positive Outcome." (2007).

17. Hofmann, Stefan G. et al. "The Efficacy of Cognitive Behavioral Therapy: A Review of Meta-analyses." *Cognitive Therapy and Research* vol. 36, 5 (2012): 427-440.

18. Hollon, Steven D. et al. "Effect of Cognitive Therapy with Antidepressant Medications vs Antidepressants Alone on the Rate of Recovery in Major Depressive Disorder: A Randomized Clinical Trial." *JAMA Psychiatry* vol. 71, 10 (2014): 1157-64.

19. Hollon, Steven D. et al. "Enduring Effects for Cognitive Behavior Therapy in the Treatment of Depression and Anxiety." *Annual Review of Psychology* vol. 57 (2006): 285-315.

20. Jorm, Anthony F. et al. "Relaxation for Depression." *The Cochrane Database of Systematic Reviews*, 4 CD007142. 8 October 2008.

21. Lazaridou, Asimina et al. "Effects of Cognitive-Behavioral Therapy (CBT) on Brain Connectivity Supporting Catastrophizing in Fibromyalgia." *The Clinical Journal of Pain* vol. 33, 3 (2017): 215-221.
22. Lewinsohn, Peter M. "The Behavioral Study and Treatment of Depression". In M. Hersen, R.M. Eisler, and P.M. Miller (eds), *Progress in Behavioral Modification Vol. 1*, pp. 19-65. New York: Academic, 1975.
23. Li, Bao-Juan et al. "A Brain Network Model for Depression: From Symptom Understanding to Disease Intervention." *CNS Neuroscience & Therapeutics* vol. 24, 11 (2018): 1004-1019.
24. McMain, Shelley et al. "Cognitive Behavioral Therapy: Current Status and Future Research Directions." *Psychotherapy Research: Journal of the Society for Psychotherapy Research* vol. 25, 3 (2015): 321-9.
25. Ochsner, Kevin N., and James J. Gross. "The Cognitive Control of Emotion." *Trends in Cognitive Sciences* vol. 9, 5 (2005): 242-9.
26. Ramachandraih, Chaitra T. et al. "Antidepressants: From MAOIs to SSRIs and More." *Indian Journal of Psychiatry* vol. 53, 2 (2011): 180-2.
27. Reynolds, Edward H., and James V. Kinnier Wilson. "Depression and Anxiety in Babylon." *Journal of the Royal Society of Medicine* vol. 106, 12 (2013): 478-81.
28. Ritchey, Maureen et al. "Neural Correlates of Emotional Processing in Depression: Changes with Cognitive Behavioral Therapy and Predictors of Treatment Response." *Journal of Psychiatric Research* vol. 45, 5 (2011): 577-87.

29. Rössler, Wulf. "The Stigma of Mental Disorders: A Millennia-long History of Social Exclusion and Prejudices." *EMBO Reports* vol. 17, 9 (2016): 1250-3.
30. Schaefer, Stacey M. et al. "Modulation of Amygdalar Activity by the Conscious Regulation of Negative Emotion." *Journal of Cognitive Neuroscience* vol. 14, 6 (2002): 913-21.
31. Tiger, Mikael et al. "Reduced 5-HT(1B) Receptor Binding in the Dorsal Brain Stem after Cognitive Behavioural Therapy of Major Depressive Disorder." *Psychiatry Research* vol. 223, 2 (2014): 164-70.
32. Tipton, Charles M. "The History of 'Exercise Is Medicine' in Ancient Civilizations." *Advances in Physiology Education* vol. 38, 2 (2014): 109-17.
33. Tolin, David F. "Is Cognitive Behavioral Therapy More Effective Than Other Therapies? A Meta-Analytic Review." *Clinical Psychology Review* vol. 30, 6 (2010): 710-20.
34. Weitz, Erica S. et al. "Baseline Depression Severity as Moderator of Depression Outcomes Between Cognitive Behavioral Therapy vs. Pharmacotherapy: An Individual Patient Data Meta-analysis." *JAMA Psychiatry* vol. 72, 11 (2015): 1102-9.

Part 1: Know the Enemy If You Want to Fight It

Chapter 1

1. Angermeyer, Matthias C. et al. "Changes in the Perception of Mental Illness Stigma in Germany over the Last Two Decades." *European Psychiatry: The Journal of the Association of European Psychiatrists* vol. 29, 6 (2014): 390-5.

2. Böge, Kerem et al. "Perceived Stigmatization and Discrimination of People with Mental Illness: A Survey-based Study of the General Population in Five Metropolitan Cities in India." *Indian Journal of Psychiatry* vol. 60, 1 (2018): 24-31.
3. Cook, Trevor M., and Jianli Wang. "Descriptive Epidemiology of Stigma Against Depression in a General Population Sample in Alberta." *BMC Psychiatry* vol. 10 29. (19 April 2010).
4. Corrigan, Patrick W., and Deepa Rao. "On the Self-stigma of Mental Illness: Stages, Disclosure, and Strategies for Change." *Canadian Journal of Psychiatry. Revue Canadienne de Psychiatrie* vol. 57, 8 (2012): 464-9.
5. Gaiha, Shivani Mathur et al. "Stigma Associated with Mental Health Problems Among Young People in India: A Systematic Review of Magnitude, Manifestations and Recommendations." *BMC Psychiatry* vol. 20,1 538 (2020).
6. Goffman, Erving, 1922-1982. *Stigma: Notes on the Management of Spoiled Identity*. Englewood Cliffs, N.J.: Prentice-Hall, 1963.
7. Ostman, Margareta, and Lars Kjellin. "Stigma by Association: Psychological Factors in Relatives of People with Mental Illness." *The British Journal of Psychiatry: The Journal of Mental Science* vol. 181 (2002): 494-8.
8. Pescosolido, Bernice A. et al. "Public Knowledge and Assessment of Child Mental Health Problems: Findings from the National Stigma Study Children." *Journal of the American Academy of Child and Adolescent Psychiatry* vol. 47, 3 (2008): 339-349.
9. Rössler, Wulf. "The Stigma of Mental Disorders: A Millennia-long History of Social Exclusion and Prejudices." *EMBO Reports* vol. 17, 9 (2016).

10. Swami, Viren. "Mental Health Literacy of Depression: Gender Differences and Attitudinal Antecedents in a Representative British Sample." *PloS one* vol. 7, 11 (2012).

Chapter 3

1. Maletic, V. et al. "Neurobiology of Depression: An Integrated View of Key Findings." *International Journal of Clinical Practice* vol. 61, 12 (2007): 2030-40.
2. Zhang, Fei-Fei et al. "Brain Structure Alterations in Depression: Psychoradiological Evidence." *CNS Neuroscience & Therapeutics* vol. 24, 11(2018): 994-1003.

Chapter 4

1. Benazzi, Franco. "Various Forms of Depression." *Dialogues in Clinical Neuroscience* vol. 8, 2(2006): 151-61.

Part 2: Thoughts Rule You, but When Twisted, They Could Fool You

Chapter 6

1. Forgeard, Marie J. C. et al. "Beyond Depression: Towards a Process-based Approach to Research, Diagnosis, and Treatment." *Clinical Psychology: A Publication of the Division of Clinical Psychology of the American Psychological Association* vol. 18, 4 (2011): 275-299.
2. Klein, D. C. et al. "Learned Helplessness, Depression, and the Attribution of Failure." *Journal of Personality and Social Psychology* vol. 33, 5 (1976): 508-16.

3. Maier S. F., Watkins, L. R. "Stressor Controllability, Anxiety, and Serotonin." *Cognitive Therapy and Research* 6 (1998): 595-613.

CHAPTER 7

1. Beck, Aaron T. *Cognitive Therapy and the Emotional Disorders*. New York: International Universities Press, 1976.
2. Davis, Blair, Anderson, Robert, and Walls, Jan (eds). *Rashomon Effects: Kurosawa, Rashomon, and their Legacies*. New York, NY: Routledge, 2016.
3. Fiske, Susan T., Taylor, Shelley E., *Social Cognition (2nd Ed)*. New York: McGraw-Hill, 1984.

CHAPTER 9

1. Beck, Aaron T. *Cognitive Therapy and the Emotional Disorders*. New York: International Universities Press, 1976.
2. Taylor, S. E. and Brown, J. D. "Positive Illusions and Well-being Revisited". *Psychological Bulletin*. 116 (1994): 21-27.

CHAPTER 10

1. Beck, Aaron T. *Cognitive Therapy and the Emotional Disorders*. New York: International Universities Press, 1976.
2. Ellis, Albert. "Rational-Emotive Therapy and Cognitive Behavior Therapy: Similarities and Differences." *Cognitive Therapy and Research*, 4, 4 (1980): 325-340.

Chapter 13

1. Beck, Aaron T., Alford, Brad A. *Depression: Causes and Treatment.* University of Pennsylvania Press, 2009.
2. Burns, David. *Feeling Good: The New Mood Therapy.* New York: Avon-HarperCollins, 1999.
3. Darley, J.M. and Gross, P.H. "A Hypothesis-confirming Bias in Labeling Effects" *Journal of Personality and Social Psychology* (1983).
4. Pucci, Aldo R. *The Client's Guide to Cognitive Behavioral Therapy: How to Live a Healthy, Happy Life… No Matter What!* iUniverse, 2006.
5. Whorf, Benjamin. L., Carroll, John, B. (ed.). *Language, Thought, and Reality: Selected Writings of Benjamin Lee Whorf.* Cambridge, Massachussetts: M.I.T. Press, 1956.

Part 4: To Start Making It Better, First, Stop Making It Worse

Chapter 28

1. Watkins, Edward R. "Constructive and Unconstructive Repetitive Thought." *Psychological Bulletin* vol. 134, 2 (2008): 163-206.

Chapter 30

1. Boden, Joseph M., and David M. Fergusson. "Alcohol and Depression." *Addiction (Abingdon, England)* vol. 106, 5 (2011): 906-14.
2. McHugh, R. Kathryn and Roger D. Weiss. "Alcohol Use Disorder and Depressive Disorders." *Alcohol Research: Current Reviews* vol. 40, 1 (2019).

3. Ramsey, Susan E. et al. "Alcohol Use Among Depressed Patients: The Need for Assessment and Intervention." *Professional Psychology, Research and Practice* vol. 36, 2 (2005): 203-207.

CHAPTER 31

1. Baxter, Leslie C. "Appetite Changes in Depression." *The American Journal of Psychiatry* vol. 173, 4 (2016): 317-8.
2. Heath, Tom P. et al. "Human Taste Thresholds Are Modulated by Serotonin and Noradrenaline." *The Journal of Neuroscience: The Official Journal of the Society for Neuroscience* vol. 26, 49 (2006): 12664-71.

CHAPTER 32

1. Armitage, R. "Sleep and Circadian Rhythms in Mood Disorders." *Acta Psychiatrica Scandinavica. Supplementum*, 433 (2007): 104-15.
2. Fang, Hong et al. "Depression in Sleep Disturbance: A Review on a Bidirectional Relationship, Mechanisms and Treatment." *Journal of Cellular and Molecular Medicine* vol. 23, 4 (2019): 2324-2332.
3. Moretto U., Palagini L. "Sleep in Major Depression". *Handbook of Behavioral Neuroscience*. Elsevier. vol. 30 (2019): 693-706.
4. Nutt, David et al. "Sleep Disorders as Core Symptoms of Depression." *Dialogues in Clinical Neuroscience* vol. 10, 3 (2008): 329-36.

CHAPTER 33

1. Klingsieck, K.B. "Procrastination: When Good Things Don't Come to Those Who Wait." *European Psychologist.* 18, 1 (2013): 24-34.
2. Steel, Piers. "The Nature of Procrastination: A Meta-analytic and Theoretical Review of Quintessential Self-regulatory Failure." *Psychological Bulletin.* 133, 1 (2007): 65-94.

CHAPTER 34

1. Clark, D., and Fawcett, J "Review of Empirical Risk Factors for Evaluation of the Suicidal Patient." In B. Bongar (ed.), *Suicide: Guidelines for Assessment, Management, and Treatment*, pp. 16-48. New York: Oxford University Press, 1992.
2. Young, M.A., Halper, I.S., Clark, D.C. et al. "An Item-response Theory Evaluation of the Beck Hopelessness Scale." *Cognitive Therapy and Research* 16 (1992): 579-587.

CHAPTER 35

1. Baumeister, R. F. "Suicide As Escape from Self". *Psychological Review* vol 97, 1 (1990): 90-113.
2. De Beurs, D. et al. "Exploring the Psychology of Suicidal Ideation: A Theory Driven Network Analysis." *Behaviour Research and Therapy* vol. 120 (2019): 103419.
3. Durkheim, E. *Suicide: A Study in Sociology*. New York: Free Press, 1897.
4. Joiner, T.E. *Why People Die by Suicide*. Cambridge, MA: Harvard University Press, 2005.

5. Klonsky, E. David et al. "Suicide, Suicide Attempts, and Suicidal Ideation." *Annual Review of Clinical Psychology* vol. 12 (2016): 307-30.
6. Lefgren, Lars J. et al. "Rationalizing Self-defeating Behaviors: Theory and Evidence." *Journal of Health Economics* vol. 76 (2021): 102407.
7. O'Connor, R.C. "Towards an Integrated Motivational-volitional Model of Suicidal Behaviour" in *International Handbook of Suicide Prevention: Research, Policy and Practice*, eds. R.C. O'Connor, S. Platt, J. Gordon, pp. 181-98. Chichester, UK: Wiley, (2011) .
8. Shneidman, E.S. *Suicide as Psychache: A Clinical Approach to Self-Destructive Behavior.* Northfield, NJ: Jason Aronson, 1993.
9. World Health Organization. "Suicide Worldwide in 2019. Global Health Estimates". World Health Organization, 2019.

Part 5: This Is How You Can Begin Your New Life

Chapter 36

1. Copeland, M. *Wellness Recovery Action Plan*. Liverpool: Sefton Recovery Group, 2005.
2. Engel, G. L. "The Need for a New Medical Model: A Challenge for Biomedicine." *Science (New York, N.Y.)* vol. 196, 4286 (1977): 129-36.
3. Hammen, Constance. "Stress and Depression." *Annual Review of Clinical Psychology* vol. 1 (2005): 293-319.
4. Hyman, S. E. "The Genetics of Mental Illness: Implications for Practice." *Bulletin of the World Health Organization* vol. 78, 4 (2000): 455-63.

5. Milbourn, B. T., McNamara, B. A., and Buchanan, A. J. "Do the Everyday Experiences of People with Severe Mental Illness Who Are 'Hard to Engage' Reflect a Journey of Personal Recovery?" *Journal of Mental Health*, vol. 35, 5 (2014): 241-245.
6. Noordsy, D., Torrey, W., Mueser, K., Mead, S., O'Keefe, C., and Fox, L. "Recovery from Severe Mental Illness: An Intrapersonal and Functional Outcome Definition". *International Review of Psychiatry*, 14 (2002): 318-326.
7. Tedeschi, Richard G., and Lawrence G. Calhoun. "Posttraumatic Growth: Conceptual Foundations and Empirical Evidence." *Psychological Inquiry*, vol. 15, 1 (2004): 1-18.
8. Williams, Simon J. "Parsons Revisited: From the Sick Role to...?." *Health* (London, England: 1997) vol. 9, 2 (2005): 123-44.

Chapter 37

1. Gilbert, P. "Compassion: Conceptualizations, Research and Use in Psychotherapy." New York, NY: Routledge, 2005.
2. Gilbert, P. "The Origins and Nature of Compassion Focused Therapy". *British Journal of Clinical Psychology*, 53 (2014): 6-41.
3. Gilbert, P. *Compassion Focused Therapy: Distinctive Features*. New York, NY: Routledge/Taylor & Francis Group, 2010.
4. Koval, Peter et al. "Getting Stuck in Depression: The Roles of Rumination and Emotional Inertia." *Cognition & Emotion* vol. 26, 8 (2012): 1412-27.

Chapter 38

1. Brody, A. L. et al. "Regional Brain Metabolic Changes in Patients With Major Depression Treated With Either Paroxetine or Interpersonal Therapy: Preliminary Findings." *Archives of General Psychiatry* vol. 58, 7 (2001): 631-40.
2. Harmer, Catherine J. et al. "How Do Antidepressants Work? New Perspectives for Refining Future Treatment Approaches." *The Lancet. Psychiatry* vol. 4, 5 (2017): 409-418.
3. Hollon, Steven D. et al. "Treatment and Prevention of Depression." *Psychological Science in the Public Interest: A Journal of the American Psychological Society* vol. 3, 2 (2002): 39-77.
4. Kennedy, S. H. et al. "Changes in Regional Brain Glucose Metabolism Measured with Positron Emission Tomography After Paroxetine Treatment of Major Depression." *The American Journal of Psychiatry* vol. 158, 6 (2001): 899-905.
5. Lambert, Olivier, and Michel Bourin. "SNRIs: Mechanism of Action and Clinical Features." *Expert Review of Neurotherapeutics* vol. 2, 6 (2002): 849-58.
6. Rush, A. J. et al. "Comparison of the Effects of Cognitive Therapy and Pharmacotherapy on Hopelessness and Self-concept." *The American Journal of Psychiatry* vol. 139, 7 (1982): 862-6.
7. Sangkuhl, Katrin et al. "Selective Serotonin Reuptake Inhibitors Pathway." *Pharmacogenetics and Genomics* vol. 19, 11 (2009): 907-9.

8. Schatzberg, A. F. "New Indications for Antidepressants." *The Journal of Clinical Psychiatry* vol. 61 Suppl 11 (2000): 9-17.
9. Siegle, G.J., Ghinassi, F. and Thase, M.E. "Neurobehavioral Therapies in the 21st Century: Summary of an Emerging Field and an Extended Example of Cognitive Control Training for Depression". *Cognitive Therapy and Research* 31 (2007): 235-262.
10. Urry, Heather L. et al. "Amygdala and Ventromedial Prefrontal Cortex Are Inversely Coupled During Regulation of Negative Affect and Predict the Diurnal Pattern of Cortisol Secretion Among Older Adults." *The Journal of Neuroscience: The Official Journal of the Society for Neuroscience* vol. 26, 16 (2006): 4415-25.

ACKNOWLEDGMENTS

It is an extraordinary debt I owe to my patients, who expressed their worst fears, darkest secrets, and lowest emotions with me over the years, keeping the faith that I could help them out of their sadness. It is they who offered me the experiential wisdom of the real world, more than any psychiatry textbook could ever teach. Their emotional pain motivated me to think out of the box and discover the light that has become this book.

I would not be able to get my work done without the continued support and vision of Jaico Publishing House and the involvement of former commissioning editor, Reena Jayswal. The team copy-edited the book with the utmost warmth, skill, and precision.

As I penned words, lines, and pages in this book, I was teleported back to my training days in psychiatry which reminded me of my teachers and professors. I thank them for their academic support and guidance. I'm thankful to my childhood friends Farida Bandukwala, Kapil Salgia, Nikhil Nasta, and Riteish Deshmukh for being my emotional buffers through thick and thin in my own formative years. I'm ever grateful to Pankaj Kothari, a "friend indeed", who responded to my enthusiasm as well as frenzy through the journey of this book, as if it were his own. Toby Malhoutra, a busy CEO, yet an all-out advocate of mental health, always reinforced my fervour and keenness for mental wellness.

Above all, I would like to acknowledge with gratitude, the support, and love of my family—my mother Smita Batra, and my late father Ashok Batra, who nourished in me the freedom to fly as high as my ambitions could soar. My sister Shilpa, her husband Sumit, and their two daughters Syna and Sysha have been my bundles of joy in my own low moments. While it may sound unconventional, my cat Hermes deserves special mention. He sat beside me throughout the writing of this book and has been by my side more than any human.

JAICO PUBLISHING HOUSE

Elevate Your Life. Transform Your World.

ESTABLISHED IN 1946, Jaico Publishing House is home to world-transforming authors such as Sri Sri Paramahansa Yogananda, Osho, the Dalai Lama, Sri Sri Ravi Shankar, Sadhguru, Robin Sharma, Deepak Chopra, Jack Canfield, Eknath Easwaran, Devdutt Pattanaik, Khushwant Singh, John Maxwell, Brian Tracy, and Stephen Hawking.

Our late founder Mr. Jaman Shah first established Jaico as a book distribution company. Sensing that independence was around the corner, he aptly named his company Jaico ('Jai' means victory in Hindi). In order to service the significant demand for affordable books in a developing nation, Mr. Shah initiated Jaico's own publications. Jaico was India's first publisher of paperback books in the English language.

While self-help, religion and philosophy, mind/body/spirit, and business titles form the cornerstone of our non-fiction list, we publish an exciting range of travel, current affairs, biography, and popular science books as well. Our renewed focus on popular fiction is evident in our new titles by a host of fresh young talent from India and abroad. Jaico's recently established translations division translates selected English content into nine regional languages.

Jaico distributes its own titles. With its headquarters in Mumbai, Jaico has branches in Ahmedabad, Bangalore, Chennai, Delhi, Hyderabad, and Kolkata.

SINCE 1946